THE
ROYAL
FORESTS
OF MEDIEVAL
ENGLAND

The Middle Ages

A series
edited by
EDWARD PETERS

Henry C. Lea, Associate Professor of
Medieval History
University of Pennsylvania

CHARLES R. YOUNG

THE ROYAL FORESTS OF MEDIEVAL ENGLAND

University of Pennsylvania Press
1979

Copyright © 1979 by Charles R. Young
All rights reserved
Printed in the United States of America

Library of Congress Cataloging in Publication Data

Young, Charles R
  The royal forests of medieval England.
  (The Middle Ages)
  Bibliography: p.
  Includes index.
  1. Royal forests—England—History. 2. Great
Britain—Politics and government—1066–1485.
1. Title. II. Series.
DA188.Y68   333.7′5   78-65109
ISBN 0-8122-7760-0

Contents

Preface

Many people know something about the royal forests of medieval England and that they were somehow important, but even most medieval historians would be hard put to direct an inquiring reader to a good book on the subject. Although the number of extant forest records is large, few of these have been published, and the subject has not attracted the scholarly attention warranted by its importance. This book is an attempt to provide a general history of the royal forests in England from their beginning (in the technical sense of the word) after the Norman Conquest to their decline in the later Middle Ages. The emphasis is placed upon the thirteenth century when the royal forest as an institution was at its height in development and significance. As indicated by the chapter divisions, the aim is to consider various aspects—political and economic as well as legal and administrative—that contributed to making the royal forest an important medieval institution, How these large areas known as royal forests (estimated at one-fourth the land of England in the thirteenth century) influenced life at the time has been a consistent interest that relieved what might otherwise have been the tedium of working out the details of administrative history and gives meaning even to those sections of the book where this interest is not made explicit. It is from this perspective that the history of the royal forests throws light upon a dimension of medieval life that was unique to the period.

Although much work in original records remained to be done, my task was lightened by several publications with information that could be incorporated into a general history. Especially valuable were the studies of Margaret Bazeley, limited as they are to a particular time or place, and the admirable survey by Nellie Neilson in the chapter she contributed to *The English Government at Work, 1327–1336*, which has value beyond the decade under examination. The pioneering introduction by G. J. Turner to the volume of forest pleas that he edited for the Selden Society remains basic to any study of the royal forests. Perhaps most impressive was the accomplishment of Charles Petit-Dutaillis, who employed the intuition of a master historian to outline in one chapter the principal stages in the history of the royal forest in England with such skill that a detailed study of the records has not made it necessary to change his outline. To these important works should be added a number of studies of individual forests as indicated in the Bibliography. However, I also found that the subject had attracted more than its share of romantic and antiquarian books and articles that contributed little or nothing, in spite of the hours spent in the British Museum tracking down sometimes obscure local publications. These have not been included in the Bibliography, which is meant to credit the studies from which I have drawn rather than to provide an inventory of publications on the subject.

Ideally a general history of the royal forests in medieval England would have been preceded by detailed studies of individual forests written by scholars with local knowledge. Lacking these studies for many forests, my procedure has been to incorporate conclusions from studies of individual forests when possible and to search for the overall pattern of forest administration buried in the detail of record sources. Individual variation and eccentricity have been avoided in the attempt to ascertain the main trends. The nature of the evidence is such that very little of it is susceptible to meaningful quantification, but some figures are given when they illustrate general trends and patterns of development. Although difficulties in interpretation underlie the selection of these figures, the application of consistent criteria should insure their comparative value even when their absolute value might be questioned. In all cases I have explained my procedures and pointed to some of the difficulties in order to allow the reader to decide what reliance to place upon my results. It seemed appropriate in a study of this scope to concentrate on the features of the royal forest that were typical. For this reason, when particular cases are cited a deliberate attempt is made to use only those representative of the majority of similar cases and to exclude the exceptional, whatever may be its intrinsic interest. This procedure also meant the exclusion of ambiguous evidence where reference to a royal forest was not completely clear and areas of special jurisdiction (such as the Duchy of Lancaster until it became merged with the crown) where forests were not strictly royal forests even when they operated on the same pattern and sometimes employed royal officials. If this method seems too modest in its objectives, it is hoped that the gains in accuracy and clarity will offset whatever losses have been incurred in terms of variety and individuality.

While working on this book, I have received assistance from several institutions and individuals, and I want at this time to express my gratitude to them. My initial research was assisted by a grant from the American Philosophical Society and a Grant-In-Aid from the American Council of Learned Societies. Additional funds for summer research and travel were provided at various times by the Duke University Council on Research, the Cooperative Program in the Humanities of Duke University and the University of North Carolina, and the National Endowment for the Humanities. I also wish to acknowledge the courteous assistance of the staffs of the Public Record Office and the Institute of Historical Research of the University of London. Virginia Ross and Jessica Dale helped comb through printed calendars of records for references to forests under auspices of the Duke University Undergraduate Research Assistantship Program, and my son, Philip, one summer provided similar assistance. I am grateful for the encouragement of my colleagues and graduate students who showed enough interest to ask how my research was progressing or had the delicacy at crucial periods to refrain from asking. In particular I want to record my debt to Betty, my wife, who continued to serve—as she has throughout our academic career—as critic, typist, and counselor during our prolonged involvement with the royal forests.

Introduction

The outstanding fact about the English landscape that greeted the Norman conquerors in 1066 was that England was still a heavily-wooded land. In spite of centuries of farming activities by the Anglo-Saxons and the Danes, vast areas were covered with ancient woods whose trees collectively produced the darkness and gloom that inspired the dread of forest depths reflected in certain types of medieval literature. What success the agriculturalists had had in making their clearings and fixing their villages within the surrounding woods is memorialized in certain English place-names ending in *den* or *leah,* and the existence of the woods contributed elements such as *hurst, holt,* and *hey* to the names of other places.[1]

The question posed by the Norman Conquest for the history of forests was whether the Norman landholders would continue the Anglo-Saxon practice of extending the fields at the expense of woods or if they would develop some characteristic practice of their own. In fact, the Normans introduced from the continent a new concept of the royal forest and thereby profoundly affected the status of the wooded areas of England and the lives of Englishmen for centuries, mostly as the quite unintentional result of a policy that had little to do directly with either trees or fields.

Literary references throughout the Middle Ages with their ambivalent attitude toward the forest reflect both the nearness of vast stretches of wooded land and the harsh reality of the royal forest law introduced by the Normans. Even in *Beowulf,* in addition to the forest as a place

1

of gloom in which was located Grendel's lair, there is also the concept of the forest as a place of refuge to which some of the hero's followers fled rather than face battle with a dragon. To the real and symbolic perils that faced Sir Gawain as he wandered in the forest of Wirral may be contrasted the descriptions of pleasant forest places in the works of Chaucer. More immediately pertinent to the royal forest as established by the Norman kings and their successors, the forest as a place of refuge for Robin Hood and his merry men is fully understandable only in reference to the royal forest laws which they daily flouted by killing the king's deer. In fact, England after the Conquest more closely preserved the Carolingian usage of the term "forest" for an area under special laws and regulations designed to protect the king's hunting than did either France or Germany.[2] This new institution came to be an influence upon English life during the Middle Ages that remained important even as the areas of uncut woods were penetrated by roads and villages with their cultivated lands. And to some extent the existence of royal forests slowed the destruction of those woods.

The key to understanding this concept of royal forest in medieval England is to start just where the contemporary writers who discussed the institution started: the king's love of hunting. Of course, William of Normandy did not differ in this regard from his Anglo-Saxon predecessors, for the Bayeux Tapestry includes hawks and hounds as completely natural to the scene where Harold Godwineson journeyed to Bosham before his ill-fated voyage to the continent. The Saxon kings also had their hunting preserves scattered throughout England, but the introduction of a special forest law designed to protect the animals important to the king's sport, thus creating the districts known as royal forests, remained for the more authoritarian Normans to establish. In this, as in the controversy over whether the Normans introduced feudalism, there were Saxon precedents that were transformed by the Conquest to create the royal forest as an institution.

When the *Anglo-Saxon Chronicle* came to summarize the deeds of William the Conqueror, the introduction of the forest law into England ranked prominently among his oppressive actions. With great foresight the writer concentrated upon aspects of the forest system that were to become the major themes in the long history of the royal forests:

> He made great protection for the game
> And imposed laws for the same,
> That who so slew hart or hind
> Should be made blind.
> He preserved the harts and boars

And loved the stags as much
As if he were their father.
Moreover, for the hares did he decree that they should go free.
Powerful men complained of it and poor men lamented it,
But so fierce was he that he cared not for the rancour of them all,
But they had to follow out the king's will entirely
If they wished to live or hold their land,
Property or estate, or his favour great.[3]

Here there is emphasis upon the brutal penalties of forest law, the arbitrary exercise of the king's authority, the potential for constitutional struggle between the barons and the king, and the oppressive burden that royal forests brought upon the ordinary people of England. One important aspect not included in the *Chronicle* was the revenue that kings obtained from royal forests, but the full import of the forest as a source of revenue did not become apparent until the reign of Henry II a century later.

As implied in this passage, the royal forest was first of all an area in which a special kind of law—the forest law—applied. Because the royal forest was based upon the king's desire to protect areas where hunting was most favorable, the area within the royal forests coincided roughly with the more heavily wooded areas of England, the same areas that from a geographical point of view might also be called forests, but this correspondence of the two areas was not absolute. From its beginning the royal forest was to some extent an artificial creation that included lands without woods and villages that were alien to the idea of a forest in any physical meaning of the term. In the later twelfth century, Richard fitz Nigel, treasurer and veteran of royal administrative service, attempted to define the legal concept of a royal forest when he introduced this exchange into his *Dialogue of the Exchequer*:

Master. The King's forest is a safe abode for wild animals, not all of them but only the woodland ones, and not everywhere, but in particular places suitable for the purpose. That is why it is called 'forest,' (*foresta*), as though the *e* of *feresta* (i.e. a haunt of wild animals, *ferarum statio*) were changed into *o*.

Scholar. Has the King a forest in every county?

Master. No, only in the wooded ones, where wild beasts have their lairs and plentiful feeding grounds. It makes no difference to whom the woods belong, whether to the King or the nobles of the realm; in both alike the beasts wander free and unscathed.[4]

Although the etymological demonstration may not be impressive, fitz Nigel did manage to sort out the main points in a legal abstraction. Perhaps the more precise definition by G. J. Turner, who applied the tools of professional scholarship as developed in the later nineteenth century to the study of forest records, might help to clarify the legal meaning of the royal forest:

> In mediaeval England a forest was a definite tract of land within which a particular body of law was enforced, having for its object the preservation of certain animals *ferae naturae*. Most of the forests were the property of the Crown, but from time to time the kings alienated some of them to their subjects. . . . But although the king or a subject might be seised of a forest, he was not necessarily seised of all the land which it comprised. Other persons might possess lands within the bounds of a forest, but were not allowed the right of hunting or of cutting trees in them at their own will.[5]

Those "certain animals" protected by forest law were the red deer, fallow deer, roe deer, and the wild boar until a judicial decision in 1339 removed the roe from the list.[6]

The *Anglo-Saxon Chronicle* was correct in the assertion that it was the Norman conqueror who introduced the forest law into England, but, as with so many institutions that developed after 1066, there were some precedents that antedated Norman rule.[7] Regulation of hunting was part of the "Laws of Cnut":

> And it is my will that every man is to be entitled to his hunting in wood and field on his own land.
>
> And everyone is to avoid trespassing on my hunting, wherever I wish to have it preserved, on pain of full fine.[8]

Of course, this provision is a long way from a royal forest in which the king's forest law superseded the hunting rights any other man may have had in his own land if it came within the bounds of a royal forest. However, the practice of the king's establishing protection for his own hunting may have made the expanded provisions of the forest law under William I seem a somewhat less drastic innovation to a people accustomed to the imposition of royal restrictions upon hunting. There is also a reference in *Domesday Book* to a forest with a warden established by Edward the Confessor, but it is going well beyond the evidence to infer that there was already an Anglo-Saxon forest law that defined the royal forest as it was known under the Norman kings.[9] On the Norman background of the royal forest, the evidence can be traced to the capitularies of Charlemagne and his successors, and, thence, to the counts and dukes who took over the royal forest during the breakup of the Carolingian Empire.[10] Charters of the Norman kings of England concerning lands on both sides of the Channel show the similarity between the ducal forest in Normandy and the royal forest in England following the Conquest.[11]

One way of suggesting the historical importance of the introduction of the royal forest is to emphasize the sheer size of the areas placed within the forest by William the Conqueror and his successors. In the thirteenth century the area in royal forest has been worked out to have covered approximately one-fourth of the land area of England, and the forests by that time were somewhat reduced from their greatest extent.[12] Obviously, with such vast areas in royal forest the economic functions of villages and the utilization of forest products did not cease as the common misconception has it, nor were the woods left to the solitary possession of deer and other beasts of the forest. Perhaps the best way to demonstrate the importance of the royal forest as a legal and administrative concept imposed upon the land is to point out that the entire county of Essex was made royal forest, including villages, towns, people, farms, and whatever else was going on in this part of England.

Without entering into disputes among historians upon the subject of the royal demesne, it should be emphasized that the royal forests were never considered part of the demesne in any strict sense. As Robert S. Hoyt put it in his pioneering work on the subject: "In simplest terms, the royal demesne consisted of all the land in England which the king held *in dominio*, 'in his own hand,' and which is not held of the king by someone else. In this sense, the forests and highways are part of the royal demesne. . . . And yet, although the royal forests and the highways are the king's, ordinary medieval usage does not include them among the *dominica regis*."[13] Often the king's own manors were located within the bounds of a royal forest, but they were administered separately from the forest administration. Even if in practice the distinction was sometimes blurred when manors and forests were placed in the hands of the same men or when financial records do not clearly show manorial revenue apart from the revenue occasioned by the enforcement of forest regulations, those instances probably worried the medieval accountants less than they do the modern researcher who likes to keep his categories clear.

Historians have given adequate attention to the effect of the forest laws forbidding the killing of the king's deer, and the ageless popularity of Robin Hood has caused this aspect of a royal forest to be known to children and adults alike. What is not so well known is the effect of the subsidiary laws and regulations intended to protect the habitat of the king's deer by restricting the use that could be made of lands that lay within the bounds of a royal forest. For example, these restrictions prevented a landowner from cutting his own woods without approval by the royal officials or hindered the clearing of additional land for farming. Although a small part of the lands within royal forests were the king's demesne, most of the lands belonged to others. When we find that the restrictions of forest law upon the king's demesne were so serious as to cause disputes between the bailiffs of the king's manors and the royal foresters that could only be settled by the king's council in the thirteenth century, it takes little historical imagination to understand that the restrictions imposed by forest law were felt even more keenly by other landowners.[14] Thus, the attempt to escape these restrictions by seeking to have particular lands exempted from the royal forest or by a general reduction in the area subject to forest jurisdiction became the goal of many barons and a continuous rallying cry in any dispute between the king and his barons, including that most famous dispute centering around Magna Carta. This conflict of interests between the king and his barons brought the question of the royal forests into the mainstream of political and constitutional history.

In order to make the laws of the forest effective over such wide areas, a large administrative machinery had to be created. Means of enforcement of forest law by courts and justices developed alongside but apart from the common law, probably from the time of the Conqueror and demonstrably from the time of his son Henry I. Because the forest law was outside the common law, it has been treated as tangential to English medieval history, and the institution of the royal forest has been considered a medieval *cul-de-sac* of interest mainly to antiquarians who might wish to explain customs like the "right of common" or curious survivals like a verderers' court. Clearly men at the time did not see forest law as inconsequential, for they complained bitterly of the harsh burden it placed upon them. The size of the administrative machinery, the influence of the chief justices of the forest upon the kings, and the propensity of the local foresters to abuse their authority were all subjects of great importance to those men who held lands within the forest or who lived there. In addition to the legal and administrative significance of the royal forest, the economic value of those areas was considerable, both for the fees that the king could collect by authority of forest law and by the economic activities on royal demesne and the lands owned by others within the royal forests. Royal forests produced timber and other forest products by royal license, but there was also farming, cattle and horse raising, mining, iron-making, and many other economic activities taking place within forest borders. Although in the next century the royal forest expanded far beyond anything William the Conqueror could have imagined, his successors' love of hunting had little to do with the influence of that institution on English life.

1
Organization by the Norman Kings

Even though the Normans introduced many changes to England and displaced the Anglo-Saxon aristocracy, the royal forest provoked more negative comments from chroniclers than any of their others acts. The hatred of the restrictive forest law introduced by the Normans is epitomized in accounts of the making of the New Forest by William the Conqueror. Chroniclers lament villages laid waste and the inhabitants being driven from their homes in order to create a forest for the king's pleasure. When William Rufus was killed in a hunting accident in the New Forest, some contemporaries saw the hand of divine retribution for the suffering brought upon the people by the excessive love of hunting displayed by the first two Norman kings and linked the death with the creation of the New Forest. One of the minor controversies among historians as they have sought to understand the significance of the Norman conquest to English history has been over whether the chroniclers were right in attributing destruction of villages in the New Forest to the Conqueror as part of the cost of consolidating the new dynasty.[1] The debate among historians based upon partial evidence from chroniclers and *Domesday Book* failed to produce agreement, but the definitive answer has now been given by combining the methods of the historian and the geographer in a monumental study of the Domesday geography of England:

The evidence of the soil is clear enough. The greater part of the area is covered by the most infertile Tertiary sands and gravels which cannot ever have supported a flourishing agriculture and a large population. In the mid-

7

dle of the Forest there are great stretches that seem always to have been virtually uninhabited. The evidence of the Domesday Book likewise shows that the making of the Forest involved no such violent upheaval as that described by the medieval chronicles.[2]

In spite of the inaccuracy of the chroniclers in these particulars about the New Forest after 1066, their accounts retain a more general historical significance as reflecting the hatred of the royal forest laws prevalent in the twelfth century when they were written.

As it happens, the entry on the New Forest in *Domesday Book* is the only one giving any detailed information about a royal forest, possibly because it may have been added to the original survey. Nevertheless, there is considerable evidence about the distribution of wooded areas in England in 1086, and incidental references also establish the existence of certain other royal forests and parks at that early date. Unfortunately, even when the dimensions of wooded areas are given it has not been possible to relate them to modern measurements, with the result that the extent of land in England covered with trees cannot be calculated and only the relative density from one county to another can be known. In *Little Domesday*, with its greater mass of detail, the extent of woodland is given by reporting the number of swine a wood could support, and this rough measurement makes possible some generalizations about woods for the several eastern counties included in that volume. A general trend that appears is the decline in area of woodlands between 1066 and 1086 in the four counties of Norfolk, Suffolk, Essex, and Cambridgeshire. The areas where trees had been cut were left as waste, which would seem to indicate the cutting was for timber rather than for bringing more land under cultivation.[3]

Although royal forests and woodlands were not the same, there is enough correspondence to use some of the evidence from *Little Domesday* to work out the implications for the forests. Unless the need for timber was of a temporary nature, the establishment or expansion of royal forests in which forest law prohibited or strictly regulated any cutting of trees produced a situation where royal policy was contrary to the needs of the population. The forest as an area off-limits for the production of timber created a problem even before the expanding agriculture of the twelfth century came up against the same obstacle. These implications of the evidence from Domesday Book suggest that the prohibition against hunting the "beasts of the forest" was not the only reason why there was resentment in England of the royal forest under the Norman kings.

The incidental references in Domesday to royal forests are sometimes of individual interest and, taken as a whole, they indicate that

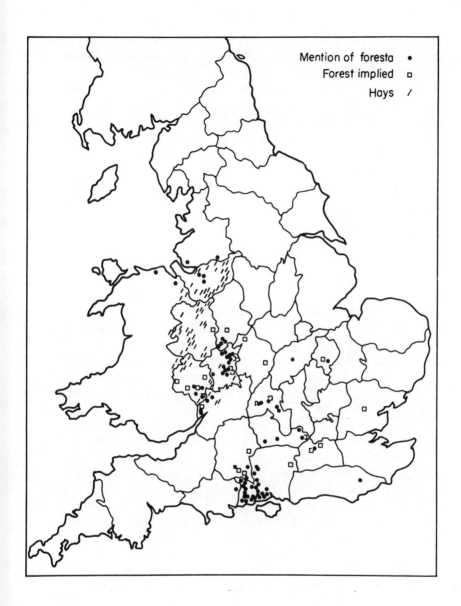

The Forest in 1086

Based on H. C. Darby, *Domesday England* (Cambridge, 1977), p. 197 by permission of Cambridge University Press.

the forests were widespread even in the Conqueror's reign. At Chelmsford in Essex a man named Robert Gernon, who had been a swineherd in 1066, had left the manor to become a forester of the king's wood (forestarius de silva regis). In Huntingdonshire it can be seen that there were royal forests in several places well before King Henry II put the whole county under forest law upon his succession.[4] Issues from Bernwood Forest are mentioned in Buckinghamshire in connection with neighboring manors.[5] The royal demesne forests within the royal forest in Oxfordshire were farmed out:

> In Shotover, Stowood, Woodstock, Cornbury and Wychwood are demesne forests of the king having 9 leagues in length and the same in breadth. To these forests belong 4½ hides, and there 6 villeins with 8 bordars have 3½ plough teams. From these and all things belonging to the forests Rainald renders £ 10 yearly to the king.[6]

In Berkshire, Windsor Forest is mentioned by name and referred to as a royal forest (foresta regis), while other entries show forests in the north and west of the county. *Domesday Book* also has references to Windsor Forest in the Surrey entry, to a forest at Dallington in Sussex, to the Forest of the Dean in Gloucester, and to forests in Lancashire. In Hereford, the hayes (as enclosures in the woods were called) appear in the area where they later became a distinct administrative unit in the twelfth century. On the other hand, there is no mention of Sherwood Forest, and its condition in the eleventh century can only be a matter of speculation.[7] Numerous references to deer parks, belonging to the king or to others, show that that method of providing for hunting was already considerably developed, in one case even at the expense of other revenues.[8]

Although the references in Domesday are sufficient to show royal forests and parks in the time of William I, there is not enough evidence from his reign and that of William Rufus to show how the forests were administered. There is some indication that forest law was enforced through the shire court, but there is no way of knowing whether that was the usual procedure.[9] However, the inference from a writ of William Rufus to his foresters forbidding them to interfere with the wood of the Abbot of Ramsey "except for beasts and assarts" is that foresters were already enforcing regulations to protect the venison and vert, to use the usual terminology of a later period.[10] Both Williams made grants of warren in surviving charters that allowed the grantees to keep dogs for hunting hares and foxes on specified lands.[11] Although the areas to which the grant of warren applied were not in the royal forest and the right to hunt there did not include the beasts of the forest, implicit in these grants is the assumption that any special privilege in reference to hunting must rest upon the royal authority. Nevertheless, the medieval kings of England never extended a claim to a monopoly over all hunting, and in areas outside the royal forest, in an established warren recognized by royal charter, or in a park licensed by the king, there was no impediment to anyone hunting freely either the beasts of the forest or those of the warren.[12]

William Rufus saw the possibility of using forest law as an instrument for other purposes than protection of hunting as shown by an incident related by the chronicler Eadmer. As a method of getting the remaining wealth of the old English nobility, the king falsely accused some fifty men of taking the king's deer and had them brought summarily to trial on this charge. The chronicler is vague about what court was used to try them, but when they denied the charge, they were forced to undergo the ordeal of hot iron as a method of proof. We are told that God preserved the hands of all the accused from being burned and thus made clear their innocence. To this setback, the king responded: "What is this? God a just judge? Perish the man who after this believes so. For the future, by this and that I swear it, answer shall be made to my judgment, not to God's, which inclines to one side or the other in answer to each man's prayer."[13]

With the extant records from the reign of Henry I, the outline of the forest administration becomes a little clearer. In his coronation charter the new king made little concession to resentment of the forest law except for the general promise that he would desist from the abuses committed by William Rufus: "I abolish all the evil customs by which the kingdom of England has been unjustly oppressed. . . . By the common counsel of my barons I have retained the forests in my own hands as my father did before me."[14] His subsequent actions show that the charter did not mean that he would restrict the boundaries of the royal forests to those fixed by William I. Although he made some grants promising that certain lands should not be afforested, it is clear that he extended the royal forests in Yorkshire, and he may have done so in Cumberland also.[15] In fact, his love of hunting was a prominent enough characteristic to be included in William of Newburgh's evaluation when he recorded the king's death: "He cared for the wild animals more than was right, and in public punishment he made too little distinction between a person who killed a deer and one who killed a man."[16] This criticism is confirmed by the harsh penalties in forest law that included blinding, emasculation, and death for violators.

Because of the unsettled conditions during Stephen's reign, the administration of the forests was not maintained as it had been under

Henry I, and the restoration of boundaries under Henry II is proof that the extent of the royal forest in Stephen's reign was also smaller than under his predecessor. To some degree, the smaller area in forest was a considered policy of King Stephen, who, in the charter of liberties for the church given at Oxford in 1136, conceded that additions to the forest made by Henry I were not to be maintained:

I reserve for myself the forests which my grandfather William and my uncle William II established and held. I return quit and concede to the churches and to the kingdom all others which King Henry added over and above these.[17]

That same year in applying this policy he ordered a jury of recognition in Hereford to determine the boundaries of the bishop of Hereford's woods that Henry I had afforested and to return them to the bishop, with the provision that no one should hunt there nor enter without the bishop's permission under pain of forfeiture enforced by the king.[18] There is some evidence for a forest eyre in 1136, but it is problematical how far the forest administration was able to function after that time.[19]

Two rather curious documents from Henry I's reign throw some light upon the operation of the forest administration as it functioned before the breakdown in Stephen's reign. There is little question that the compilation known as the "Laws of Henry I" contains a reasonably accurate account of Anglo-Norman law in the early twelfth century, and even the forgery known as the "Constitutions" of Cnut has some value in reflecting the practice of Henry I's time.[20] The seventeenth chapter of the "Laws" is a severely condensed version of the forest law:

1. The plea of the forests is embarrassed with too many inconveniences.
2. It is concerned with the clearing of land; cutting wood; burning; hunting; the carrying of bow and spears in the forest; the wretched practice of hambling dogs; anyone who does not come to aid in the deer-hunt; anyone who lets loose the livestock which he has kept confined; buildings in the forest; failure to obey summonses; the encountering of anyone in the forest with dogs; the finding of hide or flesh.[21]

A comparison of this chapter with the Assize of the Forest of 1184 makes it clear that there was little new added later by the forest regulations of Henry II.[22]

This chapter contains many of the items found in later instructions given to itinerant justices for forest pleas, and it may represent a similar set of instructions used under Henry I. In any event, the surviving Pipe Roll for 1130 does have entries relating to forest pleas both in the main body of the account for a county and under the heading of "New

Pleas." If there is any significance in the method of recording, it would mean that the fines came from more than one forest eyre, but little reliance can be placed upon an argument based on the form of the one isolated Pipe Roll that survives from this period. Of course, a forest eyre was not necessary for enforcement of the forest law, which could have been enforced in the shire court in the normal procedures as was probably the case in the reigns of Henry's predecessors. Perhaps this is reflected in the Gloucester entry where a sheriff who had just taken office owed £100 from the debts of his father as sheriff for pleas of deer in Caermarthen in Wales, but there is no indication of what court had levied the fines for which the sheriff was made responsible.[23]

Whatever may have been the usual procedure, the Pipe Roll of 1130 has clear evidence for a forest eyre carried out during the preceding twelve months. A number of justices were at work: Ralph Basset and Walchelin Visdelow in Surrey, Robert Arundel in the southwestern counties, Miles of Gloucester in the bishop of Gloucester's forest, Geoffrey de Clinton in Huntingdonshire, and William de Albini in Essex. Miles of Gloucester and Pain fitz John heard forest pleas and ordinary pleas in Staffordshire, Gloucestershire, and Pembroke. Apparently, the king himself held forest pleas on some occasions during the year.[24] By issuing royal pardons, he also intervened in other cases to spare the Earl of Leicester and others from paying the fines that had been levied upon them by the justices. Odd bits of information from the lists of fines in the Pipe Roll help to illustrate the human dimension of a forest eyre. One of the convicted men paying a fine in Dorset and Wiltshire was himself a forester, and two foresters in Gloucester had to be pardoned a fine of twelve marks because of their poverty. The largest fine incurred by an individual was the £72 16s.8d. and two warhorses owed by the Earl of Warwick. In one county the king pardoned fines amounting to £17 from the £88 recorded for forest pleas for the bishop of Lisieux, the monks of Bermondsey, the Earl of Gloucester, and the royal chancellor.[25] Both in these pardons and in other lists of fines it is clear that forest law applied to the clergy as well as to laymen.

No systematic description of the forest administration under the Norman kings is possible because references to foresters and other officials are only incidental in the extant sources, all of which were produced for other purposes. A few foresters are mentioned by name in the Pipe Roll of 1130, but the identification as foresters is only coincidental to the main point of the entries. For example, a list of men who were pardoned for Danegeld in Dorset and Wiltshire included

Warin the forester. Several foresters owed money they had promised in obtaining the office: Henry, son of Herbert the forester, owed one-half mark in gold for the land and *ministerium* of his father in Hampshire; Odo fitz Godric accounted for four marks of silver for the land and office held earlier by Husbond the forester in the same county; and Hansculf the forester owed seven marks of silver for the office of forester in Rutland.[26] Among several entries of fines owed by foresters who had failed to perform their duties properly, only one includes some supporting detail. Walter Croc, forester in Warwickshire, paid rent for the forest for the last five years, but he owed three marks for having been reinstated in his office and for two hundred pigs he took in the forest that did not belong to him but to the other foresters.[27] A charter of Henry I concerning a serjeanty in an Essex forest transferred the land forfeited by the forester to Eustace of Barenton, who was to undertake the duty of keeping the forest in return for the land, and a charter of Stephen later confirmed the inheritance of land and office to Eustace's son.[28] Other men who had some duties in the forest in addition to the foresters were hunters, hawkers, falconers, and archers.[29]

With the introduction of royal forest law into England something had to be worked out to allow those who held land within areas encompassed by the forest to continue to use their land and to live under the restrictions necessary to protect the forest. Some exceptions had to be made from the general intent of the forest law to protect the "beasts of the forest" directly and, indirectly, by protecting the trees and undergrowth needed for them to flourish. The theory seems to have been that the king suffered damages from activities by those who lived in the forest that altered the natural conditions and that he should be compensated for these losses. Thus, the "Laws of Henry I" stated "If *wudehewet,* that is, cutting of wood, is committed in the king's park or forest, compensation amounting to twenty mancuses shall be paid, unless a stricter prohibitive rule demands a greater penalty."[30] Evidence from many charters that grant exemption from the prohibition of cutting wood or from fines for cutting wood bears out the law in practice.[31]

By 1130 some of the income from those with lands in the forest (perhaps including payments for cutting of trees) had been farmed out to the foresters at a fixed rent for which they accounted at the Exchequer. For example, Waleran fitz William paid £25 for the New Forest partially in cash and partially by claiming allowances for his payments and services on behalf of the king during the year: for fixed tithes and alms that the king had granted from the income of this forest, repairs, and the cost of transporting venison and cheeses from Clarendon to Southampton.[32] Although the Pipe Roll does not always give the name of the forest, it does list rent payments in other forests as follows: Shotover in Oxfordshire; Marlborough in the account for Dorset and Wiltshire; Pickering in Yorkshire; the forests of Huntingdonshire, Northamptonshire, Buckinghamshire, and Warwickshire; Cirencester, the hayes of Hereford, and Dean in Gloucestershire; and Windsor Forest in Berkshire.[33] Within the New Forest there were seven cattle farms (*vaccaria*) that were farmed separately from the forest. Each was to have twenty cows and one bull, and the farmer was expected to pay a specified amount of cheese as a yearly rent.[34]

Comparison of the names of several foresters who made their accounts for rents in 1130 with those in the Pipe Rolls of Henry II and his sons indicates that certain families became established as foresters and continued for generations. Waleran fitz William in the New Forest was succeeded by Walter Waleran, who continued to farm that forest for the same rent of £25 throughout the reign of Henry II and until the year 1200. In 1130 Baldwin Rasor paid £10 in Oxford, and Alan Rasor paid that amount for Cornbury Forest in Oxford from 1155 until he was succeeded by his son in Richard I's reign. Probably the Raoul Croc in Wiltshire or Walter Croc in Warwickshire was the ancestor of Matthew Croc who accounted for several small forests in Wiltshire from 1155 until 1183 and of Elias Croc who accounted for the same forests from 1190 to 1209. Perhaps they all descended from Croc the huntsman, who in 1094 received a charter from William Rufus that shows he was involved as a forester.[35] It would seem likely that the Henry Esturmy of 1130 was the same man or father of the Henry Esturmy who farmed Savernake Forest in Oxford from 1155 to 1163 and was the remote ancestor of Henry de Sturmy who was hereditary forester of Savernake from 1292 to 1339.[36] The continuity of certain forests held within families agrees with other evidence that the basic pattern of forest administration had already been set by the reign of Henry I and that the pattern that appears more fully in the records of Henry II was nothing new. The well-known claim of the second Henry that he wished to restore conditions of his grandfather's time was accurate as it related to the administration of the forest.

Even under Henry I a factor that softened somewhat the oppressive force of the royal forest was that exemptions and modifications of forest law were frequent. The clergy often fell afoul of forest law, but they also benefited from special privileges contained in many royal charters. When the king and his party hunted deer, various monasteries and bishops near the particular forest benefited from a tithe of meat and hides.[37] Henry I favored Eynsham Abbey by releasing its men from the obligation of serving as beaters in the royal hunt while his household was being entertained at the abbey.[38] The monks of Chertsey were given the right to make parks or to have warrens where they could use hounds for hunting foxes, hares, wild cats, and pheasants. They could also take all the wood they needed for their own use from the woods without getting specific permission from the royal foresters.[39] Of course, nobody could make a park without the king's license, and one man was fined forty marks and forced to forfeit the park for trying to do so.[40]

Practice allowed a modification of the law against cutting trees or undergrowth in the forest, for the king often gave permission to do just that in the process of making assarts and bringing forest land under cultivation. The simplest form of permission to assart set forth the specified land where the assart was to be made without having to answer to the king through his officials for having done so.[41] An interesting grant concerning assarts is contained in the charter of the Empress Matilda to Geoffrey de Mandeville, Earl of Essex, which confirmed the bargain struck between them when he switched sides in the civil war in 1142. It provided that he and all his men should be free from any penalties for waste or assarts made before he became the Empress's man and that the assarts might be cultivated in the future without threat of forfeiture.[42] Similarly, in 1153 the future Henry II was willing to recognize all the assarts made by the bishop of Lichfield prior to that date to be held in free alms wherever they might be located in the royal forest.[43] Other persons found it profitable to offer money to the king for the privilege of making assarts in the forest.[44]

The founding of monasteries within the bounds of the royal forest was accompanied by charters that exempted them from forest law as it applied to cultivation of land, pasturing of livestock, or use of timber or firewood, provided these activities were solely for use of the monks and not for the market.[45] In addition to the obvious benefits of these exemptions, grants like these had the substantial value of exempting certain lands from interference by the royal foresters. Perhaps it is an evidence of the efficiency or rapaciousness of royal foresters that exemption from their jurisdiction should have been the main benefit sought in other charters. The year before he became king, Duke Henry recognized the liberties of Malmesbury Abbey including custody of its forests to be held just as King William I had granted them without interference within them by any royal forester.[46] If anything should be taken from the woods belonging to the abbey at Colchester, the monks and all their tenants were freed from all pleas of the forest and from interference by royal foresters. The abbot could also keep dogs for hunting hares for the use of the infirmary and did not have to have his dogs conform to forest law by having toes cut on their forefeet.[47]

The picture that can be pieced together of the royal forest by the reign of Henry I is that of an administrative system fully developed and functioning in a routine manner. There are enough pieces of direct and indirect evidence to prove that forest law was administered under the last of the Norman kings in a systematic fashion that anticipated the forest under Henry II. Some precedent for a royal forest established before the Norman Conquest may have made the concept seem less foreign to the English, but the chroniclers testify to the ruthlessness with which the Norman kings imposed the forest law they brought with them from Normandy upon their new subjects. There is even some evidence that each of the three kings manipulated the forest administration as a matter of conscious policy when it could be to his advantage, and grants of exemption from the forest were used by both sides during the civil war in an attempt to win support.

2
Reorganization Under the Angevin Kings

The administrative system of the royal forest that had been developed during the reign of Henry I was one of the casualties of the struggle for the throne that followed his death. A system that existed for the benefit of the king had little chance of continuing to function during a period in which the throne itself was a matter of dispute among shifting alliances of the leading men. The increasing *de facto* authority of the feudal lords in the time of King Stephen, dramatized by the construction of private castles, affected the jurisdiction of the royal forest also. Surviving charters of the Empress Matilda, Stephen, and Duke Henry all weakened the forest administration by granting exemptions in order to attract military and political support to the various factions. In addition, the forest administration depended more directly on the authority of the king than the Exchequer did, and that body barely managed to continue its work at a reduced level in spite of its institutional strength and more fully developed procedures and traditions. When Henry II succeeded to the throne, he was faced with the task of re-establishing a royal authority that had dissipated during the struggle for power, and that meant the reorganization of the royal forest, as well as the destruction of adulterine castles in the hands of lords who might defy the king.

Because the civil war had ended without a clearcut victory—leaving Stephen's followers in possession of some lands and Henry's supporters holding other lands they had taken during the fighting—there was considerable confusion about many legal rights. As far as the royal rights were concerned, Henry's announced policy was to restore the situation to what it had been at the death of Henry I.[1] Even so, when this standard was applied to the royal forests, there was uncertainty as to whether a particular area was subject to the forest jurisdiction because of conflicting grants of exemption, the absence of perambulation of the boundaries for many years, and the probable breakdown of the local forest courts. The complaints by the chronicler of Battle Abbey about the chief forester and the inquests he used to determine these questions of jurisdiction are indicative of the resentment caused by the restoration of the royal forest in all its strength.[2] Of course, restoration of forest or extension of boundaries through additional afforestation was always opposed by the landed classes who found forest law oppressive.

Because Henry II during his long reign extended the royal forests beyond the area they had attained under his grandfather, the question of what was legitimate royal forest was not settled by the restoration pushed through by his ministers of the forest. The issue of the extent of the forests was revived by the barons in the war against John until a settlement was reached and included in Magna Carta and, later, in the separate Forest Charter of 1217. In fact, the area of royal forest reached its greatest extent during the reign of Henry II, for there were disafforestments under both Richard and John, and both the standard adopted in the Charter of the Forest and the practice of the early thirteenth century did not recognize the additions made by Henry II during his own reign as being legitimate.[3] Even the efforts of Edward I after 1277 to restore the royal forest as it had been at its height were doomed to failure, for his subsequent efforts reflected in the perambulations of 1300 did little more than delay a process of disafforestation.

The evidence for enlargement of the forest under Henry II is mostly either indirect or retrospective, but there can be no doubt of the general policy of expansion. Contemporaries particularly complained of the activities of Alan de Neville as chief forester, and the amounts recorded in the Pipe Rolls from fines assessed by him are evidence of the vigor with which he pursued his task.[4] It is remarkable to find that the memory of the afforestations carried out by Alan and his colleagues was still alive fifty years later in the minds of the juries who carried out the perambulations in accordance with the Forest Charter of 1217.[5]

Whether the afforestations made by other ministers of Henry II were made at the same time as those by Alan de Neville was not given by all the juries of the thirteenth century, but the jurors certainly attributed the extensions to the reign of Henry II. Counties in which the jurors said additions had been made after the first coronation of Henry

II were Nottingham, Huntingdon, Leicester, and Derby. In Yorkshire the royal chamberlain had placed his foresters in Galtres and Pickering to supplement the foresters in fee, and Alan de Neville and Robert Puher had taken a woods into the king's hand and placed it in the forest because the owner had committed waste there. Alan had also afforested lands in Cumberland, Northamptonshire, and Buckinghamshire. In the latter county the king also ordered William de la Rokele to place some areas in regard that had formerly been common pasture. The jurors in Oxfordshire responded that all the woods of knights and free men had been placed in regard at the time of Henry II and, thereby, added to the royal forest that had previously consisted solely of the king's demesne woods. Areas afforested in that county by Alan de Neville included the park at Woodstock that the king had obtained through an exchange of lands with the Templars.[6] Another method by which Henry added to the royal forest was to afforest lands when they came into his hands through forfeiture or escheat by treating them as his own lands.[7] Probably more than a mistake was involved, and covert resistance to royal policy revealed, when the jurors for Yorkshire were forced to admit that they had misunderstood their instructions and had mistakenly disafforested lands that had been forest before the coronation of Henry II and, therefore, should have remained forest.[8]

Although neither Richard nor John adopted any formal change in policy about the royal forest, the area under forest law was actually reduced in both reigns. The ministers who ruled England for Richard and, later, King John found that the sale of forest privileges and exemptions was a profitable venture. The same pattern in both reigns by which the sovereign's need for money led to a sale of privileges (illustrated by the remarkable traffic in borough charters) was also established in relation to the royal forest, and the cumulative effect was that large areas were disafforested in order to raise money. The results of these piecemeal disafforestments in the Pipe Rolls, shown in Table 1, are instructive.[9] Subsequent entries usually show that the amounts offered for disafforestment were only paid gradually over a period of years. In addition to these large disafforestments, the Pipe Rolls also list substantial sums from individuals for the disafforestment of their woods or manors or to confirm previous exemptions.[10] In the reign of John, the nascent Chancery enrollments provide more details on all the major disafforestments listed above from the Pipe Rolls and for many exemptions of smaller areas to monasteries or individuals.[11] The most sweeping exemption was part of John's confirmation charter for the Templars when he allowed all their lands to be quit of regard, waste, view of foresters, and all other customs of the forest, thus, in effect re-

Table 1. Disafforestments During the Reigns of Richard I and John

Disafforested	Amount Paid	Date
That part of the county of Bedford that Henry I afforested	£200	1190
The wapentake of Ainsty in Yorkshire	£100	1190
Entire county of Cornwall	2200 marks	1204
Part of the forest of Essex	500 marks and 5 palfreys	1204
County of Devon	5000 marks	1204
Forest of Hertfordlythe in Yorkshire	100 marks and 2 palfreys	1204
County of Surrey	500 marks	1207

moving their substantial holdings from the forest wherever they might be located.[12] Although the number of areas disafforested is impressive, the evidence has the inherent bias of recording change, whereas areas that remained in forest would be less likely to appear in the type of records extant from this date. For example, it is only by chance that a perambulation of Savernake Forest in the first year of King John can be compared with one from the time of Henry II to demonstrate that the boundaries had remained the same throughout the years.[13] Nevertheless, after allowing for this inherent bias, the records do emphasize that the major trend was that the area in royal forest was being decreased by royal actions from the extent it had reached under Henry II.

The men who administered the royal forest for King John lost no opportunity for raising money even during the process of disafforestment. In 1209 they managed to place the cost of making a perambulation to determine the boundary between a private forest and the royal forest of Pickering in Yorkshire upon the owner of the private forest.[14] Another indication of an attempt to wring every last penny from the forest administration in the same year was the fine of three hundred marks imposed on the men of Devon because they refused to allow Hugh de Neville to make the regard in Devon and to perambulate the boundaries between the king's forests and their lands. In view of their payment in 1204 to secure the disafforestment of the entire county, this fine appears to have been a bit of sharp practice under the guise of forest law.[15] The imposition of a requirement that men who lived outside the royal forest could still be required to attend forest courts if they lived within two leagues of a royal forest is an example of a similar concern for interpreting forest regulations in the broadest possible way.[16] The burden caused by this particular policy was sufficient to cause its removal to be one of the demands of the barons during the negotiations for Magna Carta.

The reign of Henry II was important in the history of the royal forest not only for re-establishing and extending the areas included in the forest but also for restating the royal policy on the forests. The basic principles that constituted Henry II's policy can be read in some passages in the *Dialogue of the Exchequer* written about 1179 by one of Henry's clerks and in the various assizes of the forest copied into the chronicles of Roger of Howden. The fundamental assumption as expressed in the *Dialogue* is: "The King's forest is a safe abode for wild animals, not all of them but only the woodland ones, and not everywhere, but in particular places suitable for the purpose."[17] From its introduction into England by William the Conqueror, forest law was directly connected with the king in a way that made the forest a subject of contention between the aristocracy and the king throughout the thirteenth and early fourteenth centuries. Richard fitz Nigel in his rather verbose way points to this connection in the later twelfth century in these passages from the *Dialogue*:

> It is in the forests too that 'King's chambers' are, and their chief delights. For they come there, laying aside their cares now and then, to hunt, as a rest and recreation. It is there that they can put from them the anxious turmoil native to a court, and take a little breath in the free air of nature. And that is why forest offenders are punished only at the King's pleasure. . . .

> The whole organization of the forests, the punishment, pecuniary or corporal, of forest offences, is outside the jurisdiction of the other courts, and solely dependent on the decision of the King, or of some officer specially appointed by him. The forest has its own laws, based, it is said, not on the Common Law of the realm, but on the arbitrary legislation of the King; so that what is done in accordance with forest law is not called "just" without qualification, but "just, according to forest law."[18]

The organization of the royal forests reflected the special place of the forest in Henry II's government. W. L. Warren has pointed out that in Henry's administration there was a household element that always accompanied the king and what might be called a provincial element, and the forest administration was no exception. What Warren called the provincial administration consisted of the central court at Westminster presided over by the justiciar and performing its financial and judicial functions through the Exchequer, its subordinate treasury, the emerging "bench," and the itinerant justices. In the absence of the king, the justiciar was in complete control. Similarly, the forest administration consisted of the chief forester and his subordinate foresters who held the regular forest courts or attended the courts held irregularly by the justices on eyre for forest pleas. What set the forest administration apart from the other elements of royal government was that the chief forester was not responsible to the justiciar and did not account at the Exchequer.[19] All parts of the administration were subject to the king's control, but the forest administration was different in being directly responsible to the king.

An illustration of the difference of the forest administration from the other parts of the royal administration can be seen in the actions of Queen Eleanor as Richard I's agent on the death of Henry II. Freed from her own imprisonment by her husband's death, she made a royal progress through the cities of England and sent messengers to all the counties to proclaim Richard's order for the release of other prisoners. All persons in prison for forest offenses were to be freed at once and persons who had been outlawed for forest offenses were pardoned to return immediately to their homes. Other prisoners being held by order of the king or his justiciar were also to be released, but the procedure for them was much more elaborate and involved provisions that imply they were not considered directly under the authority of the king to deal with summarily in the way that prisoners for the forest were.[20]

Henry II was particularly fond of hunting, and his favorite resting places as he travelled ceaselessly around England were constructed within royal forests where he could indulge the sport amidst the cares of governing England.[21] However, it would be superficial to leave a description of his interest in the forests at that, for the records leave no doubt that he was quite aware of the advantages to be gained by a strict enforcement of the forest law. In 1166–67 Alan de Neville as chief forester carried out the first comprehensive forest eyre of the reign to the consternation of those affected and to the profit of the king.[22] In 1170 when Henry II returned to England after nearly four years on the continent, he commissioned a broad inquiry into the conduct of royal officials, usually known as the Inquest of Sheriffs. The eighth chapter of the inquiry concerned the forest with questions about the receipts from office for foresters and their subordinates, the number of pardons and forfeitures for forest offenses, and the record of forest officials in bringing alleged trespassers of forest law to justice or in releasing them without judgment.[23]

With respect to the forest law, Henry's harshest and most arbitrary actions took place in 1175 after he had put down the rebellion of his sons and their followers. The harshness with which he used the forest administration to exact the last penny contrasts with the leniency he showed his sons. The fullest account is found in the chronicle of Roger of Howden, who himself served as a justice in eyre for forest pleas, but it was Ralph Diceto, who normally took little interest in administrative details, who reflected the shock of the king's actions.[24] In June, Henry II opened his campaign at Reading when he impleaded the earls and barons for killing deer and other forest offenses, and on August 1 at Nottingham he extended the charges to include knights, villeins, and even the clergy. It was at Nottingham that the justiciar, Richard de Lucy, felt compelled to rise in protest to point out that during the rebellion he had received the king's own writ (which he now displayed) ordering the suspension of the forest laws during the rebellion. Apparently Henry had considered the suspension nothing more than a tactic when he found himself hard-pressed and the loyalty of some of his subjects wavering. Now, fully again in control, he refused to honor his previous commitment. Later in the month at York the king renewed his efforts to enforce the forest laws retroactively in all their vigor, and the payments recorded in the Pipe Rolls demonstrate the energy, if not the vindictiveness, with which he pursued that policy.

One of the side issues raised by the policy of rigorous enforcement was whether clergy should be treated the same as laymen. Ralph Diceto was incensed at the idea of clerks being arrested for hunting and then being dragged by the sheriffs before lay courts. Some of the clergy simply avoided the issue by offering money to the king to evade prosecution for forest offenses. However, Henry settled any possible complaints by coming to an agreement with the new papal legate who arrived at court in October in which the legate specifically agreed that the king had the right to implead clerks for forest offenses and, specifically, for taking venison. When Roger of Howden described the agreement, he called the legate an agent of Satan for entering into the agreement that turned over to the wolf the lambs that it was his duty to guard as a shepherd.[25] In point of fact, the agreement only put in writing the current practice, and the king explicitly acknowledged that a clerk might not be brought before a secular court except for a forest offense. The Pipe Roll of 1130 contains fines paid by clerks for forest offenses, and the rolls earlier in Henry II's reign prove that clerks had continued to answer for forest offenses long before the agreement of 1175. In spite of the difference between forest law and the common law in regard to criminous clerks, the periods of maximum attention to the enforcement of both laws coincided. Implementation of the Assize of Northampton in 1176 came at the time when Thomas fitz Bernard as the new chief forester intensified the application of forest law in another widespread eyre.

When the chronicler William of Newburgh came to sum up the reign of Henry II at his death, he compared his forest policy to that of his grandfather in many of the same words he had applied to Henry I. Because of their love of hunting, both were more zealous than just in punishing forest offenses, but Henry II was inclined to punish the offender by imprisonment or exile, whereas his grandfather had made little distinction between the crime of killing a man or killing a deer.[26] Whether the chronicler was really in a position to make a valid comparison, he presumably reflected the general opinion, and it is probably more than a stylistic form that he thought their policies on the royal forest important enough to receive emphasis in a brief evaluation of their careers.

The policy on the royal forest underwent little change with the accession of Richard I to the throne so long occupied by his father. Richard differed from his father in showing very little interest in governing and, in any event, spent less than a year in England during the decade in which he ruled. The forest administration developed by Henry II, like other aspects of the royal administration, demonstrated its strength by continuing to function with little attention from the king. The secret lay not only in the strength of institutions but also in the quality of the ministers who continued to serve the new king and who were replaced, in turn, by younger men who had apprenticed in the household of Henry II or one of his powerful officials. After the death of Alan de Neville in 1176, he had been succeeded by Thomas fitz Bernard, who was chief forester for almost a decade, and, then, in the reigns of Richard and John the chief foresters were Geoffrey fitz Peter and Hugh de Neville, a nephew of Alan.

The theme of King John's forest policy was the effort put into efficient administration in order to obtain the maximum profit from the royal forest. The fact that, unlike his father and brother, John was in England regularly after the loss of Normandy in 1204 made it possible for him to give his personal attention to the royal forest. Historians have noticed that John had an interest in administrative and judicial matters, but his recurrent need for money might well have suggested close attention to the operation of the forest whatever his personal interests. As in other matters, the complaints against King John made by the barons in 1215 about the royal forest were directed against an entire administrative system as it had developed from the time of Henry II and not just against any new policies begun by John himself.[27]

In the Pipe Rolls, changes in the method of recording fines from the forest and the numerous entries listing gifts made to the king for confirmation of forest privileges are evidence of strict attention being paid to the financial possibilities of the forest from the beginning of the new reign. In 1204 when John was in England, the number of gifts for disafforestation increased, and the king seems to have been systematically using this means of raising money. The other half of John's policy was rigid enforcement of the forest law, a policy that brought in revenue and provided incentive for more and more offers of money to avoid the rigors of the law. One of his biographers, W. L. Warren, caught the tone of John's policy nicely:

> Petty infringements were visited with heavy penalties, and when John was in urgent need of cash he would send round a commission of forest justices. It can be said in his favour that he did not extend the bounds of the forest, as his predecessors had frequently done; but perhaps he had no need to: he made a lot of money out of what there was.[28]

When in 1208 the king ordered all buildings, fences, and ditches within the borders of the forest to be removed, his action appeared especially severe because many of these had been tolerated for so long that they had been considered to exist legally.[29] In addition to the economic motivation implied by this and many of his actions, John also understood that the forest law could be applied as a tool to overcome opposition in the way his father had used it against the aristocracy in 1175. John used the forest law against the Cistercian order by applying pressure through his foresters when the Cistercians refused to grant him the money he tried to get from them. In November 1200 no fewer than twelve Cistercian abbots threw themselves at the king's feet to dramatize their complaints against the royal foresters and to plead that they and Christ's poor would be ruined if he did not order the foresters to allow them to pasture their animals in the royal forests as they had been accustomed to do. Although a reconciliation was worked out through the efforts of the archbishop of Canterbury, the incident provided an especially clear case of using the forest as an instrument to force the king's will upon reluctant subjects, because the Cistercians were suddenly deprived of rights to which they had been accustomed under John's predecessors as well as earlier in his reign.[30] On the other hand, the king's presence sometimes made it possible to control private exactions made by royal foresters acting on their own because he was no more anxious than his subjects for the foresters to abuse their offices in ways that were not to his advantage. In 1212, for example, when the foresters attempted to collect money by applying new rules, the king cancelled these exactions and compelled the chief foresters to swear that in the future they would require only as much as they were accustomed to collect in the days of Henry II.[31]

Royal policy in regard to the forest had a continuity from Henry II to the last years of John's reign with the policy established by the father, continuing under Richard I, and manipulated more carefully by John. Similarly, the definitive form was given to forest law during the reign of Henry II and, especially, by the Assize of the Forest, also known as the Assize of Woodstock, promulgated by the king in 1184. The royal forest needed attention that year because Thomas fitz Bernard, who had succeeded Alan de Neville in 1176, died in 1184 and the office of "magister forestarius et justitiarius per totam Angliam" was vacant.[32] The forests were divided into four groups for administrative purposes, and two clerks and two knights were appointed as justices of the forest for each group. The king also appointed two members of his household as keepers of the venison and vert in each of the four parts and gave them authority over all royal foresters and foresters appointed by barons or knights. Having set in motion this administrative reorganization, the king then required all the justices of the forests and the keepers appointed from the household to take an oath to keep the assizes of the forest.[33]

The provisions of forest law that were in force in 1184 were those embodied in the Assize of Woodstock. Because the royal records were not preserved systematically at this time, this assize and the other forest assizes must be studied in the form given by Roger of Howden in his chronicles. In all there are three forest assizes, and the relationship of these documents has been carefully worked out in the textual studies of Professor J. C. Holt, who described it as follows:

> The forest assizes are relatively straightforward. They are three in number: the *prima assisa*, the Assize of Woodstock, and the assize of 1198. Caps. 1–3, 5, and 6 of the Assize of Woodstock repeat the *prima assisa*, and the assize of 1198 repeats the Assize of Woodstock *in toto*. Howden is the earliest authority for the second text and the sole authority for the first and third. The three texts he preserves are independent of each other. . . . It is equally clear that the later documents cannot have been drawn directly from the earlier; each exhibits textual variants peculiar to itself.[34]

The document which Holt calls the *prima assisa* probably represents the articles of the eyre of 1166–67 or that of 1175–76, but it is only certain that Howden knew it to be earlier than 1184.

The authenticity of the Assize of Woodstock has been called in question because of the way Howden handled the assizes in his two chronicles and because of the way William Stubbs edited and published the text.[35] Part of the problem is that both the Assize of Woodstock and that of 1198 accumulated chapters in use. The flexible attitude in the twelfth century toward documents of this nature has been explained by Professor Holt:

> None of the surviving texts may be taken as 'original.' Some, like the forest records or perhaps the Inquest of Sheriffs, may originate in articles used by justices or other officials. The men of Howden's age were not working in the circumstances of the mid thirteenth century when Magna Carta provided a pattern for embodying legislation in royal charter, or even in the circumstances of John's reign when procedural assizes or changes in the law might be announced to the shire courts in letters patent. Their background was both less sophisticated and less formal. That the texts survive imperfectly is understandable.[36]

Although chapters 13 through 16 of Stubbs's text represent accretions, Holt concluded that only chapter 16 is clearly apocryphal and that the others represent genuine forest regulations, even if they were not part of the original Assize of Woodstock. From the constitutional point of view it is significant that this assize is said to have been made "with the advice and assent of the archbishops, bishops, barons, earls, and magnates of England."[37] The forest law was put forth in a manner that would have answered any doubts that Richard fitz Nigel, the author of the *Dialogue of the Exchequer*, or anyone else might have had that it was not really law because it rested solely upon the king's will.

Because the Assize of Woodstock incorporated the fundamental law of the forest as it had coalesced under Henry II, a summary of its provisions might be useful:[38]

1. Forest offenses will henceforth be punished not just by fines but by full justice as exacted by Henry I.

2. No person shall have a bow, arrows, or dogs within the royal forests.

3. No wood is to be given or sold from any woods within a royal forest, except wood may be taken for the owner's use.

4. Persons who have woods within a royal forest must name their own foresters and give security that they will commit no acts against the king.

5. Royal foresters shall have a care for the woods of knights and others within a forest.

6. All royal foresters must swear to uphold the assize of the forest.

7. In each county with a royal forest there shall be chosen twelve knights to keep the venison and vert and four knights for agisting the woods and collecting pannage.

8. A forester responsible for demesne woods of the king shall be arrested for any unexplained destruction.

9. No clerk shall transgress in hunting or by breaking other forest regulations.

10. Assarts, purprestures, and waste in the forest shall be inspected and recorded.

11. All men shall heed the summons of the chief forester to come and hear the pleas of the lord king concerning his forests.

12. For the first two forest transgressions safe pledges shall be taken, but for a third offense the person of the transgressor shall be taken.

The three additional chapters that probably represent authentic forest customs attached to the original assize provide that all men over the age of twelve shall take an oath to keep the king's peace, that dogs in the forest must have their toes clipped to prevent them running after deer, and that no tanner or bleacher of hides shall dwell in the forest outside a borough. The final chapter in Stubbs's edition is not found in any medieval document and cannot be considered earlier than the sixteenth century copy of the assize from which the editor took it.[39]

In Roger of Howden's chronicle, the Assize of Woodstock is immediately followed by another document listing the articles of the regard—the questions put to juries whenever the regard was taken about the condition of the trees and undergrowth in the forest as included in the general term "vert." In contrast to the Assize of Woodstock, the form of the regard did not become fixed (as can be determined from a number of lists of questions in the thirteenth century or as reconstructed from some of the responses in the twelfth century), but the basic concerns expressed in these questions remained the same. Howden's list has only nine articles and these deal with old assarts, new assarts since the last regard, whether the assarts were sown, purprestures, waste committed in the demesne or other woods, hayes enclosed for the king, mines, eyries, and forges.[40] By copying the Assize of Woodstock and the articles of the regard into his chronicle, Roger of Howden, who was a justice for forest pleas beginning in 1185, recorded the basic elements of the forest law as administered by forest officials and justices in eyre alike.

In 1198 in preparation for a new forest eyre, another Assize of the Forest was made that incorporated the Assize of Woodstock but that had some additional provisions. Writing about that year, Roger of Howden complained that the itinerant justices had just reduced all England from sea to sea to destitution when another kind of torment was begun by the justices of the forest to the confusion of all men. King Richard had ordered the chief forester, Hugh de Neville, along with Hugh Wac and Ernis de Neville to convene in all counties to which they went the archbishops, bishops, earls, barons, all freeholders, and the reeve and four men of each vill to hold forest pleas and hear the king's orders. Additions to the Assize of Woodstock were: the regard was to be taken every third year, free tenants and all men of the king's lands were added to those summoned previously to forest pleas, and carts were prohibited from the roads and pigs from the woods from 10 June to 8 July.[41]

The principal difference from the Assize of Woodstock was in the punishment for killing the king's deer. Although Henry II had declared his intention of administering forest justice according to the practice of his grandfather, the twelfth chapter of the Assize of Woodstock had provided for physical punishment (probably the death penalty) only for the third offence. In contrast, Richard's Assize of 1198 set the penalty for killing deer as mutilation by removal of the offender's eyes and testicles, but offenses against the vert continued to be penalized by fines. It would appear that Richard had reverted to the savage penalties that had given the forest law its evil reputation in Henry I's day. However, the interpretation of legal codes is notoriously difficult, and the long lists of fines for venison in the Pipe Rolls indicate that in practice mutilation must have been regarded as the possible maximum punishment and that fines continued to be the usual punishment as they had been in the time of Henry II. There are other indications that the assizes were mostly a codification of practice and not new legislation. How this worked may be illustrated by a passage in the *Dialogue of the Exchequer* that discussed the common rent for assarts as a perpetual rent of one shilling per acre for wheat and six pence for oats, and also mentioned that the regard was held every third year.[42] Although the context of this discussion was probably concerned with events in 1167, and the *Dialogue* was probably written about 1179, both these provisions first appear in a forest assize in Richard's Forest Assize of 1198.

Most scholars writing about English law deal only with the common law and ignore the forest law, but there necessarily has been some discussion about the relation between these two jurisdictions. The older view that areas designated forest, amounting to about one-fourth of England in the thirteenth century, were jurisdictional immunities from the common law must be discarded. The basic work to present this revision was the thesis by Mrs. Elizabeth Wright published in 1928 and the article which gave her conclusions wider circulation during the same year. From records of the thirteenth century, she was able to select places that were subject to forest law at certain dates, and then found evidence of the common law operating in those places at the same period. Her basic conclusion was:

We have found that, in ordinary course, forest pleas were heard in forest courts, and the criminal or civil pleas which originated from the same districts were heard in common law courts. We have found, for the most part, that the exceptions to the rule . . . caused little difficulty.[43]

Because there are few records of forest proceedings before the reign of Henry III, the relation between the two legal systems cannot be worked out so methodically for the twelfth century. There seems to have been some overlapping in terms of pleas being intermingled and in terms of judicial personnel hearing both forest pleas and those of the common law. Although the fines from a forest eyre are generally grouped in the entries in the Pipe Rolls under separate rubrics listing the names of the justices, the sheriffs collected forest fines along with those resulting from other judicial proceedings with no indication that there had been a forest eyre.[44] If the entries of forest fines reflect procedures accurately, justices of the forest must also on some occasions have heard cases arising from causes other than forest violations.[45] Indeed, the Pipe Rolls from the twelfth century indicate a nonspecialized and only partially differentiated procedure, where forest offenses were principally tried by special forest eyres, but not exclusively, and where justices of the forest could deal with other cases during their eyre. This somewhat remote evidence agrees with what seems to be implied in the eleventh chapter of the Assize of Woodstock of 1184 when the general summons by the chief forester was made to "hear the pleas of the lord king concerning his forests and to transact his other business in the county court.[46] There are a few cases in the early printed Curia Regis rolls of John's reign where the impingement of the two types of law was significant.[47] In spite of the theoretical differences between the two laws that Richard fitz Nigel correctly emphasized, practice in the twelfth century had not yet reached the degree of separation with two parallel jurisdictions effective in the same area that Mrs. Wright found to have been the usual practice in the thirteenth century.

Although a comparison of justices who held forest pleas with the lists of royal justices published by Lady Stenton shows that most justices of the forest did not hold other pleas and most other itinerant justices did not hold forest pleas, there was a significant degree of shared personnel for the two types of pleas.[48] During 1167, there was a pause in the enforcement of the Assize of Clarendon while the chief justice of the forests, Alan de Neville, conducted a full-scale forest eyre. In other years both Alan de Neville and his son of the same name helped enforce that assize. When another member of the family, Ernis de Neville, first appears in the records as a justice in 1185, he served with a panel of common law justices headed by Rannulf de Glanvil, and in the same year he acted also as a justice holding forest pleas. However, Hugh de Neville, who continued the family tradition as chief forester and justice of the forests during the reign of King John, does not seem to have been a justice in other cases. After the death of Alan de Neville, Thomas fitz Bernard was chief forester, and in 1178 he also served as an itinerant justice until he became justiciar at the beginning of John's reign and no longer held forest pleas. Of the total of forty-four justices for forest pleas identifiable by name during the Angevin period, at least nineteen also served as common law justices. These include the chronicler Roger of Howden, who began as a forest justice in 1185 and was a justice for forest pleas in the first year of King Richard for the northern counties of Cumberland, Northumberland, and York. At least eleven justices seem to have been administering both kinds of law at the same time, but this kind of duplication ceased early in the reign of Richard I with the exception of Geoffrey fitz Peter, who continued to hold both kinds of pleas until he changed his office of chief forester for that of justiciar in 1198. Slightly more justices started in the common law (nine) and moved over to forest law than the five whose experience in forest law led them into the common law.[49] The flexibility exhibited by the justices is a good deal greater than might be anticipated from the dichotomy between the forest law and the common law described by Richard fitz Nigel or implied in the complaints about the forest law by the chroniclers. Whatever may have been the legal theory, the historian needs to test any hypothesis about the forest jurisdiction against the evidence of how the forest administration used the forest law in practice.

3

The Angevin System at Work

Because there are no forest records for most of this period, the efforts of justices for forest pleas to enforce the forest law as laid down by the assizes of Henry II and Richard I can only be studied indirectly. To be sure, there is considerable information about royal forests in the Pipe Rolls, but the clerks responsible for these records were primarily interested in getting down the sums that made up royal revenue, and their interests in the forest assizes extended only to whatever revenues were produced. Nevertheless, except for a few general statements by chroniclers and the remnants of a handful of forest rolls dating from the reign of King John, the system of administering the forest in the Angevin period has to be reconstructed from these rather unpromising materials.

For the first seven years of Henry II's reign there are only a few entries in the Pipe Rolls with any relation to the royal forest, but, at the minimum, these do show that the sheriff was responsible for collecting the small amounts that came from forest pleas. In practice, the amounts were reduced even further by the freedom with which the king granted pardons for forest offenses. For example, in 1160 the sheriff of Wiltshire accounted for £24 in forest pleas, and the actual payment was cut to £8 because royal pardons had been granted for offenses that carried amercements amounting to £15. Those pardoned included an earl, a bishop, several monks and nuns, and a number of other laymen whose names are given.[1] The only significant pattern in forest entries before the first forest eyre is that the sheriffs in ten counties in the north and central parts of the country in 1162 began claiming allowances for waste.[2] These figures point to neglect and a fairly widespread flouting of the forest law, perhaps going back even further than Henry's reign. In any event, a forest eyre would have been the most effective means of investigating and correcting the situation, and the amounts listed for waste in the forest may provide a hint as to why Henry II did commission his first general forest eyre in 1166. Of course, that forest eyre was only a part of a general policy of improving the efficiency of law enforcement, as exemplified also in the Assize of Clarendon and the first general eyre of Henry II's reign that was being arranged at the same time as the forest eyre, but this independent evidence indicates that the royal forests needed urgent attention.

Only a few of the amercements for forest pleas had been completed in time for the September accounting at the Exchequer in 1166, but the Pipe Roll of the following year is filled with entries resulting from the work of Alan de Neville and his fellow justices of the forest. He appears to have continued his activities for at least two more years, and payments resulting from this eyre continued to be paid in installments over a period of four years. In 1167 there was a pause in the enforcement of the Assize of Clarendon while the forest eyre was being carried out by the justices.[3] From entries in the Pipe Rolls a pattern emerges that shows that Alan was enforcing all the provisions of Roger of Howden's *Prima Assisa* plus some chapters of the regard as they were listed by Howden under the year 1184.[4] After a brief introduction, there were only five provisions in the *Prima Assisa*:

1. No person shall transgress against the king's hunting rights in his forest.
2. Bows or arrows and hunting dogs are prohibited in the forest.
3. No person shall cause waste by giving or selling anything beyond his own needs from his own woods that lie within the forest.
4. Royal foresters shall have responsibility for the forest of knights and others who have woods within the royal forest.
5. Royal foresters shall swear to maintain the assize.

Although the manner in which Howden handled the *Prima Assisa* in his two works only indicates that he knew it to be earlier than 1184, the entries in the Pipe Rolls confirm that its provisions were at least as early as the eyre of 1166–67.[5] In addition to placing the assize and eyre together, the Pipe Rolls contain a few hints about the procedure being followed in the forest courts.

One of the problems with the available evidence is that sometimes the revenue from forest pleas is simply listed as a total without any breakdown as to the violations that occasioned the penalties. In fact, there are very few entries listed separately for violations in hunting the king's deer; the clerks list only trespass against the vert in most entries in which the offenses are specified. In considering all the entries that are itemized, it appears that poaching the king's deer did not occupy the first place that might have been expected. Because it seems unlikely that most violations against the venison are concealed in the combined totals where they cannot be identified, the conclusion must be that hunting offenses were relatively less important in the twelfth century than those offenses involving use of forest land for purposes prohibited by the assize of the forest.

Among the offenses against the venison that are listed there are two examples of technical violations of the forest law. One man brought a dead hart to Clarendon without first having obtained a witness that it was dead when he found it, and another man gave a hart to the infirm without having first obtained a royal warrant to do so. Neither man seems to have attempted to make a profit from the deer, but both had to pay for their failure to follow the letter of the forest law.[6] A curious case resulting from the ban of bows and arrows in the forest was one in which a clerk was amerced forty marks for attempting to steal a bow from some of the royal foresters.[7] Even during the forest eyre, full or partial pardons continued to play a part in reducing the actual sums collected from the increased effort to enforce the forest law.[8]

The most prevalent offense listed against the vert was that of waste, best described in its technical sense in the graphic manner of Richard fitz Nigel:

> But if woods are so severely cut that a man, standing on the half-buried stump of an oak or other tree, can see five other trees cut down round about him, that is regarded as 'waste,' which is short for 'wasted.' Such an offence, even in a man's own woods, is considered so serious, that he can in no way be quit of it by his session at the Exchequer, but must all the more suffer a money penalty proportionate to his means.[9]

Other references to shiploads of timber being taken from royal forests without authorization may help to explain the temptation for owners of woods within the forest to sell timber even at the risk of being amerced for having committed waste.[10] The demands of agriculture might also put pressure on owners to turn their lands within the forest to greater profit by bringing them under cultivation, and amercements for assarts confirm that lands were being brought under cultivation without license from the king in spite of the forest law.[11] Other encroachments upon the forest brought penalties for building houses and mills and for developing a salt pan.[12] Possibly some sort of mining was involved in the digging within the forest that was recorded in Devon.[13] Various other chapters of the regard are reflected in assessments made for farm animals straying into the forest, the sale of bark, payments for pannage, and small sums reported for honey found in the forest.[14]

Only a hazy reconstruction of the procedure followed by Alan de Neville during the eyre of 1166–67 is possible. The problem is how to work backward from the last stage of the procedure—payment for forest pleas as made by the sheriff at the Exchequer—to a picture of the earlier stages. There is evidence that there were written records of this forest eyre, even though none have survived from this or any other eyres earlier than the reign of King John, and that the sheriff had a record of the proceedings in his county or an extract of the amercements of the eyre that he should collect. In one instance, because the itemized record given by Alan de Neville to the sheriff was too long to be fitted into the space left on the Pipe Roll, the barons of the Exchequer allowed parts of it to be grouped into one total in the Pipe Roll entry. It was also noted that the sheriff had delivered Alan's list to the Treasury where the individual amercements could be found if needed.[15] There is no indication whether the list would have been delivered to the Treasury if all items could have been transcribed into the Pipe Roll.

In forest proceedings, alleged violators were presented to the justices by witnesses who had seen the violations, and the brief entries do not tell whether the witnesses were royal foresters acting in an official capacity or ordinary people who happened to be present when the crime was committed.[16] In addition, there are amercements for false presentations that may point to a presentation jury, but the entries are inconclusive.[17] Another payment for retracting an accusation of having seen the alleged violator kill a deer certainly had an ordinary person making the accusation.[18] A preliminary stage before the coming of the justices of the forest is implied in the penalty of two marks for a man who had been surety for a violator of forest law and yet failed to produce him before the justices as he had pledged to do.[19] Because local forest courts are clearly documented in the thirteenth century, there would be nothing surprising if they were in use earlier, as this entry implies.

The evidence for local forest courts is confirmed in other entries referring to men accused of forest violations who fled rather than appear in the local forest courts and had their chattels confiscated and placed in the hands of local men who would account for them when the justices for forest pleas next visited the county.[20] In another instance, the sheriff himself pledged one mark for the stray farm animals that had been found within the forest and had been surrendered to his care.[21] When some men accused before the local forest court could not obtain reputable men to stand as surety for their appearance before the justices, they were kept as prisoners.[22] One entry deals with an approver who received payment until he could fulfill his task of accusing his fellows in crime.[23]

Once the accused had been brought before the justices, the ordeal by water was a method of proof used according to the macabre evidence listing the chattels of men who had perished during the ordeal.[24] This method of proof is consistent with the new emphasis upon the ordeal by water in common law cases after the Assize of Clarendon in 1166 where it became the prescribed method for all persons indicted by juries of presentment and was substituted for the use of oath-helpers or the ordeal by hot iron.[25] Although the ordeal by water had earlier been reserved for serfs, its use in forest law at this time shows the concurrence of the two legal systems. Further, just as in the common law, trial by combat could also be used in forest law as a method of proof for those men of higher social class.[26]

For some men, once they had been found guilty, the penalties continued to be pardoned by the king in whole or in part. One particularly interesting pardon from the eyre of 1166–67 was in favor of the bishop of Salisbury for £72 7s. for killing a roebuck. The pardon had been granted by the justiciar, Richard de Luci, on the basis of a writ from King Henry II, who was absent on the continent.[27] The interest of this pardon lies mainly in that it establishes the practice of pardoning by the justiciar that became an issue between the justiciar and the king in the next forest eyre held in 1175 after the rebellion of Henry's sons and their supporters had been put down by the king.

The record of the forest eyre of 1175 as it is spread over the Pipe Rolls provides dramatic emphasis to the possibility of using strict enforcement of the forest law to raise money. Henry simply brushed aside the objections of Richard de Luci, who protested that as justiciar he had suspended the enforcement of forest regulations on instructions from the king himself.[28] It is no wonder that the chroniclers interpreted the reversal of this policy in 1175 as arbitrary and unjust when the eyre was ordered to apply to offenses committed since the last eyre. Whether his motivation was simply to reassert royal authority or, perhaps, a real need for money, it is clear that in commissioning a forest eyre Henry II made no attempt to seek popularity once he felt himself firmly in control again. In fact, the amercements from the eyre were usually high and ranged as high as five hundred marks.[29] Because his chief supporters in the late rebellion as well as his enemies were penalized, the forest eyre cannot be interpreted as a means of punishing those who had proved disloyal.[30]

The Pipe Roll is burdened with sums produced from both a common law eyre and one for forest pleas. Adding all the sums certainly attributable to forest offenses gives a total of £12,345, which was a very large amount to come from this one source. This amount can be compared to the total annual revenue of approximately £21,000 entered in the Pipe Roll seven years earlier when there was no judicial activity or to the total theoretical value of the sheriffs' farms before any deductions of about £10,000 during Henry II's reign.[31] Another sign that the penalties were unusually heavy is that for most of the larger amounts only half was paid the first year, and considerable unpaid balances from this eyre continue in the Pipe Rolls for the next four years. The justices—Alan de Neville, Robert Mantell, and William fitz Ralph— worked hard the first year, but several counties remained to be visited the following year in order to complete the job. One entry that may help to explain some of the large sums is, "Geoffrey Ridel accounts for three hundred marks of amercement for the forest and because the lord king relaxes his wrath toward him."[32] How much of the amercement should be credited to the offense against the forest and how much to return to the king's good graces is anybody's guess.

To the unpaid balances from the eyre of 1175 were added new amercements from another forest eyre in 1179. The justices were led by Thomas fitz Bernard, who had succeeded Alan de Neville as chief forester the previous year. In all he visited twenty-five counties and perhaps set a precedent for an incoming chief forester to begin his term with a forest eyre, since his successor Geoffrey fitz Peter in 1185 visited sixteen fewer counties on eyre. Unlike Geoffrey fitz Peter, who later rose to become justiciar in 1198, Thomas fitz Bernard was never heavily involved in enforcing the common law, but he did serve on one common law eyre in 1183 in which he visited twelve counties, including Leicestershire where he administered both the common law and forest law that year. Whether a comprehensive eyre had become a precedent at the beginning of each new chief forester's term is obscured by the circumstances in 1198 when Hugh de Neville succeeded to that office. Geoffrey, accompanied by Hugh, had already begun the enforcement of the Assize of 1198 when the change in office took place, and Hugh merely continued the eyre along with other justices in the remaining counties where there were forests. In addition, he returned to five counties which he had previously visited with Geoffrey. The only general forest eyre during the reign of King John was in 1212, and the amount of amercements collected probably indicates that the justices were particularly diligent in an attempt to raise money from that source.

The sums raised from forest eyres (Table 2) vary a great deal, but the exceptionally large amount from the eyre of 1175 confirms the complaints about the severity of Henry II's demands on that occasion.

Table 2
Revenue from Forest Eyres

1166	Pipe Rolls 12-13 Henry II: "Prima Assisa" Alan de Neville, Chief Forester	£502
1175	Pipe Rolls 22-23 Henry II Alan de Neville, Chief Forester	£12,305
1179	Pipe Roll 26 Henry II Thomas fitz Bernard, Chief Forester	£1007
1185	Pipe Roll 31 Henry II: Assize of Woodstock Geoffrey fitz Peter, Chief Forester	£2403
1198	Pipe Roll 10 Richard I–1 John: Assize of 1198 Geoffrey fitz Peter and Hugh de Neville, Chief Foresters	£1980
1212	Pipe Roll 14 John Hugh de Neville, Chief Forester	£4486

When the revenue from the eyre of 1212 is compared to the earlier eyres, that eyre of King John stands out as exceptionally severe except for the eyre of 1175. The oppressive effect of the eyre was greater than the totals show because extensive disafforestment had taken place under Richard and John before 1212, and the £4486 came from amercements based upon a substantially reduced area under forest law in comparison with the eyres of 1185 and earlier. Even so, John was less oppressive than Henry II had been in 1175 when he personally and deliberately used the forest law to assert his authority and raise money.

The actual revenues collected from the various forest eyres were somewhat less than the totals recorded because of the persistent problem of collecting the money. A note added to a long list of amercements in 1181 illustrates the problem: "Of the amounts above nothing could be had this year nor for many previous years because some are dead, some are fugitives, and some have nothing."[33] Two years later the clerks who made up the Pipe Roll began to refer to the amounts levied sixteen years earlier by Alan de Neville as the "old" wastes and pleas to distinguish them from returns from subsequent eyres.[34] The most frequent reason given for failure to collect the amounts set by the forest justices was the poverty of those who should have paid them. In 1189 the sheriff of Wiltshire continued to account for five shillings eight pence in pleas held by Alan de Neville, but by that time he did not know what particular amercements were included.[35] The last reference I noted to one of Alan's amercements was in 1199, some thirty-one years and two reigns after Henry II's hated chief forester had visited Essex as head of a forest eyre.[36] Whether the burgesses of Colchester ever paid the fine of ten pounds they made for postponing the pleas of Thomas fitz Bernard in 1179 is not recorded, but that debt continues in the Pipe Rolls through 1199, and a note in the Memoranda Roll of that year may indicate that the barons of the Exchequer intended to discuss the debt or, as it seems, cancelled it.[37]

The usual proliferation of entries in the Pipe Roll of 1185 for new pleas of the forest signals a new forest eyre, and this eyre has exceptional interest because it was based on the Assize of Woodstock. Geoffrey fitz Peter led the panel of justices in eight counties in a year of exceptional judicial activity for him when he also served as an itinerant justice administering the common law in nine other counties. Forest pleas were also heard by three other panels of justices. Because of the intermingling of entries in the Pipe Roll, there is some question whether certain items ought to be assigned to forest pleas, but, omitting all doubtful items, the total revenue from this eyre was £2403. When amounts owing from the earlier eyres are considered, the Pipe Roll records a substantial amount of revenue attributable to the enforcement of forest law.

Although the Assize of Woodstock contained more than double the chapters of Henry II's *Prima Assisa,* which had probably been the basis for eyres since that of 1166–67, there is no doubt that the additional chapters were being enforced. At least four of the new chapters are specific enough that any penalties for violations should be identifiable if they were being applied. In this group is chapter seven, and the income of £4 17s. 1d. for pannage in Cannock Forest from Staffordshire provides the verification.[38] Chapter nine prohibiting clergy from transgressing in the forest made more specific the previous practice and brought an amercement of twenty marks for the bishop of Chichester for hunting in the king's woods without license. Even more explicitly, the bishop and prior of Winchester were amerced one hundred shillings for "transgression of the assize."[39] Although they are specified as penalties for forest offenses, these amercements of the clergy are often listed separately from the regular forest pleas. Amercements for assarts, purprestures, and waste in the forest were not new with the Assize of Woodstock, but they are more carefully listed as separate items in accordance with the provision in chapter ten that amounts for these transgressions should be kept separately. One township failed in the compulsory attendance for forest pleas enjoined by chapter eleven and paid the sum of one hundred shillings for the omission.[40]

Chapter fourteen, which has been shown to be an addition to the Assize as promulgated at Woodstock, deals with dogs and required that they have the toes on the forefeet clipped in order to cripple them from chasing deer, a practice generally called the "lawing" of dogs. As might be expected, there are penalties for having unlawed dogs within the forest, but this was nothing new because of the general prohibition of dogs in the forest in chapter two of the *Prima Assisa,* which was copied in the Assize of Woodstock.[41] Probably chapter fourteen was added sometime after the Assize of Woodstock with the intent of clarifying the general prohibition, but entries for unlawed dogs in the Pipe Roll cannot be used to prove that the chapter was added almost immediately because the more general prohibition in the earlier chapter could have been sufficient justification for the entries. No examples were found to illustrate chapter fifteen concerning tanners in the forest, and, presumably, that chapter had not yet been added, but an amercement for stripping bark from oaks may point to the activities of tanners.[42] Penalties assessed for the discovery of a cache of sharpened palings, possibly intended for an unauthorized park, and other penalties for a park might illustrate the provision of chapter sixteen not otherwise known in a medieval document, but the violations could equally well come under some more general provision for the protection of the vert.[43] The evidence on this point is certainly too ambiguous to go against the evidence of the manuscript texts and conclude that the chapter antedates the sixteenth-century copy from which the original editor of the Assize of Woodstock took it.

Business having to do with the Assize of Woodstock takes up a large amount of space on the Pipe Roll, hardly needing the confirmation of explicit references to amercements "for transgression of the assize" to show the influence of the forest eyre during the year. Especially noticeable are the large number of fugitives from forest law and the penalties for sureties who had not been able to produce the defendants for whom they had pledged before the forest justices. Of course, the nature of the record would preclude direct evidence as to whether Henry II's justices revived the severity of death or mutilation for forest offenses as expressed in the first chapter. However, to become a fugitive meant that a man feared the severity of the forest law more than the loss of property he incurred by fleeing justice. Perhaps the two men in a case where venison had been found in their homes had been executed for their crimes, but the interest of the Exchequer was only in the value of their chattels which were confiscated and sold.[44] Chattels of men outlawed for the forest and of a man who killed deer and then fled to a church for sanctuary were also sold and duly reported.[45] Even the men who held a prisoner accused of forest offenses were amerced when they failed to prevent his escape to sanctuary.[46] Among the fugitives, some had second thoughts and payments of five marks and of ten marks represent their efforts to return to the county which they had fled.[47] A payment of ten marks to postpone the amercements of the last regard until Easter fixes the relationship of the regard carried out before the coming of the justices to the forest eyre.[48]

The most noteworthy new trend during the reigns of Richard and John was the great increase in payments offered the king for partial or full exemption from the forest. For an example of this kind of entry, the abbot of Dore in Hereford offered the unusually large sum of £333 6s. 8d. in 1199 to obtain exemptions from King John as a repetition of an offer he had made but not paid to King Richard before the latter's death.[49] What the abbot sought was a charter with the right to bring the three hundred acres in woods that he held within a royal forest under cultivation without being liable at the regard to the penalty for committing waste and without owing any secular service for it.

Occasional entries in these reigns illustrate an administrative principle or a feature of forest administration known fully only from the forest proceedings of the thirteenth century. For example, it is clear from the Pipe Rolls that officials were fined for neglect of duty: a forester for guarding the forest badly, three parkers for the same neglect of their parks, five foresters for improperly caring for the deer, the regarders of Pickering Forest for some unspecified fault, and a forester for making the attachments of offenders carelessly.[50] The problem of enforcing attendance before the justices had many variations, several of them having implications for the responsibilities enjoined by forest law. The earl of Clare was fined one hundred marks because he did not have present before the justices his men accused of forest offenses for whom he had pledged, and another lord had failed in his responsibility of producing his private forester who had been indicted for an offense against the royal forest.[51] One man was amerced three shillings four pence when he failed to attend the county court for the purpose of electing the four verderers.[52] In other instances, men exceeded their authority in releasing an accused offender against the forest from his pledge and in releasing prisoners held for forest offenses from prison without license to do so.[53] It cost another man a penalty of three shillings four pence when he unjustly harassed the jurors, who presumably did not return a favorable verdict in his case.[54] Even without a formal indictment, two other men paid sums of five and ten marks because they were suspected of having killed deer.[55]

The earliest surviving forest roll for 1208–9 supplements the Pipe Rolls on the proceedings before the justices hearing forest pleas with some background information on defaults that led to penalties: William son of Simon of Barton arrested for false accusation, failure to produce hunting dogs that had been taken while chasing a hart for later presentation before the justices in a case against the owner, and failure to produce the price of two horses seized from their owner in payment of a forest offense.[56] Several tithings were amerced because a man from the tithing had fled from justice. In addition, the practice was to seize the property of the fugitives and then outlaw them.[57] Money could also be used to avoid an inquiry, as exemplified when a man paid a fine of twenty shillings in preference to allowing an inquest into whether he had bought the fresh skin of a buck which he had been caught carrying as he alleged or whether he had killed a deer.[58]

Many of the payments in the Pipe Rolls resulted from the efforts of individuals to avoid the shortcomings of the ordinary operation of the forest courts. In the thirteenth century, defendants who were not able to obtain men who would pledge surety for their appearance before the justices of the forest were kept in prison until the coming of the justices, who set an amercement as the condition for release or waived it in case of poverty This procedure probably explains the payment of £23 1s. 4d. entered as paid to get release from a royal prison where the man was being held for forest offenses.[59] Another man, without leaving the church where he was in sanctuary, paid five marks for the privilege of taking an oath to clear himself of the charge of killing a deer.[60] There was apparently a problem of delay in the ordinary process of the courts, and some payments were made in an attempt to speed up the process. Several men were willing to pay twenty marks to get an inquest jury to settle the question of forest offenses with which they had been charged.[61] In another case, Ralph de Andevill offered ten marks to have his case tried before the king or his chief forester for the alleged offense on which he had been arrested.[62] Carrying the practice of offering money in order to speed up forest justice one step further, Peter fitz William offered sixty marks and one palfrey for having the good will of the king and to be quit of an alleged violation of forest law.[63]

Records of the proceedings of the justices for forest pleas continued to be kept by the chief justice of the panel as his own property, and this practice made the records subject to the circumstances affecting the justice involved and possible loss upon the retirement or death of the justice. Rather more unusual circumstances lie behind the payment of two marks by Hugh de Loges for the records of Robert del Broc concerning the forest which were left by him (presumably at his death) and which Hugh said had been taken by Peter del Broc with him when he entered a monastery.[64]

The effect of the many exemptions from the forest law granted by the Angevin kings was a softening of the burden of the royal forest system for certain favored groups or individuals who were able to obtain these exemptions. Under forest law the clergy were treated no differently from laymen, and clergy of various types are found listed in the Pipe Rolls as owing amercements for all kinds of violations of the forest. If the Third Lateran Council in 1179 had been somewhat more successful in changing the habits of some of the clergy, the number of violations for hunting would have at least been reduced, for the council included a prohibition on prelates taking hunting dogs and birds with them on visitation in an attempt to limit various excesses during episcopal visitations.[65] More important from the standpoint of reducing the number of clergy who might run afoul of the forest law was the special treatment given them by the king. Monasteries that were established in the midst of a royal forest needed special exemption if they were to function. When Henry II issued a charter granting land to the abbey of Flaxley within the Forest of the Dean, the monks were also given pasture for their animals, timber for their houses, a tithe of chestnuts in Dean, a grange at Westdean, a forge to make iron, and half of a particular royal woods within the forest.[66] Most monastic charters for houses established within a royal forest contain exemptions that allowed land to be brought under cultivation, flocks to be kept, and products of the woods to be used as specified in similar exemptions.[67] Another privilege was the right of warren allowing the monks and their men to hunt animals other than deer, and this privilege was frequently granted to monasteries. King Richard in his charter to Abingdon Abbey added the right to hunt the roe deer, while reserving the right to hunt other types of deer except by his license.[68]

In addition to the specific exemptions granted in the various monastic charters, many charters placed restrictions upon royal foresters and other ministers of the forest in operating on the manors belonging to the monasteries and these restrictions meant that the intangible burden of forest law and the opportunities for harassment by royal foresters were thereby decreased. The abbot of Ramsey was willing to give

Richard I one hundred marks for a charter that conceded free use of the abbey's own woods and the prohibition of royal foresters from raising any questions about the use of those woods. He apparently felt these privileges worth the money even though the charter explicitly reserved royal rights over the venison and in preventing waste in the woods as determined by the regard held every third year.[69] In a general confirmation of privileges to the bishop of London, King John specified that the bishop might have view of frankpledge in his own court, that various amercements including some from the forest might go to the bishop, that his woods could be used however he pleased without interference from royal foresters, and that his lands were exempt from pannage and various other dues.[70] Another way of getting exemption from the forest law was to seek exemption from the regard as the monks of Bristol succeeded in doing in their charter from Henry II.[71]

In addition to charters of exemption, the clergy were also sometimes favored by the king's granting a tithe of venison taken in the royal forests either to monasteries or to bishops.[72] Richard fitz Nigel repeated an explanation he had heard for another kind of tithe based on the rents for a woods or forest, as a means of atoning for forest revenue that arose from pleas or imposts that might be considered unlawful because of the arbitrary nature of forest law.[73]

Although charters containing exemptions from forest law had the effect of modifying the forest law, a more radical modification occurred when influential lay or spiritual lords were allowed to take land from a royal forest and make it into a park.[74] As far as being available for hunting, the establishment of a park produced a radical change, but the responsibilities of protecting the venison within the park and the vert that sustained the deer continued. The owner of a park was required to appoint parkers or other officials to keep the park and to keep its fences in repair in order that deer could not wander into the park from the surrounding royal forest. Of course, the king himself also had enclosed areas or parks within some forests for the easier management and hunting of the deer.[75] Before a lord could establish a park he needed a license from the king, and payments for this purpose did not seem to have been standardized. For example, the abbot of Coggeshall paid forty marks to King John for this privilege, whereas Roger de Torpel had paid one hundred shillings for making a park in the previous reign.[76] Of course, the failure to obtain a royal license could cause trouble, as exemplified three years later when a woman paid one hundred marks to regain seisin of her lands that had been confiscated because she had made an unauthorized ditch.[77] Licenses were also granted to enclose lands in order to protect crops, presumably from domestic animals, because the enclosing ditch and hedge had to be constructed in a way that would still allow the king's deer to enter and leave freely.[78]

Sometimes a king granted the right of a chace (or chase) to one of the lords, and this kind of grant differed from a park in transferring the forest regulations into the hands of a private individual.[79] King John's charter to the earl of Leicester allowed him to take venison in the woods previously granted to him and provided that the woods would be free of any penalty for waste or supervision at the regard.[80] Unfortunately, the right of chace, which essentially established a private forest, was not always described in consistent terminology, and there is considerable confusion even in the records as to whether a given area should be called a chace or a forest or even a park. As Margaret Bazeley pointed out, the terminology made little difference to the ordinary Englishman because the restrictions were approximately the same as far as he was concerned, whatever the correct legal status and whoever had prime responsibility for enforcing these restrictions.[81] It also appears that the meaning of a chace in terms of the special jurisdiction conferred changed over the years, and it would be hazardous to assume what the term may have meant in detail in the twelfth century beyond the meager information supplied by the grants themselves.

The grant of free warren on the demesne lands of a manorial lord, which gave that lord control over the hunting of animals not considered beasts of the forest, had no necessary connection with the royal forest. In fact, most grants of warren specified that the grant applied only to lands outside a royal forest, but grants of warren do imply a general recognition of the right to hunt freely except where restrictions had been imposed by the warren.[82] An exceptional case where a warren existed within the royal forest may explain three examples of men taking hares within a warren that were reported during the forest eyre in Shropshire in 1209.[83]

The right of common by which domestic animals could be pastured within a royal forest was another exemption from the rigor of forest law. In the Forest of the Dean, the earliest record referring to the right of common is the charter of Henry II, which he gave to the monks of Flaxley Abbey early in his reign, but neither the charter nor other references in the twelfth or thirteenth centuries explain fully what the right of common meant at the time.[84] Yet this was a valuable privilege for which the men of Mannesfeld were willing to pay King John fifteen marks in order that they could continue to have common in

Clipston Park as they had been accustomed to have it in his father's reign before the construction of the park.[85]

Privileges and exemptions granted either to groups or to individuals modified the royal forest in its legal and administrative sense but, with the exception of the establishment of a park, meant no observable physical change in the forest. Development of assarts in the forest with the introduction of cultivation was a different matter. There is sufficient evidence to prove that even in the twelfth century the kings followed a practice of accepting and approving assarts made in the forests by which lands were put under cultivation. Richard fitz Nigel casually mentioned the penalty for making an assart—the perpetual rent of one shilling per acre sown with wheat and six pence for oats—in a manner that indicates a long-established policy.[86] Another principle of forest law allowed the barons of the Exchequer *ex officio* exemption from these rents for any assarts they had made before the death of Henry I. This principle became an issue during the forest eyre of Alan de Neville in 1167 when the justiciar, the earl of Leicester, decided to protect himself from having to make any payments for assarts by obtaining a special charter from the king. However, the other barons of the Exchequer objected to this on the ground that his special exemption in the charter might be construed to imply that the customary exemption for all the barons was not valid. The earl accepted this reasoning and withdrew his request for the charter.[87]

The practice of granting similar charters to other men not enjoying the special status of a baron of the Exchequer was common, with numerous examples of provisions that particular assarts are to be free from the customary rents, not to be listed among the assarts for which the sheriff must account, and exempt from penalty for waste of wood and from the regard.[88] Some of these charters are licenses that permit the recipient to make an assart from his lands as specified and exempt from all penalties of the forest, and these licenses could be obtained by payments to the king.[89] Nevertheless, most assarts meant a perpetual rent, and the few surviving records of the regard from the reign of King John have figures that show they were then being assessed at a rent double that mentioned by Richard fitz Nigel. One of these records lists a total of 384 acres as having been assarted in Pickering Forest in Yorkshire.[90]

The substantial sums paid to obtain exemptions from the forest law provides indirect evidence of the burden that the royal forest placed upon anyone who held land there. When Richard fitz Nigel wrote that the justiciar sought his charter exempting his lands from the regard because he wanted "to escape the very pressing demands (unknown to the King) of Alan and his gang," it was an indication of the fear and hatred caused by the chief forester and his eyre even for the greatest lords and high officials, as well as for the ordinary man in Angevin England.[91] Because of his responsibility for heading an eyre proposing to restore the king's forest rights that may have slipped from his hands during Stephen's reign, Alan de Neville would have almost inevitably been unpopular, but he seems to have provoked stronger feelings than any of his successors. The chronicler of Battle Abbey wrote with special venom:

And since he feared neither God nor man, he spared no men of rank whether ecclesiastics or laymen. . . . This Alan so long as he lived enriched the royal treasury, and to please an earthly king did not fear to offend the king of Heaven. But how much gratitude he earned from the king whom he strove to please, the sequel showed. For when he was brought to his last, the brethren of a certain monastery, hoping, it seems, to secure something of his substance for their house, besought the king to allow them to carry away his body to their burial place. Whereupon, the king revealed his sentiments towards him in these terms. "I", he said, "will have his wealth, you shall have the corpse, and the demons of hell his soul."[92]

Although he was himself a member of King Henry II's court, Walter Map extended his low opinion of foresters beyond Alan de Neville and condemned them all as "hunters of men" characterized by their harshness. He related an incident in which Hugh, then prior of Selwood and later bishop of Lincoln, made an unflattering pun on the word foresters when he met some of them outside the king's tent to the effect that they would also be kept outside of heaven because of their ways. When the king, who had overheard the remark, appeared at the door of his tent, the fearless saint went on to warn the king that he would also be kept outside with the foresters while the poor whom they oppress would enter the gates of heaven if he did not control his foresters. However, Map relates that the king did not take the comment seriously or curb the foresters, and the courtier lamented "no, even now, after his death, they eat the flesh of men in the presence of Leviathan, and drink their blood. They set up high places, which will not be taken away unless the Lord destroy them with a strong hand. They fear and propitiate their lord who is visibly present; God, whom they see not, they fear not to offend."[93]

Both the chronicler of Battle Abbey and Walter Map stressed the loyalty of the foresters to Henry II, and their actions were fully supported by the king. The oppressive enforcement of the forest law in 1175, even though the king had himself earlier authorized a moratorium on enforcement during the revolt of his sons, was a policy that was personally endorsed by the king in the face of resistance among his counsellors and opposition by the justiciar. Another incident that happened at the same time is interrelated with his decision to authorize a rigorous forest eyre and also illustrates the direct support the king was prepared to give his agents the foresters. In the July council at Woodstock, four knights in chains were brought before the king charged with killing Gilbert the forester and his companions. The king ordered the four put in prison, and then the court moved on to Nottingham. At Lichfield, on the way to Nottingham, he heard of the bad reputation of the four knights and changed his previous order to decree that they and all their associates in the crime be hanged at once. Arriving at Nottingham on the first of August, the king was consistent when he overruled the protests of Richard de Luci, the justiciar, and ordered a new forest eyre.[94]

This eyre in 1175 was headed by Alan de Neville, who had been the principal official in administering the royal forest since 1166. The title for this position as chief forester might also be translated as "master" forester from the form used in the Assize of Woodstock (*magister forestarius*) or the chronicler Roger of Howden (*magister forestarius et justitiarius per totam Angliam*).[95] Alan de Neville was succeeded in this office by Thomas fitz Bernard and Geoffrey fitz Peter. When the latter became justiciar in 1198, Hugh de Neville, a nephew of the infamous Alan, became chief forester and remained in that position during most of the reign of King John. The influence that came with the office was emphasized by Professor Sidney Painter: "The central government of England was headed by four non-hereditary active officials: the justiciar, the chancellor, the treasurer, and the chief forester."[96] The Assize of Woodstock in 1185 provided that in each county where there was a royal forest twelve knights were to be chosen to guard the king's venison and vert, and these officials were later referred to as regarders. The Assize also provided for four other knights in each county with the responsibility of arranging the pasturing of the king's woods and collecting the pannage paid for this privilege. There is sufficient evidence to show that each royal forest was headed by a forester, but the Assize only refers to these foresters rather indirectly and in general terms. Their subordinates within each forest are even more elusive, but scattered references are made to foresters and other officials among those called "ministers" in the royal forests. In addition to the various types of royal officials who administered the royal forest, the owners of land within the royal forest that was exempt from the forest administration were required to have their private foresters or woodwards, but these officials would rarely find their way into the type of royal records available for the twelfth century.[97] Still, when the archbishopric of York was vacant and in royal hands, allowances were listed in the Pipe Rolls for the payments made to private foresters of the archbishop.[98] Amercements for failure to produce the parker to answer for his custody of a park within the royal forest are reminders that the exemptions granted to private persons carried with them the responsibility of maintaining the park in a state that would not adversely affect the royal forest.[99]

The chief forester was obviously a very powerful official with authority over all the other foresters and officials who made up the forest administration, and his authority extended as widely throughout England as there were forests. Professor Sidney Painter, who wrote the standard book on the government of King John, made the interesting observation that "A strong argument could be advanced for the thesis that the royal official who wielded the most actual power during John's reign was the chief forester, Hugh de Neville."[100] Hugh had been on the Third Crusade with Richard before being named as chief forester, and he was one of those officials who continued in office after the death of Richard to become one of King John's close companions.[101] He held forest courts, operated the administrative system, and collected all the revenues from the forests into his special exchequer at Marlborough Castle for which he accounted directly to the king and not to the royal Exchequer.[102] When the king was in Normandy in 1203, de Neville sent large sums from the English forests to meet the needs of the king on several occasions, including one shipment amounting to forty thousand marks. A year or two earlier he had loaned John 3350 marks against future revenues from the forests.[103] As chief forester, he was able to exercise complete discretion in managing the sale of wood, leasing of assarts, and negotiating gifts offered for exemptions and privileges—all with the complete approval of the king.[104] Although the chief forester did not usually account at the Exchequer, there are two accounts by Hugh for £450 and for £2000, showing that in his position he handled large sums of money collected from the royal forest.[105] However, in 1213 Hugh de Neville fell from favor with the king for some reason that was never made clear in the surviving records and was assessed a penalty of six thousand marks for allowing two prisoners to escape and for other failures not specified. Although the king later pardoned one thousand marks of this amount, Hugh continued to owe the remainder.[106] The coincidence of time when an eyre was being held to inquire into the behavior of various officials and when the king was putting a great deal of pressure on the forest administration to raise money suggests that the additional reasons for Hugh's downfall may have been related to his conduct as chief forester.[107] As it happened, the breach with the king was never healed, and Hugh joined with other Northerners in their revolt against King John in 1215, forfeiting his office as chief forester as a result.[108]

The rise and fall of Hugh de Neville as chief forester is only one example of the ambitions and struggles of many men which gave a dynamic quality to the administrative system of the royal forest. At no time was the organizational pattern as static as a description of the various officials in the forest might make it appear, because the career of a forester was subject to the will of his superior who held his office at the pleasure of the king. The procedure for naming a new forester was for the king to notify the chief forester that he should deliver the forest in question into the keeping of the new man. In this way on 2 June 1216, King John notified Hugh de Neville that he had committed the Forest of the Dean to John of Monmouth and ordered Hugh as chief forester to deliver the forest to John. At the same time another letter patent informed all the verderers, foresters, sergeants, and others in the Dean of John of Monmouth's appointment as forester and ordered them to obey his commands.[109] At a higher level than the individual forest, King John named Brian de Lisle as chief forester (*capitalis forestarius*) over all the forests of Nottingham and Derby to serve under Hugh de Neville.[110]

Letters to this same Brian provide a glimpse of a forest official caught in the midst of the political crosscurrents of the Magna Carta crisis. On subsequent days in August 1215, letters informed him that the king had granted the castle and forest of the High Peak in Derby to the earl of Derby and ordered him to deliver possession to the earl. Almost a year later the king expostulated with Brian, saying that he marvelled that his order had not been obeyed. He emphasized his interest in the matter by sending his chaplain along with the letter to prove by him, as well as by the letter, that the delivery of the forest should be made. To this the king attached a warning that if the castle were not delivered freely, the earl had been ordered to take it by force.[111] The problem in carrying out the original order in the disrupted period between the issuance of Magna Carta and the Barons' Revolt obviously lay with the control of the castle to which the forest became incidental. However, this combination of forest and castle was not unusual, for castles often were the administrative centers of royal forests. In July of 1215 John committed the castle of Carlisle to Robert de Vallibus, along with the county and the forests of Cumberland, and ordered all men in the county to obey Robert as sheriff, constable, and forester. Robert, in turn, was responsible for the forest to Hugh de Neville as chief forester and to the king.[112]

When there were manors and castles attached to the office of forester, it could only increase the value of that office, and there was a keen interest in forest offices for what they meant in terms of property. In 1204 Richard de Luci offered the king nine hundred marks and five palfreys on behalf of his wife for having the lands and the office of forester over all the forest of Cumberland in the same way that her father Hugh de Morevill had held them.[113] A different and more unusual example in which the office of forester was treated as property occurred in the same county when William fitz Adam of Hotton established a kind of lay corrody or retirement scheme for himself by granting custody of the forest to Roger de Belchamp for ten years during which he would provide the necessities of life to William and answer to the king for the forest. By working through Hugh de Neville, Roger then offered the king ten marks to ratify this private arrangement.[114] In a more normal arrangement Michael Columbières gave the king two hundred marks for permission to marry the daughter of Elias Croc and to obtain the office of forester and her inheritance after the death of Elias.[115] Other examples of the office of forester being treated as valuable property include a payment to obtain the office, to keep the office under Richard on the same terms the incumbent had held under Henry II, and to get possession in a dispute with another man over the office.[116]

Disputes were quite common because the minor forests were held as forests in fee and subject to all of the arguments that might arise over any feudal title. In 1201 one man claimed that the forest of Langstrothdale in York was attached to his land of Buckden, which he held of the countess of Warenne, and contested the right of another man who had inserted himself into the office of forester unjustly.[117] That same year the manor and forest of Danby in Yorkshire was noted as held by one knight's service, and another manor in Northumberland held by the same tenure is specified as being held in forest sergeanty.[118] The feudal aspect is also prominent in the sums of sixty to one hundred marks that were paid as relief in order that sons might assume the office of forester previously held by their fathers.[119] What dispute lay behind William of Wrotham's loss of his forestership is unknown, but the men of Dorset and Somerset were willing to give the king one hundred pounds to have him back as forester, only one of the posts in which he served King John. A few years later when he was reinstated as forester for all Somerset and Exmoor in Devon, his brother Richard performed the duties of the office for him.[120] A forester of Dean claimed in 1200 that the right of presentment to the church of Ruardean belonged to his office and offered to prove it by oath of twelve men of the neighborhood.[121] These examples of transfers and disputes over a forest illustrate the demand for these offices, but the office also brought responsibility, and one man offered twenty marks in order to be relieved of the office of forester, provided that he would respond for pleas and amercements during the time he held the office.[122]

The internal administration of a forest can only be seen as the result of a detailed study such as Margaret Bazeley's work on the Forest of the Dean. When there are sufficient records for this study early in the thirteenth century, she found that Dean was held by an official who had the title of warden and who was also constable of the castle of St. Briavels. He was appointed by the king to serve either for a term or at the king's pleasure, but the actual duties of the office were usually performed by a deputy whom the warden himself appointed. There were also local landowners who served as foresters in fee over particular districts or as sergeants in fee holding their positions by hereditary right but not restricted to any one district. Subordinate to the warden and also to the foresters or sergeants in fee were the ordinary foresters and boys who were removable at will by their immediate superiors. Other officials with duties in respect to the forest were the verderers and the regarders, and these officials were chosen in county court under the supervision of the sheriff.

The main features of this network of officials go back to the reign of Richard I and perhaps to that of Henry II, but there is practically no evidence as to how the forest was administered prior to 1154. Domesday Book did record a royal preserve in Dean, and at least one man is known to have had duties connected with the preserve in late Anglo-Saxon times. Nevertheless, it would be a mistake to assume that the administrative system existed before records are extant because the office of warden itself only developed from the turbulent years of King Stephen when the forest came into the hands of Miles of Gloucester, who had been sheriff in the latter part of Henry I's reign. When Miles switched his allegiance to the Empress Matilda in 1139, she granted him the castle of St. Briavels and the entire Forest of the Dean. Although Miles died in 1143, and Henry II in 1155 exempted the forest and the castle from the possessions that he confirmed to Miles's son, the forest and castle continued to be treated as an administrative unit to be held by the man who was named warden of the forest. Only Roger of Powis and William de Neville appear in the Pipe Rolls by name as wardens. In the thirteenth century there were nine foresters in fee in Dean, but only two are named in the records of the Angevin kings.[123]

The warden had the general responsibility for administering the forest law in Dean, and this involved many specific duties that had little to do with judicial proceedings. Of course, any grants of exemption from the forest or pardons for men who had violated forest law were sent by the king to the warden for execution. In protecting the venison, he was expected to hold inquests into any illegal acts, to arrest and place in safekeeping anyone found breaking the law, and to receive the remaining evidence from any beasts of the forest found killed. He also had to take charge of any cattle found illegally in the forest, to take possession of any private woods when the owners failed to enforce the assize, and to inspect the forest for any unauthorized cutting of wood, making assarts, placing weirs in the streams, or operating forges. Of course, most of these functions were carried out through the ordinary foresters whom he appointed. The warden also collected rents, other payments due the king from persons dwelling within the forest, and amercements. The transfer of any lands within the forest became official when acted upon by the warden.

More specific duties including supplying the deer with sufficient food in the winter, managing the slaughter and preparation of venison for the king and court, supervising the maufacture of arrows, and executing the royal orders when the king made gifts of timber or venison within the forest. Auxillary duties came from his position as constable of the castle and holder of the manor of St. Briavels. Some of the warden's many responsibilities were shared with the sheriff, who helped in producing defaulters living in the forest and in collecting amercements for forest offenses, and who joined with the warden in executing some of the semi-judicial functions of the forest. The sheriff alone was responsible for holding the election of verderers and regarders and for holding the regard.[124]

Among the many responsibilities of the Warden of the Dean and of other foresters, only a few were directly related to the stated purpose of the royal forest of preserving the venison and the vert for the king's hunting. Perhaps that traditional formulation of the purpose had been true at the time of William the Conqueror, but it had become misleading by the time of Henry II. The major change was that the royal forests had come to have an economic value independent of their value as hunting preserves. In spite of the fact that Henry II was an avid hunter who made maximum use of the royal forests for the sport, there were other royal forests maintained in areas where the king never visited or used for hunting which contributed their share to the royal coffers. A rather obvious illustration that economic factors could out-weigh hunting in policy decisions is the routine policy for dealing with assarts by assessing fines and collecting rents rather than requiring that the assarts be abandoned in the interest of keeping the area undis-turbed for the beasts of the forest.

The forest eyres, in addition to their judicial aspect, had the poten-tial of producing large amounts of revenue, and the policies of Henry II and of John were to exploit this source. In the last chapter, where the policies that governed the forest eyre were discussed, it was found that an eyre in the later twelfth century might be expected to raise nearly two thousand pounds, that in 1175 Henry II raised more than twelve thousand pounds, and that in 1212 John raised nearly five thou-sand pounds from this source. Although it is not possible to calculate total royal revenues from the Pipe Rolls because not all revenues were accounted for at the Exchequer, a comparison of these amounts raised from a forest eyre with the total revenues on the Pipe Rolls as calcu-lated by Sir James Ramsay gives some perspective. His figures would place the average annual revenue as something less than twenty thou-sand pounds for Henry II and from thirty to thirty-five thousand pounds for John with much greater fluctuation from year to year than in his father's reign.[125]

Although the money raised for forest eyres is impressive, the eyres could not be considered a regular source of income because they were held irregularly during this period. In fact, the most extensive financial entries dealing with the royal forests are the payments made for rent (*census*) of a forest. The explanation of these rents in the *Dialogue of the Exchequer* is interesting if rather imaginative in the use of etymol-ogy as an explanation:

Scholar. I am surprised at your calling some fixed rents "farms" and others "cesses." [census]

Master. Manors have farms; only woods have cesses. For the income from manors, since they are renewed and come back every year by cultivation, and besides have fixed rents established by ancient custom, is rightly called "farm," from being firm and unchangeable. But that due annually from woods, which are daily cut down and perish, from which there is no firm and unchangeable profit, but a constant, though not annual, ascent and descent, is called "cess," and by a similar dropping of the first syllable those rents are said to be "sessed" (*censeri*).[126]

To what extent the cutting and sale of wood was included in the forest rent cannot be determined from the Pipe Rolls. But it is clear that the rent was not necessarily a comprehensive figure entitling the renter to all revenues from the forest, for the accounts from the New Forest in addition to the rent list income from cattle farms (vaccaries) within the forest, sale of hides, cutting of turf, and making of salt which was paid at the Exchequer along with the rent.[127] An entry in a Memoranda Roll may indicate that the author of the *Dialogue* was correct that sales of timber made up the rent, for when the king cut most of the trees in a forest, the forester could not pay his rent and asked to be excused from this obligation.[128] However, the *Dialogue* is mistaken in emphasizing the variability of forest rent in contrast to the farm of a manor. In fact, the rent for the New Forest continued year after year at twenty-five pounds from the earliest Pipe Roll of Henry II until the latest entry under King John, and the rents of other forests were similarly fixed. Perhaps the profits of the renter varied according to the amounts of timber sold and any other items included in his rent, but the amount he paid at the Exchequer was unaffected.

Naturally some forests were worth a good deal more than others, and the rents ranged from the high of twenty-five pounds paid annually for the New Forest to the ten shillings for Pamber Forest. The practice of renting many royal forests was well established throughout the reign of Henry II except for a decline in the number rented immediately after the rebellion of his sons in 1173 and a sharp decline in the last five years of his life. Omitting those last five years, there was an average of fifteen forests rented each year for an average of nine forests and sixty-eight pounds during the last five years. Although there were fluctuations year by year during the reigns of Richard and John, the averages mark a recovery from the last years of Henry II (although failing to reach the average of the earlier part of his reign) and demonstrate the essential stability of the policy of renting forests. For the ten years of Richard and the fifteen for which there are Pipe Rolls under John, the average of each reign is the same: eleven forests rented each year for a total average income of ninety-three pounds.

The continuity of forest rents is underscored when the names of the men who rented the forests are examined. Walter Walerand was already renting the New Forest when the first Pipe Roll of Henry II was compiled, and he continued to do so until the second year of King John for a total of at least forty-four years. During the long reign of Henry II, the following men paid rents over extended periods: Richard de Luci in Windsor for twenty-three years, Henry Sturmy in Savernake for eight years, Fulk de Lisoriis in the forests of Northampton for thirty years, and Robert Poher in Galtres for nineteen years.[129] Alan Rasor held Cornbury for thirty-three years, and his son continued paying the rent for seven more years until the chief forester took over that forest. Matthew Croc was responsible for Andover, Digherle, and Chippenham in Wiltshire with some interruptions for twenty-eight years, and Elias Croc replaced him in Chippenham in Richard's reign.

Pannage paid for pigs permitted to feed in the forest provided the most consistent series of entries in the Pipe Rolls other than rents, but the method of administration differed because the pannage was not farmed out. The usual policy was for this revenue to be collected by the chief forester of all the forests in England, who accounted for pannage at the Exchequer. Table 3 shows the collections for the pannage of all the forests of England as given in the Pipe Rolls. The

Table 3
Collections for Forest Pannage

Year	Accountant	Total		
		£	s.	d.
1170	Alan de Neville	91	6	1
1171	Robert Mantel and William fitz Ralph	56	4	—
1172	Robert Mantel and William fitz Ralph	22	10	7
1178	Thomas fitz Bernard	58	14	1
1179	Thomas fitz Bernard	36	13	8
1181	Thomas fitz Bernard	20	8	4
1182	Thomas fitz Bernard	21	2	2
1183	Thomas fitz Bernard	36	—	8
1185	Geoffrey fitz Peter	62	15	11
1186	Geoffrey fitz Peter	30	16	11
1187	Geoffrey fitz Peter	48	3	5
1188	Geoffrey fitz Peter	33	19	3
1196	Geoffrey fitz Peter	48	4	7

variations in the totals show that pannage was not collected as a fixed farm but changed according to the number of pigs being fed in the forests each year. Similar variations occur within the amounts for individual forests and confirm this. Some of the missing years may be due to the vagaries of accounting or payments being made to the chief forester who then did not account at the Exchequer in all instances. However, some of the gaps may have been occasioned by years in which the oaks did not produce mast, for forest records in the thirteenth century often contain several years with notations giving this reason for the absence of pannage.

None of the other revenues from the forests occurs as systematically as that from pannage, but other sources do occur in the Pipe Rolls. Some of the royal forests—most notably the New Forest—were the locations of cattle farms called vaccaries. The fixed amount of fifteen pounds for the ten vaccaries in the New Forest was paid year after year by Walter Waleran, the forester, and may be compared with the twenty-five pounds he paid as rent for the New Forest itself. The collection of the various revenues from royal forests meant that the officials involved often had in their possession large sums of money. A case from 1206 concerned the robbery of forty marks of forest dues by a man who broke into the house where the money was being kept at night in custody of a servant. The servant was held prisoner for two days by the robber, who also shot the owner of the house in the hand with an arrow when the owner returned and attempted to raise the hue.[130] Many incidental references to the transport of venison for the king's use are reminders that the forests were all valuable as a source of meat and were exploited for that purpose beyond whatever hunting for pleasure the king might do. Two entries stand out for the quantities involved: a total of 105 harts sent from the forests of Yorkshire by water to Lincoln and then on to London by road, and a second account allowing expenses of over nine pounds for providing six ships that in 1168 carried harts and bucks to the king who was on the continent at the time.[131] Other products from the forest were timber for buildings and for military purposes, iron, hides, grain, salt, and peat.[132]

The picture that emerges of the Angevin forest system from contemporary records is strikeningly different from the overly romantic view of the forest as a royal hunting preserve uninhabited except for a few outlaws like Robin Hood and his merry band. At the same time, the stereotyped view is not completely wrong, for Henry II was an avid hunter who stayed by preference in his hunting lodges while he moved about England. Several of his contemporaries commented on this aspect of the king's character. According to Gerald of Wales:

> In times of war, which frequently threatened, he gave himself scarcely a modicum of quiet to deal with those matters of business which were left over, and in times of peace he allowed himself neither tranquillity nor repose. He was addicted to the chase beyond measure; at crack of dawn he was off on horseback, traversing waste lands, penetrating forests and climbing the mountain-tops, and so he passed restless days.[133]

And Walter Map described him as "a great connoisseur of hounds and hawks, and most greedy of that vain sport."[134]

The forest as a place of refuge for the outcasts of society at a time when the stranger was treated with suspicion and could only be allowed to spend one night, and that only within a borough is true as far as it goes.[135] Given the outcast status of such refugees from society, it is not surprising they rarely found their way into the official records.

The law-abiding men within the forest would have been reluctant even to acknowledge the existence of any outlaws because any help or sympathy extended to fugitives could bring a fine on the entire township.[136] It is only by coincidence that we learn of a knight who fled into Knaresburgh Forest in Yorkshire to live as a hermit during the reign of Richard I because he happened to be joined in his refuge by a man who was later canonized. Robert of Knaresborough, the saint whose life became the subject of a biography, lived with this fugitive knight in what was described as a "place of terrors and vast solitude" until King Richard's death made it safe for the knight to return to his family.[137] The setting of the legendary tale of Fulk fitz-Warin, which must have been believable to its audience, was in a forest. Having quarrelled with King John, Fulk fled to Braden Forest in Wiltshire. In a later episode he tricked the king into an ambush in Windsor Forest by disguising himself as a charcoal burner, whose occupation explained his presence in the forest.[138] Here fiction reflected real life, for Fawkes de Breauté terrorized the abbey of St. Albans in 1217 and then fled to Waubridge Forest where he seized about sixty men in his continued warfare against the invasion by Louis of France in support of the rebellious barons.[139] In spite of the elements of truth in the romantic views of the forest, it was not the king's inordinate love of hunting or the occasional danger to law-abiding men from the outcasts who had fled to the forests for refuge that caused the royal forest to become an issue between King John and his barons. The barons sought relief from the much more pressing burden of the forest law and the economic pressure of a system that operated totally for the king's benefit and prevented other men from using in a way advantageous to themselves their lands that happened to lie within a royal forest.

4
The Forest Becomes
a Political Issue

Discontent with the royal forests and how they were being administered was nothing new in the reign of King John, but the open rupture that developed between some of the barons and the king in the years before Magna Carta caused perennial complaints about the forest to be formulated in specific demands for reform. Although the motives of the "Northerners" who led the revolt against John are not clear, they shared a dislike for forest law, and that dislike may have served as one provocation for their revolt and a common link among those who joined it.[1] Certainly the likelihood that the royal forest might be a source of friction was greater in the North where the extensive forests interfered more with the baronial lands than in other parts of the country. Some of the actions against the royal forests taken by the rebels in the North during the civil war provide clear evidence that forest grievances were strong in that section, and the demands for reform as they can be traced in the documents associated with Magna Carta, the Forest Charter of 1217, and disputes over confirmation of the charters later in Henry III's reign kept alive the issue of the royal forest for more than two decades.

Just as the baronial struggle for Magna Carta can best be understood as a reaction to the Angevin government as it had been developing since the time of Henry II, rather than directed solely at the evil acts of King John, so demands for changes in the royal forest during this period were responses to the entire Angevin forest system. The barons in 1215 were no more interested in doing away with the royal forests than they were in overturning most of the legal and administrative innovations of Henry II, but they felt strongly that there were abuses that must be curbed in order to bring the royal forest back under the "good customs" of an earlier period. Just what that standard meant for the royal forest was a matter of dispute throughout the last years of King John and the minority of Henry III.

The forest eyre of 1212 insured that the royal forest would become a political issue along with all the other issues that divided the king and the barons. In addition to the severity of that eyre as seen in the total amount of revenue it produced and the gifts listed in the Pipe Roll for exemptions from the forest, there were foresters who were abusing their positions at the expense of the landowners. Probably warned of trouble brewing over his forest policy, King John backed off from the harshness that had characterized that eyre and attempted to bring the minor tyrannies of the royal foresters under control by forcing them to swear that they would limit their exactions to those customary in his father's reign. In addition, he ordered a general inquiry into the administration of the forests north of the Trent, and in May 1213 he extended his personal intervention by ordering four knights in each county in the region to come to meet with Brian de Lisle, a royal servant who was deputy to the chief forester, and to carry out what Brian should tell them about the king's business.[2] The king's conciliatory attitude at this time even won the grudging respect of one chronicler who wrote: "Amid so many hazards he did something which should be remembered in his honour. For the foresters were levying novel and burdensome exactions on almost all England, and the king showed pity for those afflicted and completely remitted them."[3]

These royal gestures were insufficient to calm the opposition, for the period from 1213 to 1215 must have been marked by claims and counterclaims as the opponents and supporters of the king elaborated their positions on the forest and many other issues. Unfortunately, few records of the negotiations and disputes prior to Magna Carta survive, and for those few the absence of dates on the documents makes it uncertain where each fits in the sequence. One of the extant documents, the "Unknown Charter," probably represents an early stage in the dispute because it contains the most radical baronial demands about the forest—demands that were later dropped or modified—and because the forest demands are prominent, as might be expected in an early stage when men from the North led the revolt before the term "Northerners" came to be used generally for all the rebels.[4] This charter (or radical demands similar to it) continued to be discussed, for the errors made by two chroniclers about what happened at Runny-

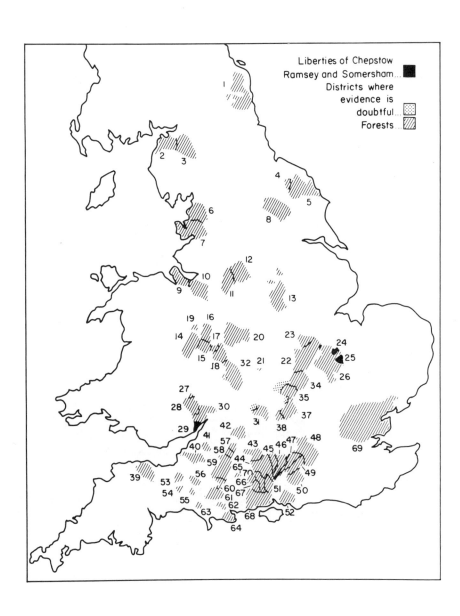

Liberties of Chepstow
Ramsey and Somersham...
Districts where
evidence is
doubtful...
Forests...

The Royal Forests
13th Century

50	Aliceholt and Wolmer	18	Kinver
2	Allerdale	14	Longforest
7	Amounderness	6	Lonsdale
49	Bagshot	11	Macclesfield
62	Bere	58	Melksham
51	Bere Ashley	40	Mendip
52	Bere Porchester	67	Milcet
37	Bernwood	17	Morfe
61	Blackmore	54	Neroche
42	Braden	55	To Neroche
70	Buckholt	68	New Forest
20	Cannock	53	North Petherton
29	Chepstow	1	Northumberland
57	Chippenham	46	Pamber
44	Chute	12	Peak
66	Clarendon	5	Pickering
30	Dean	63	Powerstock
10	Delamere	64	Purbeck
69	Essex	24	Ramsey
47	Eversley	22	Rockingham
39	Exmoor	23	Rutland
4	Farndale	34	Salcey
32	Feckenham	43	Savernake
45	Freemantle	59	Selwood
8	Galtres	13	Sherwood
60	Gillingham	15	Shirlet
65	Groveley	38	Shotover
19	Haughmond	25	Somersham
27	Haywood	56	Somerton
26	Huntingdon	35	Whittlewood
3	Inglewood	48	Windsor
28	Irchenfield	50	Wolmer and Aliceholt
21	Kenilworth Park	16	Wrekin
41	Kingswood	31	Wychwood
		9	Wyrral

Based on Margaret Bazeley, "The Extent of the English Forest in the Thirteenth Century," *Transactions of the Royal Historical Society*, 4th ser., 4 (1921): 165 by permission.

mede in June 1215 can only be explained by the confusion caused by the sudden dropping of certain radical positions in the course of negotiations.

A comparison of chapters on the forest in the "Unknown Charter," the Articles of the Barons, Magna Carta of 1215 and of 1216, and the Forest Charter of 1217 will show how demands for forest reforms survived the compromise of Magna Carta to reappear as the Forest Charter.[5] Whether the first two documents in this series are in reverse chronological order does not affect the argument, and there were probably other demands of which we have no record. The "Unknown Charter" represents the barons as seeking the liberties promised in the coronation charter of King Henry I. As far as the royal forests were concerned, the coronation charter would have provided little specific guidance because it simply stated that Henry retained the royal forests by common consent of his barons as his father had held them. However, there was the implication that Henry recognized a standard by which a king was expected to exercise his control of the forests and that the abuses of William Rufus, having fallen beneath that standard, would be corrected. Another possible argument from the coronation charter that might have appealed to King John's barons would be that Henry I's charter set a limit to the extent of the royal forests to include only those forests of William the Conqueror before his death in 1087. Whether anyone made that argument is not reported, but chapter nine of the "Unknown Charter" on the extent of the forests would in itself have meant radical change if accepted by King John by having him agree to disafforest all areas brought into the forest by his father, brother, and himself, thus setting the test date for which forests were legitimate as 1154. The extensive afforestation by Henry II became an issue with this chapter. The following chapter of the "Unknown Charter" provided that knights who held woods within the ancient royal forests might have pasture and firewood and that they could have a forester to preserve the royal beasts. The final chapter aimed to reverse the provisions of the Assize of 1198 by specifying that no man should lose life or member because of the beasts of the forest.

The radical demands of the "Unknown Charter" for changes in the royal forest did not appear in the "Articles of the Barons," a document containing the provisions incorporated later in Magna Carta except for minor changes in wording. The thirty-ninth article asserted that men who lived outside the forest should not be compelled to appear before the justices of the forest unless they were involved in a plea or as a pledge for someone who was involved. It also provided for the election of twelve knights in each county whose task it would be to reform the evil customs of the forest and practice of the foresters. Stated with more precision, these articles became chapters forty-four and forty-eight of Magna Carta with the sole substantive change being the stipulation that evil customs were to be changed within a period of forty days after an inquiry had been made by the knights. Similarly, the forty-seventh article became a chapter in Magna Carta with the same number and almost the same wording. It provided that all forests afforested by King John should be disafforested, and Magna Carta added "at once."

The provisions for an inquiry into evil forest customs in the "Articles" and Magna Carta seem to fall far short of the prohibition of life and member contained in the "Unknown Charter." In practice the difference was probably not very great because the usual punishment for forest offenses had remained the imposition of monetary penalties even though the Assize of 1198 had reasserted the principle of corporal punishment for these offenses. However, the provision of the "Articles" applying disafforestment only to new forests created by King John was a major difference between that document and the "Unknown Charter" and a major concession by the barons. In fact, this provision was virtually meaningless because King John had decreased the area of forest by his sale of exemptions that removed lands from the bounds to which Henry II had pushed the royal forest. Although the "Articles" has nothing more on the extent of the forests, there is a recognition in Magna Carta of the problem of areas afforested by Henry II and Richard between 1154 and 1199. Any decision on this problem which basically involved the afforestations of Henry II was postponed by the fifty-third chapter of Magna Carta which applied the respite due to King John's vow as a crusader to the question of the extent of the forests.[6]

While the forest as a political issue was not resolved by Magna Carta, the provision in Magna Carta for a general inquiry into the administration of the forests practically guaranteed that the issue would not go away. King John's specific concessions about the forest at Runnymede cost him very little, and, in comparison with some of the radical demands that had surfaced during the controversy, it could be said that the king had won at least a temporary victory on the forest question. However, that victory proved to be short-lived, and the king's admission that persons other than the king and his officials might inquire about forest boundaries and administration had damaging consequences for the royal position that King John could not have anticipated.[7] No longer could the forest be considered something apart from the ordinary legal and governmental system because it was entirely dependent upon the king's will. This admission undermined the unique status of the forest as it had existed in the reign of Henry II as described by a contemporary authority: "The forest has its own laws, based, it is said, not on the Common Law of the realm, but on the arbitrary legislation of the King; so that what is done in accordance with forest law is not called 'just' without qualification, but 'just,' according to forest law."[8] The royal forest was no longer untouchable and was revived as an issue several times later in the thirteenth century and the early fourteenth century.

Just four days after Magna Carta, King John issued letters patent at Runnymede on 19 June 1215 to his sheriffs, foresters, and other officials informing them of the agreement with the barons and setting into motion the machinery for choosing the knights who would inquire into various problems postponed by Magna Carta including the administration of the forests.[9] However, the issue of the forests was not to be settled by legal procedures, for the Runnymede settlement between the barons and king began to break down very quickly, and there may never have been good faith on either side from the beginning. In the North some of the dissident barons raided the king's manors and destroyed royal forests by cutting timber and slaughtering the animals that the forest law was meant to protect.[10] These flagrant acts gave King John an opportunity to strengthen his position among the more moderate barons. It was probably in this confused period of political maneuvering that Archbishop Stephen Langton with the archbishop of Dublin and six English bishops issued an undated letter in an attempt to clarify the meaning of chapter forty-eight of Magna Carta that provided for an inquiry into the forests.[11] Addressing themselves to all who might read the letter, the prelates affirmed that all parties to Magna Carta understood the chapter to mean that the king should retain all forest customs without which the forest could not be preserved. Extremists who had taken it into their own hands to destroy the royal forests were matched by King John who by the middle of July appealed to the pope for release from the oath he had taken at Runnymede. By the end of September when the papal bull nullifying Magna Carta arrived in England, that document had lost its value in providing a framework for settling the issue of the forest and the papal decision merely provided legal sanction for the existing situation. The question of the forest, along with other issues between the king and the barons, had to await the outcome of civil war.

The death of King John during the night of 18 October 1216 brought a fundamental change to the political situation. The new king succeeded as a boy of nine to a divided inheritance supported by some ecclesiastical and lay magnates loyal to his father and opposed by others who had transferred their allegiance to Louis of France with the territory of England itself divided along similar lines. Within a month (on 12 November) the men about the king formally stated their political position by reissuing Magna Carta in a carefully re-written form with appropriate omissions but with a commitment to most of the baronial demands that John had accepted at Runnymede and later rejected when he asked Pope Innocent III to quash the orig-inal document.[12] Of the chapters of 1215 concerned with the forest, only chapter forty-four was retained with its provision that men living outside the forest would not have to appear before the justices of the forest by a common summons. The whole remaining question of the forest and the conduct of foresters were among the matters of a "grave and doubtful" nature reserved for further deliberation. This reissue of 1216 bore the seal of the papal legate along with those of the protectors of the king, thus circumventing the papal nullification of the original charter. Even though the major questions about the forest were not settled by the reissue, it meant that the forest would continue as a political question and would continue to be raised within the context of Magna Carta.

The continuity of the charters was insured by the treaty of Kings-ton which ended the civil war in September 1217. That treaty by which Louis agreed to withdraw his claims on England included a promise that Henry III would grant the liberties that his barons had demanded and set the stage for yet another reissue of Magna Carta, perhaps in that month and certainly before November.[13] The reissue of 1217 omitted all reference to the forest because the whole question of the royal forest was the subject of a separate charter sealed on 6 Novem-ber.[14] From that date there were always two charters to be considered, and the question of the forest was given thorough attention for the first time since it began to emerge as a political issue after the unwonted severity of the forest eyre of 1212. Of the seventeen chapters in the Forest Charter only the second was carried over directly from Magna Carta of 1215 where it had appeared as chapter forty-four and had exempted men who lived outside the forest from appearance at forest courts. Chapter ten of the Forest Charter echoed the twelfth chapter of the "Unknown Charter," that no man should lose life or member for breaking forest law. The remaining chapters were all new, or at least not borrowed from the extant documents surrounding the baronial revolt, but the period of controversy very likely helped to lay the groundwork for the comprehensive provisions in the charter. J. C. Holt makes the very plausible suggestion that the commissions of inquiry authorized by King John in 1215 may have gone about their work (even though none of their findings have been preserved), and that they provided some of the information on which the Forest Charter was based.[15]

Along with Magna Carta, the Forest Charter became part of the law of the land cited in courts of law and appealed to in disputes over rights.[16] Only a decade after the Forest Charter was first granted, a jury in Lancashire in the process of making a perambulation rested its findings on the Forest Charter as a fixed point of departure that was accepted without dispute by all parties.[17] Its provisions, which remained the framework of forest law throughout the thirteenth century, may be summarized as follows:

1. All forests created by Henry II shall be inspected. Any woods he afforested, except his own demesne woods, are to be disafforested.

2. Men who live outside the forest do not have to appear before justices of the forest except when they are personally involved.

3. All woods afforested by Richard and John are to be disafforested at once except for royal demesne woods.

4. Men holding woods in the forest are to hold them as they were held at the first coronation of Henry II and exempt from any fines for purpresture, waste, and assarts made from that time until the second year of Henry III's coronation, but they shall answer for anything after that year.

5. Regards shall be held in the forests as held at the first coronation of Henry II.

6. An inquest for lawing of dogs shall be made along with the regard every third year. The amercement for unlawed dogs is three shillings. Three toes are to be cut from a front foot, but lawing is required only where customary at the first coronation of Henry II.

7. Foresters shall no longer collect forced exactions, and the number of foresters shall be set by the twelve regarders at the regard.

8. Swanimote courts will be held just three times a year. Foresters and verderers will meet every forty days to view attachments of venison and vert.

9. Every free man can agist his woods within the forest at will and have his pannage. He can drive his pigs through royal demesne woods for this purpose.

10. No man shall lose life or member for taking venison. He shall be fined unless he cannot pay, in which case he will be imprisoned for a year and a day. Then he may be released if he can find sureties. If not, he must abjure the realm.

11. Every archbishop, bishop, earl, or baron travelling through the forest may take one or two beasts by view of the foresters or he may blow a horn to give notice if they are not present.

12. Every free man without fear of prosecution can make a mill, fishpond

dam, marlpit, ditch, or arable land outside the covert on arable land in his own wood or land if his action does not damage a neighbor.

13. Every free man shall have eyries of hawks and any honey found in his woods.

14. No forester except a forester in fee shall take cheminage to allow transportation through the forest.

15. Men outlawed for forest offenses committed from the time of Henry II to first coronation of Henry III are pardoned, but they must find pledges for future conduct.

16. No warden of a castle or anyone else may hold forest pleas. A forester in fee who makes attachments must present them to the verderers, who will enroll them and present them to the chief forester when he comes to hold and terminate forest pleas.

17. The king grants to all persons the liberties of the forest and free customs they previously had within forests and without. All must observe the liberties and customs granted in this charter.

Most of the provisions of the Forest Charter are clear, but it left the question of the legitimate extent of the forests unclear. There could be no doubt that the new forests created by Henry II were to be disafforested, but whether that policy applied to other areas which he restored to the forest after their loss by King Stephen was ambiguous. The instructions given to the men who were to survey all royal forests in 1219 continue to be ambiguous.[18] They authorized not only an inquiry but also the disafforestment of any areas made forest by King John, but a different procedure was outlined for forests dating from the time of Henry II. The men making the inquiry about areas afforested by Henry II or through Alan de Neville or his other foresters should report their findings to the justiciar and royal council in order that immediate disafforestments might be made by that body. This difference in procedure seems to imply that the council might exercise some discretion about disafforestment in those areas created by Henry II. The instructions also provided for a survey of forest lands held by royal foresters, wardens of castles, and other bailiffs except foresters in fee; these forest lands were to be placed temporarily in the hands of two knights and a clerk until decisions could be made about their permanent custody. In addition to these instructions for a general survey of forests, there are a few letters sent in the king's name in the first few years after the Forest Charter was granted that deal with the boundaries or custody of particular forests as the administration of the royal forests returned to normal after the disruptions of rebellion and civil war.[19] As late as April 1220, the guardians of the king were prepared to order a return to the *status quo* under King John for the forest between the

Derwent and Ouse rivers in Yorkshire until it could be determined whether the perambulation was correct or not.[20] Perhaps because no grants in perpetuity could be made during the minority of the king, the legitimate extent of the forests remained an unsettled question.

The two charters of 1217 continued to have a place in political history after that date partially because there were still unanswered questions about the forest. The surprising thing about Magna Carta was the acceptance of its provisions after John's death by the men who had supported him against the rebels. Nevertheless, demands for reform after 1217 took the form of asking that King Henry III confirm the "liberties and free customs" over which a war had been fought against his father and which he had sworn to uphold when Louis left England. When some barons made this demand at Christmas 1223, only William Brewer among the king's advisors objected that the "liberties" had been extorted by violence and should not be observed as a matter of legal principle, and he was immediately overruled by the young king.[21] Even so, there might be room for differences about what the liberties meant for the royal forests, and in October 1224 Hugh de Neville as chief forester was ordered to have regards made within the same boundaries as had been customary in King John's reign before the war with the barons. This order was in clear contradiction of chapter five of the Forest Charter.[22] That Christmas the barons demanded a formal confirmation of the charters in return for their agreement to a tax of a fifteenth on movables. The chronicler reports that two charters were sealed and sent to counties in which there were royal forests—"one of common liberties and another for forest liberties"—and the charters themselves state that the *quid pro quo* for confirming the charters was a fifteenth on movables.[23]

The old question of the extent of the forests remained even after the confirmation of the charters, and Hugh de Neville, along with his deputy Brian de Lisle and others, set out with the aid of local juries in 1225 to perambulate the forests and determine which should be disafforested.[24] One man's simplistic interpretation of their task in a monastic annal was "All new forests throughout England were disafforested."[25] The reality proved more complicated, for the juries sometimes contradicted their predecessors who had made perambulations a few years earlier after the Charter of the Forest was granted. In addition, the legal status of any boundaries which may have resulted in reducing the king's forest rights during his minority could be questioned by applying the principles of feudal wardship to the case of a minor king and his guardians. Explicit recognition of the tentative nature of any settlement impinging on royal forest prerogatives is found in an agreement between the king and Waltham Abbey in which certain of the abbey's woods were to remain within the forest, even though the perambulation showed they should have been disafforested, in return for an agreement to allow the abbey to make parks in other woods. The agreement provided that the king could reverse both parts of it when he came of age if he wished.[26] The same restrictions had been applied in 1221 when the forest of Berkshire had been granted to the men there to be administered as it had been under royal foresters and with regards every three years. All the sealed rolls of these regards would have to be presented and impleaded when the king came of age and the men of Berkshire would have to answer for their custody of the forest. At that time, the king would make a firm decision whether the area should be disafforested or returned to the royal forest as it had been prior to the grant.[27]

In February 1227 Henry III declared himself to be of legal age and proceeded to cancel charters granted during his minority. Although Roger of Wendover wrote that this action applied to the Forest Charter, his account is rather garbled and Henry's own letters at the time prove that his actions applied neither to the Forest Charter nor Magna Carta.[28] Nevertheless, he did reopen the question of the extent of the forests by having new perambulations made in a number of counties. Juries in Northamptonshire, Leicestershire, Rutland, Huntingdonshire, Lancashire, Staffordshire, Surrey, Shropshire, Worcestershire, and Yorkshire all admitted that they had made errors during the perambulations of 1225 in declaring that various areas should be disafforested.[29] In contrast, the perambulation for Hampshire was still being used as authoritative by Richard II late in the fourteenth century.[30] The instructions of 1225 had certainly been ambiguous in reference to afforestations by Henry II, but the number of "errors" found in 1227 when the king was asserting his mature authority points to some coercion in favor of the king.

This assertion of royal authority was more explicit in some areas than in others. On 15 January 1228, the king ordered a searching inquiry into claims for exemption from the forest in Surrey and Warwickshire with orders to the sheriffs to have all foresters in fee and all others claiming any liberties of the forest to appear before him to prove "by what warrant" they and their ancestors held the privileges now being claimed. The inquiry also was to name the perambulators to answer why they had disafforested parts of the forest that had been forest before King Henry II's coronation when they had been ordered to retain those parts as forest and to show which parts of the royal demesne had been disafforested without warrant.[31] Later in June there was concern that the sheriff of Northumberland should proclaim publicly that part of a manor had been found by the perambulation of Hugh de Neville to be within royal forest and that it should remain so.[32] The bishop of Bath found it to his advantage to obtain charters from the king securing the disafforestment of certain of his lands that may well have been in question under the stricter policy being followed in 1228.[33] The Bishop of Worcester and others holding land within the forests of Ombersley and Horewell in Worcestershire paid four hundred marks for a charter disafforesting these two areas, and some men of Lincolnshire paid 250 marks for a similar charter in their area.[34] In Nottinghamshire men dwelling in areas disafforested by the perambulation of 1225 found it prudent to pay twenty marks to insure that they would be exempt from courts hearing pleas of the forest.[35] As late as March 1231, the king was still hounding the men who had made the perambulation in Northamptonshire to answer charges about their work.[36]

A letter close in April 1228 to the sheriffs posed the issue of disafforestment in terms of those areas afforested by Henry II that were areas previously in forest but that had been lost to the forest during the reign of Stephen. The royal position was that those areas should remain forest in 1227 and that they had erroneously been disafforested along with the new areas brought into the forest by Henry II.[37] The men of Leicestershire gave a fine of one hundred pounds in order to have a new perambulation to clear up the differences between that of 1225 and the "errors" acknowledged by their jurors in 1227. The jury in 1235 making the new perambulation reported that they were ignorant of the extent of the forest under Henry I and Stephen and that the woods in their county had been afforested under Henry II. The problem remained because they did not know whether the woods had been afforested before or after the first coronation and whether all or part of the covert was afforested. In the event, the king granted that woods belonging to others be disafforested and vigorously maintained his rights to forest in his own demesne when there was a question a year later whether these had been disafforested, too.[38] However, the royal orders in 1228 were much more sweeping than merely dealing with the particular error about areas first brought into the forest by Henry II. The sheriffs were to proclaim that all forests be kept with the boundaries as they had been in the time of King John before the war with his barons and that forest law would be enforced within those bounds.[39]

The enforcement of this policy would have meant that the Forest Charter had been annulled as far as its provision on the extent of the forest was concerned. Areas created forest by Richard and John would have returned to forest, a change in wording that might have had some negative psychological effect even though the whole trend in both those reigns had been toward disafforestment. But restoration to the forest of areas created by Henry II and disafforested by perambulations after the Forest Charter or in 1226 would have meant a major change in trends since Magna Carta in 1215. Although there is little about the forests in the sources for the next few years, the barons did not accept this reversal, and their demands concentrated on obtaining a confirmation of Magna Carta and the Forest Charter that would be binding upon the king without the legal doubts of the confirmation of 1225 made in the name of the minor king, even though that confirmation had stated it was to be "in perpetuity." The opportunity for action came in January 1237 when Henry III sought an aid against the opposition of the barons. This gave the barons their opportunity, and, in return for the tax of a thirtieth, the king confirmed the charters which were then read publicly in county courts.[40] However, the ambiguity about the afforestation under Henry II still remained. By a letter directed to a problem that arose in Hampshire, the king left no doubt that he did not understand that confirmation to mean a return to the disputed boundaries of the 1226 perambulations in place of the revised boundaries he had obtained the following year.[41] The question of the extent of the forest was one in which the interests of the barons and the crown were fundamentally opposed, with pressure from the barons to reduce the area in forest that hampered how they could use their lands. On his side of the argument, the king returned in 1251 and 1252 to the standard of the time of King John prior to the barons' war to measure the legality of claims about pannage and rights of common. One inquest into whether men of the royal demesne had usurped rights of common during several wars was to be resolved by returning to the situation that had prevailed "in time of peace of our father King John when his forests were kept better."[42] The forest as a political issue had entered English history and was to remain an issue until the fourteenth century. The Forest Charter brought a new period in the administration of the forests by providing a fixed body of law for the guidance of the justices in place of the more flexible and less defined approach of the assizes of the latter twelfth century, but it did not resolve the political issue of the royal forest.

5

The Forest System
at Its Height:
Law and Administration

The Charter of the Forest provided the framework for the administration of the forests and the application of forest law in the thirteenth century, but what the royal forests meant in practice for the subjects of Henry III and Edward I depended equally upon the royal officials who applied the forest law. Until 1229 the forest administration continued to be headed by an official known variously as chief forester, master forester, and chief justice of the forests. Then two jurisdictions were created with the appointment of Brian de Lisle as justice of the forests in thirteen counties in the North and East and John of Monmouth to a similar office in the remaining counties. This division lasted a few years until Peter d'Airvault was appointed in 1236 as the sole justice over all the counties. In 1239 the jurisdiction was permanently divided between a justice for the forests north of the Trent and one for the forests south of the Trent. The title of "gardien" was adopted for these officials in the forest ordinances of 1311, but in 1397 the older usage of "justice" was revived without any real change in the office on either occasion.[1]

The appointment of a justice of the forest proceeded in a very businesslike way that insured the accountability of the justice for his conduct in office and that all parties who needed to be informed were informed of a new appointment. The appointment itself came directly from the king in the form of a letter patent, and the justice held office at the pleasure of the king. The perquisites of office included seisin of the king's demesne houses pertaining to the forest, frequently an appointment as constable in the chief royal castle in the area, and jurisdiction over various parks and warrens attached to the houses or castle.[2] Before the new justice assumed his responsibilities the sheriff held an inquest into the state of the forest by means of four knights of the county along with the foresters, verderers, and regarders, who inspected the forest and delivered a sealed report to the king. When a justice left office, he was required to make a final accounting for the "exits" of the forest at the Exchequer, which he could make by attorney with the king's permission, on penalty of seizure of his property into the king's hands for failure to do so.[3] The seriousness of the obligation to account is illustrated in the case of William de Leyburn whom Edward I pardoned for any arrears his father had left from any of the many offices he held, including his term as justice of the forests north of the Trent, and in the fact that the pardon was granted because of the intervention of the queen on William's behalf.[4] Another example was Geoffrey of Langeley, who was paid two hundred marks a year as justice of the forests south of the Trent from 1249 to 1252, with the question of possible liabilities in office not finally settled until he obtained a charter in 1255, which acquitted him and all his agents of any liabilities in any forest office, including that as justice of the forests, and ordered the charter itself to be read by the justices for forest pleas during their eyres.[5]

The two justices of the forest had a general responsibility for the custody of the forests that included both executive and judicial functions. The scope of these responsibilities was set forth in the letter patent appointing a justice of the forests north of the Trent in 1267: to hear all pleas of the forest outside of those heard at an eyre; to hold inquests about vert and venison, purprestures, assarts, trespasses, and lawing of dogs; and to do justice and take amends for these cases according to the law and custom of the forest.[6] He also was responsible for hearing pleas for trespasses within or without the forest that occurred in parks, warrens, stews, and the king's prohibited rivers and to answer for the fines and amercements arising from them.[7] Even the coming of the justices on eyre did not entirely relieve him of his responsibilities because the justice of the forest was usually named as one of the justices to hold an eyre. Only the king or one of the justices of the forests had the authority to release a man imprisoned for an offense against the venison, and the warden of a particular forest was not allowed to accept the fine of his release.[8] However, the deputy of the justice was expected to perform this function in the absence of the justice on the king's business overseas.[9]

The responsibility for all the forests within his jurisdiction was clarified in 1270 by a royal order that any writ having to do with the vert or venison must be addressed to the justice of the forests and not to any subordinate warden or forester.[10] When the warden of a forest resigned, that forest came into the direct custody of the justice of the forest until the king decided to make other arrangements.[11] Because the wardens were directly responsible to one of the two justices, serious disruption could occur with the death of a justice in office, and in 1255 the king attempted to alleviate the consequences in this situation by writing to remind the wardens and foresters that they were responsible for safeguarding their forests until he could name another justice to whom they could respond.[12]

One jurisdictional problem that arose concerned the bailiffs of the royal demesne manors and woods that lay within forests. In 1237 the king's council attempted to draw a clear line between the jurisdiction of a justice of the forests and a bailiff by a general statement that the justice should have care for all the forests including those with woods belonging to the royal demesne. However, the bailiff should have the proceeds that belonged to the king's manor: nuts, honey, pannage, agistment by view of the agisters and foresters, and herbage for the king's animals by view and counsel of the justice of the forests. Although the bailiff could provide his own foresters without bows and arrows, the justice should appoint those who carried bows and arrows. In addition, the justice of the forests should safeguard any woods within the forest that did not belong to the king's manor or to anyone else who might have been enfeoffed with it. For this reason, the bailiff of the royal manor in Feckenham Forest had to cut trees by view of the foresters and verderers when he was ordered in 1234 to take timber for repairing the king's enclosure for animals on the manor. It was further provided that in case of any conflict between the justice and the bailiff the conflict was to be settled by the *curia regis*.[13]

With these far-reaching responsibilities the justices of the forest in the thirteenth century were men of substance, and many of them held other royal appointments and otherwise took an active part in events of their time. Occasionally, some of the justices of the forest performed their duties by deputy, but the use of deputies as a regular practice did not develop until the following century.[14] Robert Passelewe provides an interesting example of a justice of the forests south of the Trent from about 1245 to 1250 who had an active career in addition to his position as a justice. He began as a royal clerk and reached a position of some influence in the train of Peter de Rivaux, who obtained control of the Exchequer with the overthrow of Hubert de Burgh the justiciar in January of 1233. As deputy treasurer, Robert's fortunes were tied to those of his patron, and he and Stephen Segrave, the new justiciar, were called to account when Peter de Rivaux lost the king's good will in a political reversal that swept him from power in 1234. All three fled to sanctuary rather than account for the receipts and expenses of their period in office, and it was about ten months before Stephen and Robert purchased their reconciliation with the king by a payment of one thousand marks.

Robert Passelewe continued in royal service and later earned the greatest unpopularity of any of the men who served Henry III with his heading an inquest in 1243–44 into encroachments upon the forest.[15] Matthew Paris wrote in venom of Robert's proposal for a forest inquest in order to raise money for the king and excoriated the manner in which the inquest was later carried out to the impoverishment of both clergy and laymen.[16] According to evidence from the next reign, Robert used this inquest to add lands to the royal forest against the provisions of the Charter of the Forest and the settlement that had been made with the perambulations earlier in Henry's reign.[17] At the same time, the canons of Chichester hoped to gain favor with the king by electing Robert to the vacant bishopric, but an examination by Robert Grosseteste, bishop of Lincoln, proved him to be unqualified, and the election was quashed.[18] Two years later he headed the justices for a forest eyre, and in the same year also served as a justice for hearing a case under the assize of novel disseisin at Chelmsford.[19] His clerical career prospered with his presentment to the church of Northampton by the archbishop of Canterbury, but that unusually scrupulous bishop, Robert Grosseteste, refused to admit him to an office involving pastoral care. The bishop maintained that the presentation was made primarily because Robert had served the king as a justice on a forest eyre and that his refusal was based on the same royal service. He pointed out that Robert had arrested and imprisoned clerks as well as laymen and that his serving in secular offices was against the canons of the church.[20]

The next level of administration under the two justices of the forests on either side of the Trent was the warden or forester in charge of each forest. Unfortunately for clarity, the titles for this official varied in the contemporary records, but warden (*custos*) was frequently used and has the advantage for the historian of being distinct, in contrast to the title of forester which was applied to men in every level of forest administration. One exception to the general administrative system was a grouping of the forests between Oxford and Stamford bridges (i.e., the forests in Northampton, Huntingdon, Oxford, and Buckingham) into an administrative unit headed by an official intermediate between the justice of the forests south of the Trent and the wardens of individual forests. Nevertheless, the forests in this area retained their separate names, and their wardens accounted separately for the income from each forest.[21]

The method of appointment and installation of the warden was parallel to that for a justice of the forest—appointment by a royal letter patent and an inquest into the state of the forest at the time of installation.[22] Most of the wardens administered other properties in addition to the forest itself as part of the bailiwick attached to the office of warden. For example, a letter patent appointing Geoffrey de Picheford to Windsor Forest in 1272 to serve as warden at the king's pleasure included the provisions that he would have custody of the castle, town, and forest of Windsor and of two royal manors with their seven hundreds and other appurtenances for which he would render at the Exchequer the same amount as his deceased predecessor had been accustomed to pay.[23] Many forest bailiwicks included the custody of a castle that became the center of administration, and the warden is sometimes referred to as constable of the castle even when he clearly was serving in his office as warden of the forest.[24] Reasons given for appointment as warden include prior service to the king, the desire to please members of the royal family or powerful nobles who supported the appointee, and inheritance of the office.[25] Undoubtedly the size of some of the gifts presented to the king for obtaining the appointment had their weight, but that is hardly the kind of reason that would be included in an official letter announcing an appointment.[26] The terms of appointment varied and were hereditary for the warden and his heirs, for life, at the king's pleasure, and for a specified term.[27]

In return for the fixed payments at the Exchequer recorded as rents in the Pipe Rolls, the wardens collected many varied types of income from the forest (usually referred to collectively as the exits of the forest) and from these made whatever profit they could manage from the office of warden. A typical letter of appointment for the Forest of the Dean listed the sources of revenue available to the warden. The warden was to collect the issues and profits from the king's demesne; the annual rent of weirs and of the manor attached to the office of warden; rents from mines, forges, coal, and customs on coal brought across the Severn; and the usual forest issues from cheminage, herbage, wind-fallen wood, loppings from oaks cut for lumber, pannage, ashes, nuts, and other perquisites of the forest not listed in detail. He also had the income from the manorial court and minor courts within the forest. For his office as warden he was to pay forty pounds annually and to keep the castle and forest at his own expense. In addition, the king's great forge within the forest was explicitly stated as being outside the warden's bailiwick and was to be managed as the king desired.[28] Nothing is said in this letter about subordinate foresters in Dean, but the warden could normally appoint his own subordinates, and these should be considered as sources of income because the warden customarily collected gifts and payments from them to secure the appointment.[29] This custom led to many abuses only partially controlled by efforts of the royal government to enforce the provisions in the seventh chapter of the Charter of the Forest that limited the number of subordinate foresters allowed.[30]

The exceptional nature of the forests between Oxford and Stamford bridges is described in an inquest held to determine whether Brigstock and Geddington were one or two bailiwicks. The return stated that they were one bailiwick held directly by the seneschal of the forests between the bridges and that herbage, nuts, pontage, cheminage, and lesser attachments of vert pertained to the seneschal, although the agisters should respond directly to the Exchequer.[31] In another dispute, the warden claimed to have the forest of Essex by gift of Thomas de Clare as farm for the several hundreds that were in the forest. He claimed the bailiwick included custody of the king's houses in Havering, the park there, all forfeited woods, and cheminage at four pence per year for each cart of lumber, brush, bark, and charcoal from 29 September to 11 November. He also claimed the trimmings from trees cut in the forest, except those cut for lumber, and the right to appoint riding foresters and to collect payments from them for their bailiwicks. They, in turn, appointed foot foresters and collected payments from them.[32] It is evident from this case and many others that both the wardens and the king approached the office as a kind of property in which the distribution of revenue was a question of vital concern. When the value of the wardenship of Windsor Forest had been reduced because the king had granted land and licenses to make purprestures in the forest to Queen Eleanor and her men of Cobham, the king ordered an inquest, and the jurors reported damages to the income of the warden over a period of seven years that amounted to a total of £20 13s. 4d.[33]

Most of the information about how the wardens administered the forests in their custody comes from the inquests made when the office passed from one warden to his successor or inquests held when there had been complaints into the conduct of the warden, but there are a few surviving rolls belonging to the wardens that record their official actions. Along with the verderers, the wardens were charged with making attachments for trespasses against the venison and vert of the forest, and a record of these attachments had to be presented to the justices on eyre for forest pleas when they came to the area. An inquest in the Forest of the Peak showed that the warden under Henry III heard and terminated all pleas from day to day wherever the trans- gressions occurred except for the cutting of oaks and pleas for venison, pleas that were reserved for the justices on forest eyre. Yet the pleas being held by the warden, later called the lesser pleas of the vert, amounted to substantial sums in this record in which the amounts are summarized by the terms of the various wardens who held the forest over a period of twenty-three years: forty-eight pounds for six years, one mark for one year, twenty-four pounds for four years, four pounds for one-half year, forty pounds for five years, forty-eight pounds for six years, and eight pounds for one year. From the sums collected the warden was entitled to eight pounds a year, but there is no explana- tion of what happened when the amount due the warden was less than that collected for a year.[34]

The few extant rolls of wardens may be illustrated by a roll of Henry Sturmy, one of several men of the same name in the family which held the wardenship of Savernake Forest. This roll covering the years 1296 to 1305 shows that the warden held inquests from one to four times a year with no evidence of a regular pattern. The verderers, subforesters and woodwards from private woods, and representatives of the neigh- boring townships were present, and presentments were made by juries, probably on each occasion when a violation of the forest came to the attention of the warden. Most of the entries concern deer taken and oaks that had been cut down, as would be expected in a warden's roll meant to be delivered to the justices on eyre. Both types of entry show a low level of violations amounting to an occasional deer and often only one oak a year up to six at the most in any year. In one case there was a notation that no attachment had been made because the defendant was dead. The only extraneous business recorded in this roll concerned the inheritance of a forester in fee.[35]

The lowest level of forest administration consisted of those foresters appointed by the wardens of the forest and the foresters in fee. The appointive foresters were usually classified as riding foresters and walk- ing foresters in that order of importance with the riding forester having responsibility for a larger area. Their assistants, if any, were simply called "boys" (*garciones*).[36] The foresters in fee had responsibilities like those of the appointive foresters, but their areas of jurisdiction were held as hereditary fees. There were also private foresters or wood- wards in forests where men other than the king had woods within the forest, and within these woods these private woodwards performed the duties done elsewhere by royal foresters subject to the overriding authority of the royal warden of the forest if they failed to perform their duty. They were appointed by the landowner, but they also took an oath of office before the justices for forest pleas, and failure to present a sworn woodward at an eyre meant that private woods would be taken into the king's hands.[37]

The routine work of protecting the forest and dealing with violators fell to these foresters, and the job could be dangerous when the violator of the forest law was an illegal hunter armed with bow and arrows for taking venison. Foresters were sometimes killed or wounded under these circumstances while attempting to make arrests.[38] In spite of the stereotyped format of an eyre roll, there are occasional glimpses of the give-and-take of actual situations that lay behind the abbreviated official record. In one case the information was given that although a forester failed to arrest some men he caught hunting deer, he did manage to capture two of their greyhounds, which he left with another man for safekeeping until the meeting of a forest court. Not to be outdone, Robert de Gernon, the apparent lawbreaker in the case, retaliated by kidnapping the forester and throwing him into a dovecot until he paid two shillings eleven pence for his release. Meanwhile Robert also regained the greyhounds by forcing them from the man who had them in his custody and entered the forest again with them to kill two deer.[39] In another case a habitual poacher named William Bukke resisted arrest when a forester found him hunting deer, and he was shot and killed while attempting to flee from the hue and cry.[40] Another forester probably had advance information about a large illegal hunting group because he had three additional foresters with him the night he caught twelve men with bows and arrows, greyhounds, and nets just after they had captured a deer in the nets. Unfortunately for the foresters, the arrest went badly when one of the poachers shot the forester in the thigh and the others beat the three other foresters before taking off with the venison.[41] In another case the forester was successful in arresting two men he found hunting at night, and he took them to his house where he planned to keep them until morning under guard of one of his servants. Before morning twenty men armed with bows and arrows and with swords came to rescue the arrested man, and they beat the servant badly and then vented their remaining anger at the forester by breaking all the doors and windows in his house.[42]

Not all foresters were so conscientious in performing their duties, and many abused their authority by using their office for personal gain in spite of the oath they swore when they entered office. It took nine pages when an editor printed the misdeeds of Peter de Neville in 1269 as warden in Rutland, and his example could be paralleled from countless other cases from the forest rolls still in manuscript.[43] When erring foresters were brought to account by the verderers or by grievances presented to justices on forest eyre by local juries, the rolls contain details with many examples of foresters failing to carry out their duties or abusing their authority. There is even an example of a warden of the forest who took possession of the rolls from the term of his predecessor in order to prevent access to them by a jury.[44] In fact, the errors of omission when foresters failed in their responsibility are less frequent than outright abuse, but these failures did include not responding for the bailiwick, concealing attachments because the forester had been bribed, overlooking unlicensed sales of wood, and allowing a man in custody for forest offenses to escape.[45]

Most of the destruction to the forest attributable to foresters was to the vert rather than the venison because it was common for them to cut trees for their own use or for sale and to pasture their own animals without regard for the regulations.[46] One forester was caught and charged with illegally cutting six hundred oaks even though he had covered the stumps with turf to escape detection.[47] The few entries concerning illegal hunting of deer include the case of a forester who took home fifteen deer that were killed by the dogs accompanying the king's hunter instead of delivering the slain deer to the hunter for use of the court.[48] Another forester attempted to hide his misdeeds by making a false presentation of a bailiff of the queen for killing deer, but his duplicity was revealed when it was found the bailiff had been for two years on the continent at the time the deer killing had taken place.[49]

In addition to explicit offenses against the vert and some against the venison, foresters were adept at inflicting payments upon the men in their jurisdiction (even resorting to torture) or in collecting illegally high amounts for fees like cheminage and pannage that in themselves were legitimate charges pertaining to their office.[50] When the regarders in one forest were making their regular inquest concerning the lawing of dogs, the forester took over the proceedings and extorted money as amercements from the owners of dogs by claiming that the law required the removal of the left forefoot if the dog had toes removed from the right (and vice versa) and that part of the ball of the foot had to be removed as well as the toes.[51] Even though expressly prohibited by chapter seven of the Forest Charter, some foresters continued to extort payments in grain and to make ale, which they forced the people to buy at scotales before they would allow the sale of any ale.[52] The accounts of the ingenious ways in which foresters abused their office fill the records, but at least one case serves as a reminder that a forester might also become a victim of a miscarriage of justice. In 1255 Hugh of Goldingham, a warden of the forest, was accused of leading a group in making trespasses to vert, venison, pannage, and other things in the forest, and he demanded an inquiry by verderers, regarders, and all knights and free tenants. The verdict was that representatives of four townships had falsely accused him out of their hatred for him.[53]

Some foresters found it profitable to burden their bailiwicks with an unnecessary number of subordinates who paid for the privilege and then attempted to collect additional money from their victims. The jurors in one area found four subordinate foresters, four boys, and two horses when they testified that one riding forester with one boy and one walking forester would have been sufficient.[54] In a list of grievances alleging acts against the Charter of the Forest drawn up in French by men of Somerset in 1278/9 the misdeeds of the foresters and the excess of subordinates who were a burden to the populace were emphasized.[55] False arrests and false presentations were other means by which foresters could use their office to extort money.[56] Even the office itself might be put up for sale to the damage of the king's right of appointment or approval of a transfer from one man to another.[57] This kind of evidence illustrates in detail that foresters continued to abuse their office as they had in the previous century even though the administrative organization of the forests had been regularized in the thirteenth century. With these abuses in mind there is no need to speculate why the forester continued to be an official especially hated by all who came within his jurisdiction.

In most forests there were other bailiwicks on the same administrative level of the appointed foresters that were held by foresters in fee.[58] Because each of these was established by a grant from the king, the specific terms varied and were subject to the vicissitudes of the same incidents that applied to other fiefs—wardship, marriage, escheat, and relief. Disputes over the jurisdiction of foresters in fee were resolved on the basis of inquests held during forest eyres. For example, in Worcester in 1271 the justices found that when Robert Streche, a forester in fee in Feckenham Forest, died nine years before, his bailiwick had been taken into the king's hands and placed in the custody of the justice of the forests south of the Trent. Because the two riding foresters whom the justice put in charge of the fee committed waste, the king then gave custody of the bailiwick to Walter Marshal, who was in the queen's service, along with the wardship and marriage of the heir of the last forester in fee. Unfortunately, Walter and his subordinate foresters continued to cause great waste by cutting and selling trees and allowing others to do so. The foresters were fined and Walter was cited to appear for trial *coram rege* wherever the king might be in England at Christmas.[59] Another inquest concerning a forester in fee produced the information that John fitz Nigel should hold Bernwood Forest by hereditary right for fifty shillings a year as his ancestors had held the bailiwick since the Conquest.[60] The question of inheritance of a forest bailiwick when the heirs were four daughters was solved by working out a rotation by which each daughter would receive the income for a year and divide equally with her sisters who would in later years receive the income in their turns.[61] The case of Roger Gernet in 1236–37 illustrates some of the difficulties a forester in fee might have in maintaining his rights against powerful men—in this case the earl of Kent, the king himself, and another forester—but perseverence and a fine offered to the king won in the long run, and the king ended by providing him the protection he needed in his holding.[62]

The simplest terms by which a forester in fee might hold his bailiwick were by his service in guarding the forest in return for the income from his bailiwick. However, many foresters paid an annual rent in addition to the service of safeguarding their bailiwicks, and others in return for the service as foresters were granted lands in addition to the forest bailiwick.[63] Various issues of the forest collected by foresters in fee are listed in inquests including dead wood and windblown trees, fees for pasturing farm animals, right of common pasture for their own animals, and a fowl at Christmas from every man holding land in the bailiwick.[64] The fourteenth chapter of the Charter of the Forest limited the amounts that foresters in fee could charge for the fee (*cheminage*) from cart or wagon loads of wood or other forest products being transported through the bailiwick.

Like the appointed foresters, the foresters in fee came under the authority of the warden of the forest in which their bailiwicks lay.[65] They were responsible for presenting malefactors at the local forest court and for making attachments on those men who were held for trial before the justices on eyre for forest pleas. They were required to keep rolls to record the attachments that had been made, to have their rolls certified by the verderers, and to present the rolls to the justice of the forest or to the justices on eyre for forest pleas. Failure to perform these duties could mean seizure of the bailiwick into the king's hands and replacement of the forester in fee if the charges were proved.[66] In Sherwood Forest some of the foresters in fee held bailiwicks large enough to need a riding forester, two foot foresters, and some boys for their administration.[67] Where the grant of the bailiwick was not recent, there was a probability that some dispute over the terms by which the bailiwick was held might develop, and in the absence of a charter the forester in fee could only rest his claims on the ground of ancient custom.[68] The foresters in fee were similar to the appointed foresters in other parts of the forest in regard to their misdeeds in office and similar also in committing many more acts against the vert than the occasional lapse against the venison.[69]

In a general sense the term forester was applied to anyone in the forest administration from the justice of the forests north or south of the Trent to the lowly walking forester appointed to his post by the warden of a particular forest or by a forester in fee. In addition to these officials there were other "ministers" of the forest whose work was essential to the management of the royal forests. The verderers (usually four in each forest) were elected to their position in the county court. They were men of considerable standing in the county, and at a minimum they had to possess land within the forest as a qualification. Unlike the various foresters, the verderers neither received salaries nor perquisites with the office, but by custom they were not liable to serve on assizes, recognitions, or juries because those duties might take them out of the county for which they were responsible, and one royal letter carried an order to a sheriff to remove a man as escheator if he were a verderer.[70] In 1290 the king ordered the sheriff of Lancashire to have another man elected coroner in place of John Gentil, who was already a sub-escheator and a verderer and could not conveniently execute any more offices and who was elected coroner because his enemies wanted to aggrieve him further by another office.[71]

As set forth in chapter eight of the Charter of the Forest, the principal duty of the verderers was to attend local forest courts along with the foresters every forty days for viewing attachments for vert and venison. In fact, in the absence of elected verderers attachments could not be made, thus effectively crippling the enforcement of the forest law for both vert and venison on the lowest level.[72] These duties were set forth in more detail in the assize of William de Vescy in 1286/7 when he was a justice in eyre for forest pleas.[73] Although the basic function of the verderers in making attachments remained the same, the assize provided that small pleas were to be decided in the local forest court instead of being referred to the coming of the justices in eyre. Various references illustrate how the system worked. When a man was caught felling a green oak, the verderers and foresters appraised the value of the oak and the verderers collected that amount and made certain that the man had obtained pledges to insure his appearance at the next forest eyre.[74] For lesser transgressions against the vert, the warden and verderers composed a court and collected the amercement for the king.[75] When the foresters found animals belonging to men dwelling outside the forest grazing in the forest without license, they captured the animals and took them before the verderers. After the value of the animals had been appraised, the verderers received that amount and responded for it at the next eyre.[76] Another function of the verderers was to view suspected damage to the forest to ascertain whether damage had been done.[77] Because of his standing in the community and his experience in forest matters, the testimony of a verderer was given special weight in the forest court.[78]

The verderers, like the foresters who made up the local attachment court, were a link between the local court and the justices in eyre for most forest cases. The assize fixed their responsibility as a group for presenting one roll to the justices concerning the attachments made for the forest instead of individual rolls kept by each verderer. In the case of a verderer who had died since the last eyre, his heir was held responsible for making the accounting before the justices and could be fined if he were unable to produce the rolls of his father.[79] Verderers themselves were fined for failing to include all pertinent details including the exact time at which the offense was committed, for contradicting orally what was in the roll, and for not having the bones of a slain deer which they were supposed to keep safely as evidence for the eyre.[80] Because the verderers were not directly responsible to the warden or any other forester, they also provided a check on the conduct of the foresters by bringing abuses by the appointed foresters and foresters in fee before the justices in eyre.[81]

Something of the atmosphere of an actual trial found its way into a record when two verderers disagreed on whether the dogs accompanying a malefactor had been brachs or mastiffs. The justices took the view that verderers should know about dogs and hunting and should not disagree in their testimony before the eyre, and they ordered both verderers thrown into prison until they could pay for their release.[82] The lot of the verderer going about his business in the forest was not always an easy one either, for there are several examples of physical assaults upon verderers by those who identified the verderer with the enforcement of forest law.[83] The following incident shows the feeling that might develop. When some foresters attempted to arrest four men in the forest of Brigstock, they resisted and shot arrows at the foresters. At the inquest, Richard of Aldwinkle, a verderer, gave evidence that William, the steward of Sir Nicholas of Bassingbourn, might have been involved. Later when the verderer was in the forest searching for his pigs, he met the steward and greeted him. "And William replied: 'I do not greet you.' 'Why not?' 'Because you stole our buck.' 'Certainly not,' he said. 'Richard! I would rather go to my plough than serve in such an office as yours.' "[84]

The only other type of forest official whose work was of general importance was the regarder. According to the sixth chapter of the Charter of the Forest, the regarders should make the regard every third year, and it was essential that a regard be made before the coming of the justices in eyre for forest pleas. The sheriff chose the regarders (usually twelve) when ordered to do so by a royal letter.[85] It is doubtful if regards were made every third year when the eyres became much less frequent, but the scanty evidence for regards is inconclusive.[86] Certainly the regarders could be fined for failure to make the regard or for doing the job incompletely or improperly. Although the foresters were expected to lead the regarders, the regarders were required to make the regard on their own initiative if necessary and to present the results to the justices in eyre.[87] No man was allowed to be a regarder and a coroner at the same time.[88]

The regard consisted of a general inspection of the forest to determine the answers to a number of specific questions known as the chapters of the regard.[89] The major thrust of these chapters was to determine whether anyone had made assarts to bring forest land into cultivation, had constructed buildings or other encroachments known by the general term of purprestures, or had cut trees and thereby created waste in the forest. Other questions concerned the royal demesne woods and pastures, whether any eyries of hawks had been found, forges or mines, seaports in which ships or boats could operate for transporting timber, whether any honey had been found, and who had bows and arrows or dogs for hunting. Supplemental questions varied from regard to regard but sometimes included an accounting for gifts of venison or oaks made by the king; whether domestic animals had strayed into the forest; and the conduct of the foresters, agisters, and sellers of wood. Because they were like the verderers in being independent of the foresters, the regarders provided another check on any abuse committed by those officials. How this worked in practice is shown by the report by the regarders of Thurgton that the forest was well kept and the foresters good and faithful, but they also called attention to the practice of the warden Robert de Eueringham in moving several appointed foresters about at will and demanding payment with each move at the rate of one mark from a forester and twenty shillings from a walking forester.[90]

The functions of all these forest officials in their more narrowly administrative aspects as well as in enforcing forest law were carried out through a system of forest courts. In the previous discussion of their duties and responsibilities it was implicit that during the thirteenth century the eyre for forest pleas was central to the functioning of the royal forest. However, even in this century when the eyre was at its height the interval between the eyres could be lengthy, and the uncertainty and delay in holding an eyre contributed to the reputation of forest law as arbitrary and capricious. Eyres that reached most forest counties were held in 1229, 1255–56, 1262, 1269–70, and 1285–86. Although some additional eyres were held in particular counties, the interval between eyres in a given forest might have been as much as twenty-five years, and the eyre rolls with their lists of essoins by death are testimony to the deficiencies caused by such infrequent eyres.[91] An interval of twenty-four years explains the extraordinary number of 247 men summoned to the eyre of 1286 in Nottingham who had died since the last eyre, but most eyre rolls contain enough essoins of this kind to illustrate the problem.[92] The work of the eyre was further complicated by persons who simply failed to appear, townships which failed to send their representatives, and men who failed to produce the defendants for whom they had pledged.[93] Toward the end of the century the eyre became less important and more reliance came to be placed on the general inquisition as a means of enforcing forest law.[94]

Preparations for a forest eyre began with the king appointing justices and directing writs to sheriffs ordering them to summon all the persons required for the business of the eyre. These included royal foresters and verderers with their rolls of attachments made since the last eyre, the regarders with the sealed record of the regard, agisters and their records, and four men from each township. The general summons also included all prelates, knights, free tenants holding land within the forest, and men living outside the forest who followed forest pleas, as well as all persons attached for violations of forest law.[95] Justices for forest pleas often served at other times as itinerant justices for the general eyre, but one limitation to the amount of interchange among justices applying the two kinds of law was that the justice of the forest either north or south of the Trent usually served as one of the forest justices.[96] The rolls of the eyre, which were vital to the business of the next eyre, were kept by the justice of the forests between eyres and transmitted to his successor when the office changed hands or a justice of the forests died.[97] Although there is considerable variation among eyre rolls, they all contain several sections of which the pleas of vert and venison are the most important.[98]

In the ordinary procedure at the eyre the foresters and verderers presented pleas of venison. Usually there is no indication that juries were used at the eyre or that any inquiry was more than a certification of the record being presented. Special inquisitions are only mentioned when townships are amerced for not having come fully. In some cases there is enough information to make it appear that there had been a deliberate refusal to cooperate, probably because of fear of the person committing the offense. If the defendant had never been attached or failed to appear or to present a satisfactory reason for his absence, the sheriff was ordered by the justices to arrest him or to distrain his property. If the accused had no property, the sheriff was authorized to exact him at the county court, where he would eventually be outlawed if he failed to appear. These duties show that cooperation by the sheriff was essential to the functioning of the eyre and that a sheriff could frustrate a decision of the justices if he refused to enforce their orders.[99]

Much of the importance of the forest eyre in the thirteenth century lay in its relation to the other forest courts: the inquisition, attachment court, regard, and swanimote.[100] The Charter of the Forest in its eighth chapter refers to attachment courts held every forty days by verderers and foresters for both vert and venison and swanimotes held in some forests three times a year to deal with the placing of farm animals in the forest. However, the term "swanimote" is a source of confusion because it was used in some counties for the attachment court, later it was applied to a special inquisition, and in the time of Edward I it was used for the general inquisition.[101] The special inquisition took place when evidence was found that might indicate a violation of the forest, and the procedure was for four representatives from the neighboring townships to inquire into the circumstances. General inquisitions on articles concerning the forest are in evidence by mid-century, and commissions of inquest into "the state of the forest" became common by the end of the century when they were used first to supplement and then to replace the eyre.

Of these various courts, the attachment court and its relation to the eyre raises the basic question of the nature of the eyre. Unfortunately, the evidence on the relationship of these two courts is not only scarce but somewhat contradictory. The Charter of the Forest in chapters eight and ten provided for the attachment court to meet every forty days and conceded that no person was to lose life or members for offenses against the venison. It provided instead for punishment by amercement. If he could not pay, the transgressor was imprisoned and then released when he could find pledges, or after a year and a day he was forced to abjure the realm. In chapter sixteen no constable or other person was allowed to hold pleas of the forest, and foresters in fee were required to present their lists of men whom they had attached for forest offenses to the verderers. The verderers, in turn, were to present their sealed rolls of attachments to the chief forester when he came into the area for holding forest pleas, and these cases listed in the attachments were to be terminated before him. The charter is not clear whether judgments were made in the attachment court or at the eyre. In 1287 the assize used by William de Vescy and his fellow justices repeated the charter but in cases of vert distinguished between "lesser pleas" that were to be pleaded in attachment court and other pleas for which the verderers were to answer before the justices in eyre. Cases involving green oaks were attached and then amercements were made at the eyre, but for dry saplings under four pence in value the amercement was paid at the next attachment court. The assize further provided that for escapes of beasts of the plow into the demesne woods and enclosures of the king and for all other transgressions against the Charter of the Forest the pleas were to be held in the future in the attachment court.[102] In his forest ordinance of 1306 Edward I further split the jurisdiction by providing that with the assent of the treasurer the justice of the forest might take fines from those indicted for forest transgressions without waiting for the next eyre.[103]

The rolls of the eyre are never explicit on this question, and even the few surviving rolls of attachment courts have little evidence on procedure in that court.[104] It may be that the jurisdiction of the attachment court was not clear at the time. The justices in eyre ruled in one case that the warden of the forest and the verderers had no power to try a man for killing a forester and nullified their verdict on the ground that they had overstepped their authority.[105] The attachment court acted to make attachments of both vert and venison, to hold inquests about venison, to arrest and imprison men determined to have transgressed against the venison, and to make inquiries about waste.[106]

Yet the attachment courts did not function independently of the eyre. There was a basic relationship in that cases in which attachments had been made were presented by foresters, verderers, and foresters in fee at the eyre; there the justices decided the amount of amercements and by their decision terminated these cases. However, the justices might investigate further and once questioned the foresters and verderers as to whether they thought a man listed in their rolls was really guilty.[107] Nevertheless, even a cursory glance at the eyre roll gives the impression that levying the amercements was considered the most important work of the eyre. This impression of an overriding financial interest is substantiated in some rolls in which the scribe kept a running total of the amounts collected.[108] The eyre as the place where amercements were set would explain why royal writs not to amerce men who had already fined with the king were directed to the justices.[109] In spite of the care taken in the eyre, mistakes did occur that had to be investigated and in some cases corrected by the barons of the Exchequer when they attempted to collect the sums assessed at the eyre.[110]

In addition to their function in assessing penalties as emphasized by the attention given in an eyre roll to amercements, the justices in eyre handled cases which the attachment court had failed to settle. When a married couple resisted attachment by the foresters and verderers for cutting oaks, the justices heard the case, ordered the bailiffs of Colchester to produce the man and wife, and collected the amercement for the offense.[111] In a more general sense, this type of case implies that the authority of the eyre was available to reinforce the attachment court and that the authority of the eyre was superior to that of the attachment court. Moreover, because the foresters and verderers who staffed the attachment court were accountable at the eyre for their conduct in office, the eyre had the indirect effect of strengthening the conscientious operation of the lower court.

There were other cases in which the function of the eyre seems to have been independent from the attachment court, but the principle by which some cases were brought directly to the eyre is never made clear. Sometimes defendants appeared before the justices to plead, or failed to appear and were ordered to be arrested by the sheriff.[112] The justices proclaimed outlawry for venison, freed men from prison, and heard the case of men found guilty by an inquisition of cutting trees by night.[113] Exemptions from the forest law were claimed before the justices.[114] At least one roll suggests that the justices were trying cases that were pending at the time of the eyre, while they were at the same time levying amercements to terminate other cases that had accumulated during the years since the last eyre.[115]

The arrangements for taking up the business of an eyre for the Forest of the Dean that had been interrupted in 1282 by the war in Wales provide a unique glimpse into the operation of an eyre. Royal orders for resumption of the eyre on a restricted basis provided that all those persons who had been indicted, attached, or mainprised and who had not made fines were to appear for terminating pleas in a three-day session. The writ noted that pleas of the vert were customarily pleaded in the swanimotes, even though that was not an authorized procedure, and added that foresters and verderers were authorized henceforth to hear pleas for vert in a reasonable manner and to enroll two pledges for each attachment. At the same time, the constable of St. Briavels, who was also warden of the Dean, was prohibited from pleading attachments for vert that should be pleaded and terminated before the justices.[116] Apparently the jurisdiction of the eyre had begun to erode in cases of vert well before the circumstances of the fore-shortened eyre forced official approval of the practice of pleading these cases in the lower court. The reservation of certain cases whether in respect to the constable acting arbitrarily on his own or, perhaps more likely, as presiding officer in the attachment court (or swanimote as it was called in Dean) may have been the division for cases of vert that was formalized five years later in the assize of William de Vescy.

In practice there was some intermingling of forest law and common law. Important officials were involved in the operations of both kinds of courts. There is evidence from the New Forest to show that pleas of the forest and common law pleas were sometimes intermingled, and the verderers of Huntingdon recognized the problem to the extent of raising the question of a division between the two laws.[117] Not only was the assistance of the sheriff necessary for arresting offenders and imprisoning them until the coming of the forest eyre, he was also ordered to read the Forest Charter in full county court and to choose the regarders and hold elections for the verderers.[118] Other studies show that in spite of the fuzzy boundaries between forest law and the common law both laws coexisted in the large area that was forest in the thirteenth century with little difficulty caused in practice by the overlapping jurisdiction.[119]

One particularly explicit royal letter was sent in 1234 to sheriffs in four counties directing them to hold inquests into hunting violations in their counties and to take pledges from violators of the forest who had not allowed themselves to be attached by royal foresters in the usual manner. The sheriffs were then to make sure that the defendants were brought before the king at Westminster on the charges. The letter also established a general procedure in which sheriffs would make arrests when foresters reported that they had been unable to do so and that the sheriffs would place the men arrested in these instances in the county jail.[120] In fact, not all forests had their own prisons and the county jail was used routinely in those areas for offenders against the forest law.[121]

The intricate intermingling of officials and jurisdictions is illustrated in a Northampton case of 1255 concerning three men arrested for possession of venison. When the trial of these men opened, the sheriff was unable to produce two of the three because they had already been hanged for theft by order of Geoffrey Lewknor, who had been acting as a justice assigned for delivering the jail at Northampton. In 1255 the same justice was present as one of the justices for forest pleas, and he acknowledged that the two men had been convicted of theft before him, but he emphasized that the foresters and the sheriff had been present and had not mentioned that the two men were being held in prison for trespass against the venison. The record concludes with the statement that because the sheriff could not deny this he was brought to judgment for neglect.[122] In another case the question whether deer had been killed within or outside the forest was determined in a common law court, and because two verderers came to this court to report they had held the inquest on the slain deer as required by forest law and determined the killing had been within the forest, the defendant later made a fine of three palfreys with the king for himself and his men.[123]

Killings within the bounds of the forest obviously caused some confusion of legal jurisdiction. One improvisation was to order the sheriff and the forester jointly to make an inquest, but in the New Forest crown pleas were included in the forest eyre. Even there, some confusion arose whether the indictment had to be made by the coroner and whether the accused had the right to a jury.[124] In 1255 the verderers in Huntingdon successfully argued that they were not required by the assize of the forest to make attachments in the case of a stranger found slain in the forest on the grounds that the law of the land should not be abolished by a forest assize and, therefore, the procedure had to be according to the pleas of the crown.[125]

As might be expected, much of the confusion between the two kinds of law resulted from the problem of whether land was within the forest or not. The issue of who had the right to a particular piece of land turned on the issue of a perambulation of the forest and whether that perambulation affected common land, and the decision was sought in a common law court by an abbot who claimed the land as granted by a charter of King John.[126] Again the alleged offense of asserting a common wood to the detriment of the royal forest was brought before a common law court and delayed on the basis of a rule of common law involving the gift by a minor.[127] The seizure of two manors belonging to the bishop of Coventry and Lichfield by the justices on a forest eyre because of purprestures there brought a petition to Parliament by the bishop who claimed an exemption by charter of Richard I. After the question had been raised whether these particular manors had been acquired subsequent to the charter and were not included in the provisions of the charter, the bishop surrendered the manors to the king and received them back exempt from the forest for a payment of one thousand pounds.[128] Other petitions to Parliament show that problems of rights within the forest could be resolved by petition either by obtaining special orders for justices of the forest or by special inquests appointed by the king, and, in either case, they represent the practice of going outside the normal operation of the forest law in order to resolve a grievance.[129] Attorneys were quick to use the confusion of laws when it was to their client's advantage, as in the arguments abstracted for the *Year Books* in 1293 when there was an attempt to block a writ of *novel disseisn* by the claim that the land was within a royal forest. The opposing attorney countered with the claim that the defendant had only a chace and that because the land was not in royal forest the only remedy was in common law, not in forest law.[130]

Although the major question of jurisdiction involved the relation of forest law to the common law courts, forest law occasionally impinged upon the privileges of boroughs and universities and regularly involved the clergy who had no exemption from forest courts by virtue of their order. The procedure for clergy accused of forest offenses differed from that used for laymen both before and after the trial because the bishop was responsible for producing a clerk for trial, and the clerk did not have to provide pledges for his appearance. After a trial, if the bishop claimed a clerk, the justices surrendered him as one convicted of forest offenses, but the clergy had to pay amercements just as laymen did.[131] In fact, an examination of the payments for forest offenses shows that they were consistently higher for clergy. Perhaps the clergy were somewhat less likely to be convicted for forest offenses simply because abbots and bishops were more likely to have obtained charters of exemption from forest law for themselves and their men than were lay lords. Nevertheless, neither respect nor fear of the clergy had any intimidating effect upon the foresters, who did not hesitate to arrest clerks for forest violations, and one group of foresters even resisted the threat of excommunication with bells and candles rather than surrender an imprisoned clerk.[132] Other disputes were caused by clergy over the right to tithes, a right that did not exist if the land claimed to be subject to tithes was within a royal forest.[133] Students at Oxford were similarly bound by forest law, and it took an appeal to the king by three archdeans, the chancellor of Oxford, a master, and the "whole university" to obtain the release of five students caught with bows and arrows in Shotover Forest.[134]

The boundaries between forest law and that of towns and manors caused some problems. In the New Forest the enforcement of the assize of bread and wine, usually under the jurisdiction of the manorial court by the thirteenth century, was regularly enforced in the forest

courts.[135] Two common features of borough charters raised the possibility of conflict with the forest law: 1) exemption of the borough from
the authority of royal officials, and 2) exemption of the burgesses from
being tried in courts outside the borough. The justices for forest pleas
recognized these exemptions but only when the town officials were
able to produce their charters in court to confirm their claims.[136]

A case from Colchester in 1277 illustrates the difficulty of putting
some of the nice legal distinctions into practice. A forester saw three
men from Colchester hunting in the forest with bows and arrows but
failed to prevent their escape into the thick undergrowth. The justices
in eyre for forest pleas then ordered the bailiffs of Colchester to produce the culprits, but they did nothing about it. Then the sheriff was
ordered to arrest the one man who had been recognized, whether he
was found within or without the town and in spite of the liberty of the
town. A week after this order had been given the forester who had
attempted the arrest in the first place came into Colchester, and one
of the bailiffs had him seized and imprisoned. When a riding forester
came to free his subordinate if he could, three bailiffs and a large group
of townsmen imprisoned him also for eight days. Shortly thereafter
Roger de Clifford, justice of the forest at Colchester, held an inquest
that uncovered the additional information that the two foresters had
earlier accidentally killed a townsman who was a flagrant violator of
the forest during an attempt to arrest him. The outcome of the incident
was that the townsmen pledged ten marks to the foresters for their
disgraceful treatment of those royal officials. Furthermore, because the
burgesses claimed the right that no forester could make an attachment
within their *banlieu* where the royal forest was within the *banlieu*, and
for this reason, the forest was allowed to be wasted and destroyed.
Because of the treatment of the two foresters, the justice of the forest
would speak to the king about the problem. The record concludes with
a copy of the Colchester charter as granted by Richard I and confirmed by Henry III with a little hand drawn in the margin opposite
the pertinent sentence that no forester should have the power to interfere with anybody within the *banlieu*.[137]

In addition to the exemption from forest law provided by borough
charters, there were several other types of exemption that lessened the
effective area of royal forest law. When King Henry III granted Lancaster to his son Edmund in 1267, the grant included the forests that
were temporarily removed from the number of royal forests even
though they continued to be administered under Edmund as they had
been when they were under the king. This arrangement continued in
the next reign, and King Edward I in 1285 granted Edmund the right

to hold forest pleas in Lancaster.[138] Edward I also used some royal forests as part of the dower that went to his mother upon Henry III's death, but this arrangement was by its nature a temporary provision and was more significant for the collection of revenue and the appointment of forest officials than it was for forest law because these forests were not removed from the jurisdiction of the royal forest courts.[139] There were several other significant modifications of the usual operation of the forests. Members of the royal household and all the barons, while not exempt from forest law, had the right to be tried before the king and their cases were not heard by the justices in eyre for forest pleas.[140] Of the many charters granting exemption of particular woods or individuals from forest jurisdiction, the charter obtained by the Templars, which allowed them to use their lands within royal forests exempt from the laws pertaining to the vert, was the most generous, but their lands remained subject to the laws about the venison.[141] When the charters of partial exemptions and exceptions are considered as a whole, the effect was to provide an amelioration of the forest law in practice.[142]

Additional modification of the forest law developed by means of the licenses granted to persons allowing them to construct parks or to establish a "chace" on their lands and by official recognition of the rights of common by which domestic animals were permitted to graze in certain parts of the forest. The essential feature of a park was the enclosure that physically set off the park from the royal forest, and the fence or ditch had to be sufficient to prevent the king's beasts from leaving the forest and entering the park where they would no longer be protected by forest law.[143] Just as breaking the gates or fence of a park was punished in royal forest courts, so failure to maintain the enclosure might be punished by the seizure of the park into the king's hands.[144] Frequently the license to construct a park was accompanied by a gift of deer from the royal forest to stock the park.[145]

Legally the license for a park brought exemption from the regard and other aspects of forest law provided the integrity of the park was maintained and the king sustained no loss to his venison from the park. Occasionally the king allowed other enclosures to be built within royal forests to protect lands under cultivation from the deer, but these were not considered parks.[146] In addition to the obvious advantage of a park in creating easier conditions for hunting deer, it can be seen from the reports on royal parks that these areas produced a variety of other income.[147] They also caused many problems that came to the attention of forest courts, including the unauthorized construction of a park, deer being hunted in a park escaping into the forest and being pursued there by hunters, parks inadequately enclosed, parkers in royal parks who failed to protect the venison, and parkers in private parks who hunted in the neighboring royal forest[148] When Henry III enclosed Plumpton Park, there were claims from residents of the forest that the king had violated their right of common in removing the area from the forest.[149]

The laws concerned with hunting within parks were changed several times in the thirteenth century, but, strictly speaking, parks were removed from the jurisdiction of forest law. The subject of penalties for trespassing in parks was raised in 1236 before the royal council, but it was not pursued when the king objected to the magnates' request to have their own prisons as part of the enforcement machinery.[150] Ten years later a procedure that brought royal assistance to the owner of a park had the following provisions: the owner should lodge a complaint of trespass within his park with the king, the king would order an inquest into the complaint, those guilty of a trespass would be imprisoned in a royal prison, and the king and owner would divide the fines paid by prisoners for their release. The assistance to owners of parks continued to be provided in a modified way throughout the century, but any action taken by royal officials was done under the law of trespass through the common law courts and not as a part of the forest law.[151] Another partial exemption from forest law was established with a royal grant of the right to have a chace on one's land, which established what amounted to a private forest. A chace placed the protection of the beasts of the forest in private hands, and the forest eyre and other forest courts no longer operated within the boundaries.[152] Another type of hunting privilege granted by the king in the form of a warren had nothing to do with a royal forest because warrens were usually granted only on lands outside the forest and because the animals concerned were rabbits and some other animals that were never considered beasts of the forest in any location. Occasionally the king himself had warren on lands within the forest, and enforcement of laws relating to these warrens brought cases into the forest records, but this was an exceptional circumstance and not technically a part of the royal forest.[153]

The rolls of a forest eyre were divided into two general sections containing trespasses against the venison and trespasses against the vert. The forest law won its reputation for severity mainly for its treatment of crimes against the venison with penalties that included death and mutilation as maximum penalties in the first half and at the end of the twelfth century. In practice, as discussed in a previous chapter, amercements were usually substituted for the rigor of the law, and the tenth chapter of the Forest Charter in 1217 explicitly stated that no person henceforth should lose his life or member for an offense against the venison. Instead the Charter provided that the offender should pay a monetary penalty and, if he could not pay, be held in prison a year and a day when he would be released if he could find pledges or be forced to abjure the realm. The satirical writer Nigel Wireker commented about both kinds of penalty as he observed the forest law at work about 1180:[154]

> And man, though in his Maker's image made
> Who all, that is, created, yet is paid
> By princes less regard than beasts of earth,
> Ay, all our race is held of lesser worth.
> How many are hanged on cruel gallows-tree
> For taking flesh of beasts! more savagely
> Sicilian tyrants could not well ordain
> Than that for slaying beasts a man be slain.

He continued with a harangue that there is no truth in princes and illustrated his point with the assertion that justice can only be obtained by purchasing it with money and the king persuaded to act only by gifts. Although his complaint was not meant to apply specifically to the forest law, it became more and more apt in the change to a system of monetary penalties and the adopting in 1217 of a payment as the normal penalty.

The crime of hunting or killing a deer could not be settled by the lesser forest courts and had to be brought before the eyre for forest pleas. Because large numbers of these eyre rolls survive, they suggest the possibility of working out the incidence of trespasses against the venison. Only the rolls in which the year of the offense was recorded can be used for this purpose because the eyres were not held regularly and the surviving rolls are by no means complete. Nevertheless, there are cases in which the years of the offenses are given for twenty-five forests, and some of the records extend over long enough periods to indicate trends. Table 4 contains the figures for the number of cases for venison from eyre rolls arranged in rough order from North to South that represent all sections of the country and for long enough periods to be significant. The remaining forests had entries in too few years to eliminate the possibility of the chance survival of a year that was the exception to the usual pattern or extended into two counties, making a roll from only one county incomplete. Of course, the figures in table 4 are only those cases in which an arrest was made and the violator brought before the justices. Sometimes several men were in-

Table 4
Cases for Trespass of Venison from the Eyre Rolls°

Forest	Years	Range of Cases per year	Average No. of Cases per year
Inglewood (Cumberland)	1263–85	4–25	7
Sherwood (Nottingham)	1263–87	1–18	8
Shropshire	1251–72	1–9	4
Cannock (Stafford)	1249–86	1–15	4
Kinver (Stafford)	1253–85	1–10	4
Feckenham (Worcester)	1261–68	2–11	5
Rockingham (Northampton)	1251–87	1–32	5
Chippenham (Wiltshire)	1246–55	1–10	4
Clarendon (Wiltshire)	1263–67	1–5	4
Melksham (Wiltshire)	1246–56	1–4	2
Savernake (Wiltshire)	1264–69	2–11	5
Essex	1277–92	1–14	5
New Forest (Hampshire)	1270–80	1–7	4

° All these rolls are in P.R.O., Exchequer, Treasury of Receipt, Forest Proceedings.

volved when one case included a group of hunters, and the cases are misleading about the number of violations when a case concerned a man listed as "a habitual malefactor in the forest" who, presumably, was not caught for most of the violations he was reputed to have committed. Years in which no cases were recorded have not been included in the averages because there are too many possibilities for error to warrant the assumption that no cases occurred in a given year just because the extant records do not list any cases. When all the vagaries of the records have been considered, the figures point to a conclusion that the number of cases of illegal hunting per year in these forests (and probably for others where the records are not extant) was quite small. Either illegal hunting of deer was not common or, more likely, the efficiency of the foresters and verderers has been highly overrated. In the light of successful cases, the forest law concerning venison had little effect on the men who lived in the royal forests, and in many years even in large forests there was only one case (and possibly none in some years) brought before the justices.

The standard rationale for royal forests was that they were established to protect the king's beasts, but in the thirteenth century the procedure for dealing with cases concerned with venison had become complex, and many subsidiary interests affected the manner in which they were handled. A case began when a man was caught in the act of hunting by foresters or by villagers who raised the hue and cry or when he was discovered by means of an inquest to explain circumstances that pointed to the death of a deer. The representatives of the four neighboring townships testified concerning their knowledge of an apparent violation at an inquest before the foresters and verderers. The defendant was arrested by the foresters if they caught him or by the sheriff when he had been named by an inquest, and at the attachment court he had either to obtain men as pledges for his appearance at the next eyre for forest pleas or he would be imprisoned until he could pay for his release and obtain pledges. With the coming of the justices in eyre, the foresters and verderers presented their rolls of attachments listing the cases and the names of pledges since the last eyre. The justices then set the amount of the amercements or made further inquiries into a case by holding another inquest. Those found guilty who could not pay the assessed amount were imprisoned up to a year and a day when they might be released because of their poverty or, in theory, made to abjure the realm. Men who could not be arrested and failed to appear before the justices were declared outlaws.

Because of the complex procedure that brought a case before the justices for an offense against the venison, most eyre rolls begin with a list of defaults. Townships were fined for not being present at the eyre, sureties failed to have the men for whom they had pledged, and verderers did not produce their rolls. Examination of the amounts assessed for these defaults shows that they were not standardized even within the same eyre, with payments for failure of a township to appear ranging from two pounds to a half mark (6s. 8d.).[155] Perhaps the amounts represent the justices' idea of the seriousness of the default, because there were reasons given (other than negligence) to explain why townships were frequently in default for not coming or not coming fully to the eyre. The rolls contain many examples of neighboring townships summoned to an inquest when a deer had been killed and reporting that they had no knowledge of the crime, only to be fined for default at the next eyre.[156] Some references of this kind give enough information to indicate that the men of the townships had pleaded ignorance to protect one of their own people, from fear of retaliation if they named a man with whom they had to live side by side, and out of contempt for royal officials who were attempting to enforce an unpopular forest law among them.[157]

There were many exceptions to the enforcement of the laws prohibiting the hunting of the king's deer, and these had to be administered by the foresters and the justices who had final disposition of cases involving the venison. Even when the king himself hunted, the justices had to be informed in order that no charges would be brought against the members of the royal hunting party or that no negligence could be charged against any official whose duty it was to guard the beasts of the forest.[158] Notification was made by a royal writ, but some writs allowing a member of the hunting party to take deer "without number" did little more than provide identification of a person hunting with permission.[159] The accounting for the deer killed by a royal hunting party at times was also rather loose, as illustrated by a day's hunt in Inglewood in 1271 reported as four hundred harts and hinds, but the succeeding days' results of thirty-two, eight, and sixteen hinds probably represent accurate counts.[160] In addition to the king's own hunts, the court employed professional hunters or local foresters to provide meat for the court or to trap deer for stocking parks, and the justices were notified to exempt these men from any possible prosecution.[161] In 1277 John de Somerset obtained a general pardon for all trespasses against the forest because he had long served King Henry III as a hunter and might easily be indicted for trespass of the forest in the course of his employment.[162]

Of course, the king could share the deer in the royal forests with other persons as he saw fit, and any gifts or permission to hunt meant exceptions to the normal operation of the forest law. A general exception was made for the justices, who were permitted to take deer for food during the course of a forest eyre, but deer taken for this purpose were duly recorded on the rolls.[163] The king shared the royal forests with members of his family by granting what amounted to free hunting privileges, and he sometimes favored visiting dignitaries or men who had served him well by giving them hunting privileges or the right to take a specified number of deer.[164] Indirectly, various monasteries benefited from deer taken by the king or under terms of a royal gift by their right to a tithe of the deer.[165] One historian studying the Forest of the Dean counted the animals listed in grants for the later twelfth and the thirteenth centuries and arrived at totals of eight or nine hundred fallow deer, two hundred red deer, and sixty wild boars.[166] When the number of deer became diminished in 1271, the king ordered that no deer should be taken in Feckenham Forest for two years notwithstanding any writs he had issued to permit hunting.[167] Whether overhunting or disease had caused the shortage was not stated, but in 1285 and 1287 there were references to hundreds of deer killed by "murrain."[168] Outside of a general epidemic, individual references to deer having been killed by disease can not always be taken at face value because that was a convenient explanation at an inquest, and the justices refused this explanation in one case and fined the four townships for "not coming fully" when they used it.[169]

In practice the inefficiencies of the eyre caused more exceptions in the enforcement of forest law than all the other reasons. Because of the long intervals between the coming of the justices, the main cause of exceptions was the death of persons indicted for crimes against the venison before their cases were brought before the eyre. It is an unusual eyre roll that does not dispose of many cases with the ominous notation of "mort" placed beside the record of the case. A case in 1277 involving years of delay by the sheriff in executing the orders of the justices was not treated as being unusual. In 1264 three men were presented as having killed a deer, but one was dead at the time of the presentment. The justices ordered the sheriff to arrest the other two who had not appeared, but he failed to make the arrests and was fined for default. Afterward the sheriff told the justices that the two men had been dead for five years and protested that he was explaining as soon as he could and that he did not have contempt for the judicial order for which he had been found in default. His explanation was accepted and his fine removed, thus terminating a case thirteen years after the offense and after all the defendants had died.[170] Even when a case proceeded smoothly to a conviction, the king used his pardoning power so generously as to provide a significant interference with the enforcement of forest law. Some men purchased pardons by gifts to the king and others benefited from the influence of persons close to the king or from their own prior service to the king.[171]

Although imprisonment was used as a procedural device rather than a penalty under forest law, there is sufficient evidence that it could amount to severe punishment even for those only awaiting trial. It could be avoided by obtaining pledges for appearance before the justices or by paying fines, and only the defendant who could not meet these conditions would be held for a maximum of a year and a day. In addition, the fines were frequently reduced or the king ordered men released because of their poverty, but the conditions of imprisonment for any length of time made it something to be dreaded.[172] The implications of one case from 1209 are chilling. Having traced the blood of a slain deer to the house of Ralph Red, the forester of Cliffe sent for verderers and good men and they found the flesh of a deer in the house. Ralph was imprisoned and appealed two other men as his companions before he himself died in prison awaiting trial. One of the men produced an alibi and the other, Roger Tock, denied all guilt. The record ends with a notation: "And because Roger lay for a long time in prison, so that he is nearly dead it is adjudged that he go quit; and let him dwell outside the forest."[173] In another case a man unable to find pledges remained in prison a year and a day and then abjured the realm. However, he was later pardoned by the king because of his poverty, his imprisonment, and the debility of his body.[174] For men who could not be arrested and brought to prison, the ultimate penalty was outlawry, and rolls with lists of men who had been declared outlaws by the justices are evidence that some offenders chose to suffer this penalty in preference to submitting to the forest courts.[175]

The usual penalty for illegal hunting in the thirteenth century was an amercement assessed by the justices in eyre for forest pleas, and it is obvious in looking at any eyre roll that the amounts for this offense varied a great deal. From the entries that contain enough information to judge, it is clear that neither the number of deer killed nor any other measure of the severity of the offense explains the variation in amounts. In fact, the forest law was a respecter of persons, and the fines were relative to the amount that the defendant could be expected to pay.[176] However, a defendant of baronial rank could not be amerced before the justices in eyre because he had the right to be tried before the king himself. A rather complicated case from a roll of 1278 turned on the question of baronage. The facts given were that John Tregor had been convicted in the last eyre of killing a deer, but he had not come before the justices nor made a fine because he held by barony and could only be amerced *coram rege*. By inspection of the earlier rolls in 1278 it was found that he had never been amerced, and he was arrested and imprisoned. Now he claimed that he was not a baron at the time of the offense and sought an inquest by the foresters, verderers, and other ministers of the forest to determine his status. They confirmed that his father had still been alive and that he was a "bachelarius" at the time of the offense, but the justices must have felt some uncertainty about how to proceed, for the case was adjourned to be heard before the king at the next parliament.[177] In any event, the privilege of being heard *coram rege* did not necessarily mean that a baron would be fined less than he might have been by the justices, for even the king's own brother, Edmund, earl of Cornwall, paid twenty pounds at the Exchequer in a case that had begun with the justices and had been referred to the king for a decision.[178]

As bishop of Durham, Anthony Bek had the right of a baron to be tried *coram rege*, but the clergy of all ranks, both secular and regular, were subject to the forest law.[179] The chief difference in procedure from laymen was that the bishop was held responsible for producing clerks before the justices, instead of using the usual attachment procedure and the sheriff, but there are instances where the sheriff attempted to attach a clerk.[180] In illegal hunting parties consisting of clergy and laymen the penalties for the clergy were consistently higher than those for the laymen found guilty of the same offense. Often the disparity was quite large as, for example, a layman amerced ten shillings and two clerks in the same party fined forty marks (£26 13s. 4d.) and fifty marks (£33 6s. 8d.) with the difference in the two clerical sums attributable to the latter having possession of the venison in his house.[181] Another list of payments for trespass against the venison usually has the amount as one-half mark, with one large payment of ten marks, but in the same list the amount assessed the abbot of Battle Abbey was sixty marks.[182]

Another case in which there was a marked disparity in the amercements included some Jews among those convicted. After a hunting party had started a deer in the forest, it ran into Colchester and both Christian and Jewish townsmen joined in a chase that caused the deer to run through a gate and break its neck in a leap beyond the wall. Because some of the defendants did not surrender voluntarily, all the amounts ultimately assessed in the case are not comparable, but the Christians were each amerced two shillings and the Jews who surrendered were amerced forty shillings, one mark (13s. 4d.), two marks (£1 6s. 8d.), and four marks (£2 13s. 4d.).[183]

The explanation for variation in the amounts listed for amercements probably is that they were set according to the ability to pay. This conclusion is consistent with the description of a forest eyre given in the lawbook known as *Fleta* in which maximum limits on amercements were fixed according to the status of the defendant. It provides that a freeman shall be amerced according to his delict, saving his livelihood as determined by his peers; and a clergyman according to his lay holdings and not by the worth of his ecclesiastical benefice.[184] Application of these limits might produce variations in payments for the same offense, and the pecuniary bias in the forest administration can be seen in the larger sums assessed for barons, clergy, and Jews as groups.

A suspicion of strangers or outsiders is another thread that runs through the records of the forest eyres. In some cases this xenophobia may have been nothing more than an attempt to blame unknown persons rather than to inquire too closely into the activities of neighbors, but even these attempts depended upon a general feeling against strangers for their plausibility. For example, a jury returned that they did not know anyone who killed a deer found by the foresters unless it might have been some unknown robbers going secretly through the countryside.[185] Rather more convincing is another case in which the culprits were named as a stranger knight and his two squires.[186] Other cases in which men had been arrested for crimes against the venison only to be released for lack of evidence reveal a general suspicion of vagrants strong enough to cause them to be arrested for forest violations even when there was nothing except their vagrancy to warrant the arrests.[187]

Of course, there were men living on the fringes of society who preyed on the king's deer in reality as well as fiction whose activities gave credibility to the suspected crimes of other outsiders. When the king was crossing through Windsor Forest toward Reading in 1234, he learned that a certain Richard Siward was hiding in the forest with a multitude of men and that only the king's presence prevented him from attacking the entourage. Letters close went to the sheriffs in ten counties urging all efforts to arrest Richard, whose present whereabouts was unknown, and warning them to be especially careful when they or their agents brought money to the next Exchequer in order that Richard should not rob them along the way. In fact, the royal justiciar suffered that fate and efforts were made to cut Richard Siward off from escape to Wales while the campaign to arrest him and his followers was intensified in England.[188]

During the next several years, Windsor Forest continued to be a problem as a haven for malefactors, but other forests were almost equally plagued.[189] In 1238 there was a plan to enlist the support of all people living in the countryside (*homines rurales*) to report the activities of malefactors who were boldly travelling around by day and night, or, at least, to prohibit the country people from selling the malefactors food and drink, on the theory that they could only operate so freely with the support of the populace. The intensity of the royal campaign is further illustrated by warnings to sheriffs that they must arrest these malefactors and hold them in prison even though they had been reluctant to do so because of the uncertainty of getting paid for the expenses of keeping the prisoners, and the clergy were told to cooperate or face the loss of their special exemptions.[190] At other times, individual malefactors or small bands were responsible for depredations upon the forest, harassing or killing foresters, and raiding travellers.[191] Trouble spots where passes or narrow roads through a forest provided cover for the bandits were identified and the king ordered clearings to provide for a greater margin of safety in these spots.[192] In 1291 a band (*societas*) of at least twenty-four men operated in Kingswood in Essex taking deer at will for at least six months in true Robin Hood fashion before the foresters began to deal with them.[193] The question of whether Robin Hood of the ballads was a real person or, at least, personifies real conditions is one on which there is no consensus, but there can be no question there were real outlaws taking refuge in royal forests during the thirteenth century and posing a threat to travellers and to those who lived in the forests.[194]

Buried among the concise summaries of cases about the venison are vignettes that evoke other living persons who tried to be law-abiding, to whom the royal foresters meant a real limitation on how they could go about their daily business and not some sort of administrative abstraction. In 1265 Walter le Monner found himself suddenly confronted with the power of the foresters and the harsh reality of the forest law. He had been crossing through the Forest of the Dean when he came upon Walter Kadel, who was skinning a buck and who forced him to assist. Unfortunately, at this point some foresters appeared and, having caught the two men red-handed, proceeded to arrest and imprison them. The case had a happy ending when Walter was able to prove his innocence.[195] Often the foresters are pictured in more active roles following up circumstantial evidence—the finding of blood and hair on a man's property—to obtain an indictment or staking out a spot in the forest where a net had been placed to secure the arrest of two men, only to have one turn out to be an innocent party.[196] The position of the foresters against trespassers was strengthened by a statute in 1293 which provided that if a forester killed a trespasser who put up armed resistance to an arrest, the forester would not have to answer for the killing before royal justices. However, the statute contained the warning that foresters would be liable if they used this statute as a pretense to kill any persons passing through their jurisdictions who were not trespassing on the forest.[197] The familiarity of both foresters and jurors with the details of hunting is illustrated in a case in which a careful description of the hunting dogs that were captured when their masters escaped was sufficient to identify the culprits.[198] Dogs figured in another arrest when a group of foresters dining with the abbot of Pipewell saw three greyhounds that matched the description of the dogs belonging to a poacher who had killed a forester attempting to arrest him.[199]

All sorts and conditions of men ran afoul of the forest law from the three men who killed a deer to provide the wedding feast for a friend to the earl of Derby whose passion for hunting accounted for more than two thousand deer killed in the forest of High Peak over a six-year period.[200] Alicia, the wife of Thomas fitz Ralph, found herself under arrest for possession of the shoulder of a hart that her husband and a friend had taken in a trap. Although her husband died in prison while awaiting trial, Alicia was released on the ground that "Thomas her man whom she could not contradict while he lived brought the said venison to her and Alicia was not guilty."[201] Other glimpses of life in the forest include jurors of one township accusing another of building a deer stall, two men who made a business of poaching and selling venison in spite of the forest law, the number of deer being transferred from one royal official to another for the king's use carefully accounted for with a receipt, the disagreeable task of removing the dead bodies of wild animals and pigs that were decaying in the park of Havering, and the assignment of one hundred pounds from the amercements of a forest eyre to help the Dominicans build a new church in London.[202]

Another darker aspect of the pervasive forest law was the climate of fear that it generated. How this fear worked in the minds of two men is exemplified in a case when the foresters found a doe with its throat cut. Nearby they discovered Henry fitz Benselin cowering under a bush, but he maintained that he was in the forest looking for a horse that had strayed. Nevertheless, he was imprisoned, and when his case came before the justices, the foresters and verderers reported that he was no longer suspected because another man upon hearing of Henry's arrest had fled and was subsequently arrested. The justices dismissed Henry upon condition that he find pledges if he were to continue living in the forest.[203] Reading between the lines of the official report several points stand out: Henry's instinctive attempt to hide when he came upon a slain deer in the forest, the harsh treatment of an innocent man, the closeness of the village where the guilty man fled immediately upon hearing of the false arrest, the interpretation of guilt that the foresters placed upon his flight, the requirement of a community evaluation of Henry's reputation implied in the requirement to obtain pledges, and, above all, the power of the foresters to ruin the life of a villager if they merely suspected his guilt. Part of the problem with forest law was that it was so easy to get into trouble unintentionally simply by being in the wrong place at the wrong time.[204]

Even for those men guilty of breaking the law, the enforcement of that law was in practice arbitrary through a court system in which many escaped punishment by inefficiency in bringing them to trial, others were exempt from trial by privileges and pardons, and those punished were assessed amounts fixed more by the status of the defendant than the seriousness of the crime. One of the conclusions of a detailed study of Feckenham Forest was that in 1270 only about one-third of the known offenders mentioned in the records had been brought to justice. Furthermore, by classifying the known offenders according to social status it appears that about half the poachers were engaged in sport and the other half needed the meat for food. Yet the forest courts did not provide an even-handed justice between the two types of poachers, for by the same criteria for social status the men hunting for need were more heavily represented among those actually punished for their offenses than were those hunting for sport.[205] These figures from Feckenham, if they are typical of other forests that have not been studied in the same way, would indicate that the higher amounts assessed those men of higher social rank in the forest rolls were offset in practice by the much larger proportion of the lower ranking men actually punished for hunting in the royal forests.

Although the forest laws directly concerned with the venison had serious effects upon the lives of men living in the forest, the laws about the vert were much broader because they regulated in detail the use that could be made of private woods and lands within the forest. The number of cases against the venison in a judicial eyre was always small, but the incidence of cases against the vert was high, and these cases dominate most eyre rolls. Even though the typical amount set for trespass against the vert was small, the total in an eyre placed a substantial financial burden upon the areas within royal forests and provided a significant income for the crown.

For an attempt to discover whether there was any pattern in the enforcement of penalties against the vert, the surviving eyre rolls contain entries from forty-four forests in which the years of the offenses are entered. However, in only nineteen forests are there entries from two or more years that can be compared, mostly for only two years from the same forest, and, thus, any conclusions that can be drawn from this evidence are extremely limited. Patterns within a particular forest could only be seen among these nineteen and patterns by comparing a cross section of forests at one time are not possible. Figures from the nineteen forests show substantial variations in number of offenses and amounts of amercements from eyre to eyre. Typical of the figures are the eyres in Braden with surviving rolls for 1257, 1263, and 1270 in which the numbers of offenses were 289, 95, and 89 and the amounts of amercements were 154, 109, and 106 shillings respectively.[206] Obviously penalties for offenses against the vert had not become stereotyped, but what little comparison with other forests is possible does not show that enforcement was greater in a particular eyre, as the large number of cases from 1257 in Braden might suggest. The other obvious conclusion is that in comparison with the average of two or three offenses against the venison per year in a forest, the number of cases for vert was of an entirely different magnitude, and other forests, like Braden, provide several examples of more than two hundred cases in an eyre. In all cases the amount of the amercement was quite small.

More often than not, the exact nature of an offense against the vert was not listed in the eyre roll, but the general run of offenses can be guessed because these cases resulted from the answers found to questions posed during the regard. In addition to the regard, there were special inquests to find out what unauthorized assarts had been made and brought under cultivation within royal forests, and the results of these inquests added to the cases ultimately finding their way into the eyre roll. Punishment for assarts varied according to cases, as illustrated by payments imposed on the abbot of Tintern for thirty-three acres that had been sown three times, forty acres sown five times, twenty acres currently sown, and fifty acres currently sown and the contrasting order by the justices that the abbot's two other assarts of thirty acres and two hundred acres be taken into the king's hands and the enclosures torn down.[207] In still other instances the king would grant someone the right to make assarts on royal land or on the petitioner's own land when the assarts had been determined not to be detrimental to the royal forest.[208] Purprestures were closely allied to assarts as a broad term that might include enclosed land, but the usual meaning of the term in forest records was to describe buildings or other construction made within the forest. The king's interest in purprestures built without license or preparatory to requesting a license was again concerned with what damage they might cause to the forest.[209] Usually an unauthorized building only brought a penalty of twelve pence. The 243 newly built houses listed on an eyre roll of the Forest of the High Peak suggest that purprestures were more the occasion for a small payment than a serious concern for the forest justices.[210] Rarely were offending houses built without authorization ordered torn down. In one case from 1255 when the justices did order a house razed, the bailiffs of the sheriff prevented the foresters and verderers from destroying the house, but they seem to have acted on their own initiative.[211]

The third major offense against the vert was the cutting of a wood so extensively as to be considered within the technical definition of waste. The procedure in respect to waste was for the wood to be taken into the king's hands until the owner paid a fine for its redemption, but the redemption had to take place within a year and a day or the land was permanently forfeited to the king.[212] While the wood was in the king's hand, it might also be rented as a means of adding to the royal revenue, in addition to the penalty for having caused damage to the royal forest.[213] Of course, the creation of waste in a person's wood was not done as wantonly as the terminology of the forest records might suggest, and usually was caused by selling timber or cutting trees for a building.[214] For example, the jurors reporting on waste in Savernake Forest during the time it was held by William Marshal said that waste had been committed over several years in the amount of forty pounds and caused the destruction of an estimated 33,673 trees of all kinds mostly for work being done on Marlborough Castle.[215]

The king's demesne woods within the forest were particularly important for the lumber they could produce in addition to their value in providing cover for the venison. Because any deterioration of these woods came under the scrutiny of the foresters and verderers, the various royal orders for the use of his demesne woods came to these officials. Among the uses brought to their notice were wood for fuel and for work on the park at Clarendon, sale of wood from clearings being made in Dean, the enclosure and renting of open places in Windsor, sale of windblown wood from a number of forests, sale of underwood in all the king's demesne woods, sale of tops from oaks used in building at Guildford, and thorn trees taken for enclosing the garden at Windsor.[216] From the demesne woods the king also made gifts of trees for fuel and for building purposes, and he often granted licenses for other owners of woods within the forest to cut trees from their woods.[217] Henry III's gift of twenty-five oaks from his demesne wood at Cheddar in 1235 had a curious sequel because the bishop of Bath was able to produce charters of King John and Henry's own confirmation granting him the manor and attached wood and leaving the king with only the usual right to protect the vert and venison there as part of a royal forest.[218] Even the demesne woods belonging unquestionably to the king were not inviolate, for there are cases where the trees were cut and shipped illegally and of forest officials using trees for their own profit in abuse of the office to which they had been appointed.[219]

One important value of the forest records about the vert is that they provide information to correct the picture of a royal forest as the solitary refuge for the king's deer to that of the forest as the background for flourishing activity with some industries and animal husbandry taking their places alongside hunting and lumbering. Charcoal making and iron smelting were two natural forest industries that frequently required the attention of forest officials. The authorized charcoal making was a source of royal income, and the illicit practice was a threat to the forest because the smaller growth was cut and destroyed in the process.[220] Most of the references to iron smelting, an industry that used much charcoal, come from the Forest of the Dean where the iron works were concentrated. Although the king gave permits for men to operate forges within the forest, the forest officials there were kept busy trying to prevent or, at least, regulate the activities of other men who worked mobile forges in that forest. In fact, the regarders reported forges being in use for as long as ten years in spite of the fines imposed upon illicit forges when found of a usual one mark (13s. 4d.) and the occasional fine as high as forty shillings.[221] In 1270 forty-three persons in Dean were fined a total of £10 17s. 4d. mostly at the rate of one-half mark each in an effort to prevent the "great damage" being done to the trees and underwood.[222] Several wardens of the Dean Forest were themselves involved in mining iron over a number of years on property belonging to Flaxley Abbey until the abbot appealed to the king for an inquest to substantiate his rights to the mine.[223] By 1282 the regulations on mining specified that the king was to receive one-half penny for every load of iron ore removed from the forest and an additional one penny a week from every workman in three named bailiwicks within the forest who took three or more loads of ore. Similar regulations were developed for coal mines, and stone quarries also came within the scope of forest law and required a royal license for their operation.[224]

Domestic animals that were in the royal forests were subject to the forest law and supervision by foresters. When farm animals strayed into the forest, the officials would take control of them until the owners paid a fine for their release or until the king pardoned the accidental breaking of the law.[225] However, in many forests farm animals were allowed by special grants from the king, and the forest officials were only required to supervise the number of animals and any payments specified in the grants.[226] Other individuals and religious institutions had the right of common for their animals at various places within the forest, but this right was the subject for many inquests because it usually rested upon "immemorial custom" or upon foundation charters that were not easily interpreted to fit changed conditions after long periods of time.[227] Even so, where legitimate right of common could be established, even a grant from the king could not introduce changes within a forest that would impede this right.[228] Other cattle and pigs were allowed in the forest by payment of fees under the supervision of royal officials known as agisters, who tallied the animals brought into the forest and allowed there except for the two weeks preceding and after Midsummer Day, a period known as "fence month," when all domestic animals were cleared from the forest in the belief they interfered with the deer while they were having their fawns.[229]

Although the eyre was essential to the administration of forest law in the thirteenth century, the lengthy intervals between eyres led to an inefficiency that contributed to an arbitrary application of the law. To some extent the failures of the eyre were corrected by specially commissioned inquests that were held in all the forests for general questions or in specific areas to remedy more local problems.[230] According to Matthew Paris, in November 1244 Robert Passelewe advised the king to hold an inquest of the forests as a means of raising money, but financial considerations were always present in the eyre and similar charges could be made about a decision to hold a general eyre. In any case, the thrust of the inquest in 1245 was to investigate and correct the conduct of the foresters that had come under suspicion. Among those found misusing his office was John de Neville, chief justice of the forests and son of Hugh de Neville, the powerful justice of the forests under King John. The chronicler could spare no pity for John in his fall from power because as a forester he had been without mercy to other men who had come for trial before him in similar circumstances.[231] Inquests with the broad purpose "to inquire concerning the state of the forests" came to be used frequently during the latter years of Henry III's reign, were regularized under Edward I, and received permanent recognition in the statute of 1306 dealing with the forest.[232] By the fourteenth century, inquests were held almost annually and they displaced the eyre as the center of forest administration. The change from eyre to inquest parallels the change in the common law from the general eyre to special commissions to deal with limited questions in limited areas.[233]

The question of the extent of the forests had been settled early in the reign of Henry III and did not become an important political issue until the end of the century, but the area designated as forest was never entirely fixed. To be sure, some forests like the Forest of the Dean underwent no changes with the same boundaries in 1282 as it had in the perambulation of 1228.[234] Royal policy worked toward the maintenance of forest boundaries, as shown by the king's order in 1266 to the chief justice of the forests north of the Trent to restore the forests to the boundaries they had before being disafforested by Simon de Montfort during his short-lived control of the kingdom.[235] During his fifth year as king, Edward I demonstrated a similar policy in ordering a general perambulation of the forests to make certain the boundaries established by Henry III were still being observed.[236] However, minor changes were made as a result of cases that raised the question whether the place under dispute was within the forest. In addition, the king sometimes made grants of lands to individuals with the provision that the lands be removed from the forest.[237] The most significant disafforestment by royal charter was on 28 December 1280, when Edward I removed all forests in the county of Northumberland from the royal forest in return for an annual payment of forty marks by the county, retention by the king of all the rents from lands already leased within the forest, and retention of the right of common where it existed prior to disafforestment.[238]

After the Barons' War against King John, the administration of the royal forest was affected very little by outside events. Some men took advantage of the disruption caused by the revolt of the barons under Simon de Montfort to break the forest law, but there is no evidence of any general breakdown of the forest administration outside of the temporary disafforestments in the North as decreed by Simon. Nevertheless, the forests were not isolated from other aspects of life for those who lived within its boundaries, as has been seen in the discussion of offenses against the vert and venison. A curious effect of the forest law was that the form for conserving the peace and swearing to arms used in 1242 (which specified the types of arms) made an exception from the arms carried by men of ordinary rank for men who lived within the bounds of a royal forest by changing the requirement from bow and arrows to bow and pellets that could be discharged from crossbows.[239] Perhaps the best way to illustrate the constant burden imposed by forest regulations is to cite a charter exempting a manor of the bishop of Bath from the forest. The bishop may enclose his woods; make parks or assarts; and give, sell, and take wood without inspection or control by foresters, verderers, or other ministers of the forest. His men of the manor were exempted from all forest pleas, the lawing of dogs, and all other things pertaining to the forest.[240] The impossibility of legally doing any of these things prior to the charter provides a partial measure of the restrictive burden imposed by the forest law.

6
The Forest System
at Its Height: Economy

The legal and administrative aspects of the royal forest can only be
separated from the economic aspect for purposes of analysis. In reality,
the two justices of the forests and the wardens of all the forests super-
vised the collection of many payments and accounted for the revenue
they produced. Fortunately, many of these accounts survive, especially
for Galtres and Inglewood among the forests north of the Trent, and
provide a valuable record of the revenue the crown derived from the
royal forests from 1257 to the early fifteenth century.

Four accounts of the justice of the forests north of the Trent for the
last half of the thirteenth century provide a good overview of the types
of income the king received from his forests. John de Eyvil accounted
for the years 1257–61, Geoffrey de Neville for 1270–79 and 1279–81,
and William de Vescy for 1288–97.[1] Although not all types of income
are represented in each account, a composite from the four accounts
provides a comprehensive picture of the income reported in the regular
accounts except for the amounts concealed under the general rubric of
"profits and issues" of the forests. Among the rents and payments were
rents from assarts, herbage paid for the pasturage of domestic animals,
farm from a turbary where turf was being cut, money collected by the
agisters for pigs feeding in the forest, other sums for retropannage
collected after the regular season for pannage from those pigs in the
forest, farms from parks and special areas rented out, and rent from
areas where there was dead wood. There were also payments for
licenses and special permissions including the lawing of dogs, use of an

114

alder grove to make palings, cheminage assessed on carts and wagons using the roads, setting up a sheep fold, postponement of a case until the next forest eyre, allowing domestic animals to run free in the forest at night throughout the year, and the mining of iron. Forest pleas brought income for defaults, delivery from prison, repossession of woods forfeited for waste until the next eyre, routine forest pleas, pigs sold after being confiscated for being in the covert during fence month, payments for recovery of domestic animals straying into the forest without license, and attachments taken for forest offenses. Sales from forest products not included in the general issues of the forest were listed separately as windfallen timber, hay, nuts, and firewood. For the four years of John de Eyvil's account, he received a salary of forty pounds per year from the receipts of the northern forests and still returned an additional seventy-seven pounds to the treasury. Although Geoffrey de Neville paid in £20 14d. for his term of 1279–81, much of the income during those years had been used for maintenance and wages: constructing and repair of houses preparatory to a visit by the king, wages of two men guarding lawn in the forest, repairs of the paling of Plumpton Park, wages for two men set to guard a new park and lawn within the park, and repair of the king's prison in Galtres Forest.

An account for the years 1343–51 by Bartholomew de Burgherssh for the forests south of the Trent deducted his annual salary of one hundred pounds and also allowed expenses for the days he was attending the king's council for a total of 137 days at the rate of 26s. 8d. per day, amounting to £184 over the period all carefully itemized by the dates he attended.[2] More details both of income and expenses can be gleaned from accounts made by wardens of individual forests in the south. In the New Forest in 1246–47 the rents from the vaccaries provided the substantial sum of fifteen pounds, and saltmaking and the sale of honey added their bit. On the debit side, riding foresters were paid from the account and tithes of £4 3d. went to the canons of Salisbury.[3] The warden in 1250–52 claimed allowances for hunting, salting, and transporting venison for use of the king's son Edward and his family and for payments to a royal hunter for his expenses. There were also expenses for making fifty thousand shingles and transporting them to Clarendon for use on the king's houses there.[4] In 1236 the warden of Windsor Forest claimed expenses for hunting eight deer and transporting them to Westminster Abbey as a gift from the king.[5] The account for Windsor a decade later is complicated by including several manors that the warden held from the king concurrently with his forest office, but the payments to Master William the painter for work in the

royal chapel at Windsor and to Master Simon a carpenter for paving
the king's chamber there can be attributed to the combined office of
warden of the forest and constable of Windsor Castle. From four to
eight chaplains at Windsor received fifty shillings a year for celebrating
mass and their expenses over a period of four years amounted to some
seventy-three pounds. Forest revenues also were used to pay the wages
of a man who made crossbows at Windsor Castle, for the wood he
needed in his occupation, and for transporting the finished crossbows
to the king. When the repair and strengthening of Windsor Castle resulted in the confiscation of lands and houses of men at Windsor, they
received compensation of £33 18s. 8d. from the warden of the forest.
Improvements to the chapel in Windsor Park and repair of royal houses
appear alongside expenses for making fishponds and hay for the deer
in the same account.[6]

Other accounts from individual forests round out the economic picture by their detail on the sale of wood resulting from a careful utilization of the timber and the sale of animals received as payments in kind
for rents. A different type of record contains the expenses of enclosing
the lawn at Plumpton within Inglewood Forest to make a park with a
stone wall around it during the years 1332–35 for the cost of £185 6s.
6d., including materials and the wages of men for quarrying stones at
three pence a day, making fences at three pence a day, carting stones
at six pence per week, and making the wall at five pence per rod of
wall.[7] This kind of detail emphasizes that development of a park with
a royal forest was a costly undertaking and that the economic picture
of the forests was not all profit.

The accounts of chief justices for forests north of the Trent provide
the best information for any long-term trends in profits from royal forests. These trends can be seen visually in Graph 1 for the total issues
from Inglewood in Cumberland and the smaller forest of Galtres in
Yorkshire for which the accounts are most complete. For the first
period in which there are records, from 1257 to 1330, there was no
trend of either increase or decrease, and the variations for both forests
followed roughly similar patterns. However, in 1360 the figures show a
startling increase in the total issues to a peak of more than £152 in
1371 in the issues from Inglewood, in contrast to the continued level
for Galtres about the same as the figures before 1330, except showing
less annual variation. Galtres continued to have issues from fifteen
pounds to twenty pounds throughout the fourteenth century and then
declined to about ten pounds for the remaining figures available to
1463. Inglewood experienced a sharp decline beginning in 1379 and
lasting to the end of the century, but the issues then returned to the

highest previous marks for the years in which figures are available up to 1423, again contrasting to Galtres where there was a decline in the first quarter of the fifteenth century. From 1425 to 1461 the issues for Inglewood became more stable, levelling off between seventy pounds and eighty pounds about half way between the low levels of the early period 1257 to 1330 and the peak years of the two decades between 1360 and 1380.[8]

The main categories into which the reports are broken down are returns for agistment and attachments in Inglewood and for farm of lawns and attachments in Galtres. (See Graph 2.) These two categories in each forest usually amounted to about half the total issues. During the period for which these figures are available (1318–78 for Inglewood and 1319–1403 for Galtres) the percentage of total issues for the two categories reversed in importance with attachments becoming larger than agistment in Inglewood after 1337 and attachments larger than farm of lawns in Galtres after 1360. The greater stability in the total issues for Galtres as compared to Inglewood resulted from the fact that lawns were farmed out from the earliest figures. The variation in income from farms was not great throughout the period, and these farms amounted to around twenty percent of the totals. In the two decades after 1360, when the total of issues from Inglewood increased markedly, both agistments and attachments almost doubled, but an important new factor was the income from sale or farming of herbage in the lawns. Once these farms had become fixed they may account for the greater stability exhibited by later totals in the fifteenth century. Because assarts were the major cause of attachments, it would appear that the high attachments from 1360 to 1368 indicate pressure upon the forest from the needs of agriculture. Because these high attachments coincided with high yields from agistment and from sales of herbage, the total income from Inglewood Forest was forced to its highest level, but only at the expense of farming operations impinging heavily upon the forest as a hunting preserve.

The figures on assarting support this conclusion by showing large increases in the number of acres being assarted by the mid-fourteenth century as compared to a century earlier. Although the forest records contain a large amount of information on assarting, not many records provide figures to make possible the comparison of total figures on assarting in one forest over an extended period, but Table 5 contains some examples in which direct comparison is possible.[9]

In addition to these few examples of comparable figures on assarting over a period of time, the scattered figures of assarting for many other forests are evidence of the tension between assarting caused by the

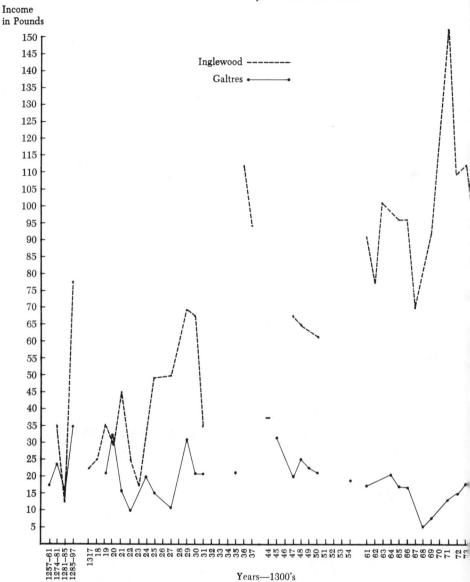

Graph 1
Total Income from Two Royal Forests 1257–1463

Income
in Pounds

Inglewood ---------
Galtres •————————•

Years—1300's

118

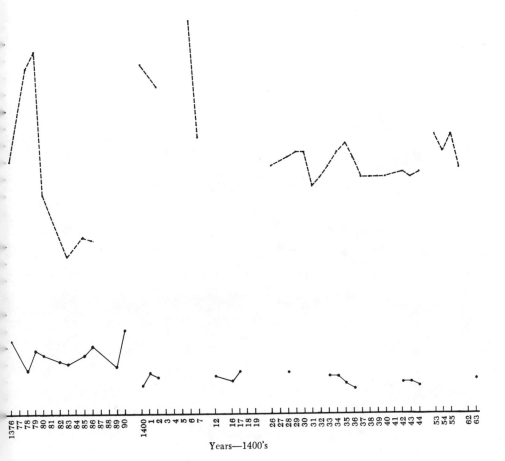

Inglewood ---------
Galtres •————•

Years—1400's

119

Graph 2
Major Items in Forest Income

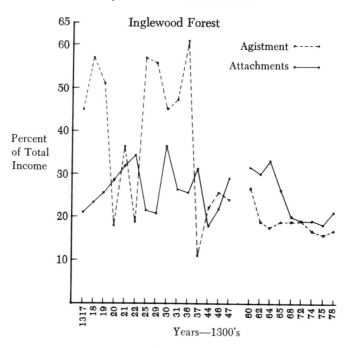

Inglewood Forest

Agistment ------►
Attachments •———

Percent of Total Income

Years—1300's

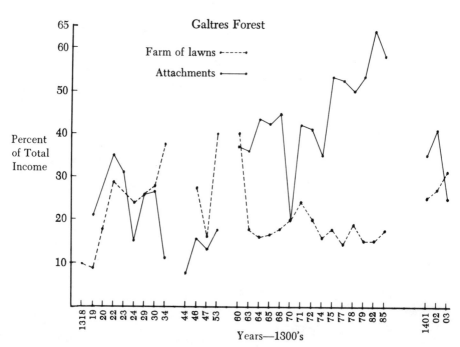

Galtres Forest

Farm of lawns ------►
Attachments •———

Percent of Total Income

Years—1300's

Table 5

Assarting (in acres)

Forest	Date	Old Assarts	New Assarts	Total Assarts
Cliffe and				
Rockingham	1253			784
	1255			780
	1272	363		—
	1339	753	487	1,240
	1346	634	554	1,188
	1355	697	486	1,183
Rutland	1344	714	236	950
	1375	283	1,126	1,409
Salcey and				
Whittlewood	1249	378		378
	1252			393
	1255			238
	1345			1,128
	1348		430	

demand for more arable land and the forest laws designed to protect the cover needed for the king's beasts. Even in the twelfth century the economic interest in rents from assarts was prominent enough that most assarting had been tacitly recognized by royal officials in return for the income assessed for the rents. Most economic historians agree with Michael Postan that demand for more arable land brought continued expansion of land under cultivation in England throughout the thirteenth century until the older lands began to be worked out toward the end of that century and marginal lands that had been farmed under pressure of demand failed to maintain productivity for any length of time. The figures on assarting within the royal forests suggest that one response to the continued need for expanded arable land in the first half of the fourteenth century was to turn more and more of the forest into farmland. In fact, the few examples where figures are available for the period after the Black Death show evidence of continued assarting in the forests. This would agree with Postan's suggestion that assarting continued later in the forests than elsewhere, but records are not available to test whether there was any contraction in assarts under cultivation in correspondence with the downtrend Postan described for the later fourteenth and fifteenth centuries.[10]

The small size of most of the assarts, two acres or less, indicates that most of the assarting in the royal forests was the result of individual initiative.[11] At times the assarts were unauthorized but were accepted when they were duly reported at the regard, but other assarts were made only after application to royal officials for permission and with prior approval from the king. In these cases, the procedure was for inquests to be held to determine whether the proposed assarts would be to the damage of the king or his forest, and the permission was granted only when no damage was expected.[12] There were occasional instances of assarting on a larger scale that must have been due to the initiative of manorial lords, and the forest records show that monasteries were usually involved when large areas were newly placed under cultivation.[13] At Windsor the king himself as manorial lord was involved in extensive assarting after it had been determined that no damage to the forest would result from that activity.[14] Numerous references confirm that the standard in deciding whether to grant a license for an assart in the forest was whether the king's profit from the assart would be greater than any damage to the forest. The only other consideration was whether a proposed assart would infringe upon the right of common held by other men in the forest.[15] Presumably, it was the neglect of this last consideration that explains the occasional destruction of ditches and fences associated with an assart in cases that came before the king to determine whether the assart was legitimate or not.[16] In fact, many of the assarts were made in his own woods by the owner and needed royal permission only because of the overriding jurisdiction of the forest law that prevented him from treating his woods as he wished. For this reason, the right to license an assart was in itself an economic factor of considerable value as shown by the gifts to the king for these licenses and the king's freely granting of licenses to men whom he wished to reward for their services to him.[17]

However, it was not the detailed mechanism of assarting that was of prime importance for the history of the royal forests in the thirteenth and early fourteenth centuries. Although the records are not adequate to support any conclusion about the amount of land newly brought under cultivation, there can be no question of a general upsurge in farming activity as a result of continued assarting. Clearly large areas of the royal forests were drawn more closely into the agricultural life of the country. When this farming activity is put alongside the other economic activity taking place within the royal forests, it suggests a thesis that the essential nature of the royal forest changed during the period. The economic importance of the forest in the twelfth century, based primarily upon the income that could be extracted by a strict enforcement of forest law, now became stabilized by the exploitation of the forests for farming and other economic activities of a permanent nature. Kings like Edward I loved to hunt, but his true understanding of the value of the royal forest that he strove to protect is better demonstrated by the massive sales of wood that he ordered when he needed large sums of money for his military adventures.

In addition to exploiting the woods on the royal demesne lands for the timber they could supply, the prohibition against cutting woods within the royal forest was turned into another source of revenue by granting licenses allowing individuals to cut their woods that lay within the forest. Before a license was granted, the king would order an inquest to determine how much cutting could be done without damage to the royal forest even in emergency appeals such as that of the nuns of Romsey who desperately needed the money they could obtain from sales of wood in order to finance the rebuilding of their abbey and to pay other debts they had incurred.[18] Other nuns in similar financial difficulties obtained licenses to sell underwood up to forty acres and to sell forty oaks from their woods.[19] In addition to placing a limitation on the amount of woods that could be sold, licenses of this type usually required the owner to construct a low hedge around the cut-over area that would allow the deer to enter and leave but would protect the new growth from cattle, horses, or pigs foraging in the forest.[20] This concern for reforestation is explicit recognition by the royal administration of the value of the woods to the future interest of the king in exercising his rights over the royal forest. A variant of the licensing practice was a royal order permitting an entrepreneur to buy woods from the owners up to a specified amount and to cut and sell the timber under terms of the license.[21] The usual punishment for men who cut woods without license, including foresters who sometimes succumbed to this temptation, was through the forest courts, which assessed amercements or confiscated the lands from their owners until adequate payment was made to the king to redeem them.[22]

The king's own demesne woods within the royal forests were important for revenue, and they were used systematically but with some care to do the least possible damage to the forest even in the face of economic necessity. The procedures with local inquests concerning damage to be expected from cutting and supervision of the actual cutting by forest officials give a picture of a managed resource rather than arbitrary exploitation. In March 1255 King Henry III appointed commissioners to sell part of his woods in fourteen counties south of the Trent as advised by his council for relief from his debts, but a month later he modified the order to include only underwood. The reasons given for the change are interesting for the insight they provide into the economics of the timber market. It had been concluded that such a large sale of wood would cause irreparable damage to the king because of the lack of money among potential buyers. It was estimated that three or four trees would bring the amount that only one tree would bring if the trees were sold more gradually in order not to flood the market and that the wholesale cutting following the original order would have caused destruction to the king's deer. In the revised plan the commissioners were ordered to inventory the trees that might be cut in the future without causing damage to the forest and to list their present value. Simultaneously they were to sell the underwood and remit the proceeds to the king as soon as possible.[23] Two years later, the followup to this procedure occurred when Philip Luvel received a commission to sell the king's woods in the forest of England to the amount of three or four thousand marks.[24]

The accounts entered in the Pipe Rolls from men entrusted with large sales of wood from the forests south of the Trent show the importance of royal income from this source. In 1223 the master mason in charge of work at Winchester Castle received eighty pounds from the sales of windfallen trees in Clarendon Forest toward the cost of work being done there, and various other items of forest income had been assigned to him for the same purpose.[25] In addition to sales of windblown trees and of underwood, types of sales that could be considered part of the maintenance to aid the growth of the more valuable trees, there were other sales of trees from the royal demesne woods and even sales of oaks under specified limits.[26] Accounts in 1261 for several forests contain the following totals: in Northampton £230 for 2545 oaks, in Rutland £123 for 1117 great oaks and 2004 lesser oaks, in Bere £28 for 319 oaks, and in Savernake £61 for 824 oaks.[27] Sales of underwood in 1251–52 involved the assistance of four knights chosen in each country, who acted under threat of distraint by the sheriff to perform this duty.[28] Although the danger of destruction of the underwood in a particular area was sufficient to allow an exemption from the policy of these sales, the records confirm an intensive effort to raise money from this source.[29]

Edward I toward the end of the century was involved in a similar effort to make effective use of the forests to raise money. In 1295 Roger le Strange wrote the royal chancellor for a warrant for the chapters on waste he intended to use in making an inquest in the forests. The reply cited the king's desire to know what waste could be found in his own land and that of others, and gave the purpose of raising money from the sale of underwood, old dead trees, and oaks in his demesne woods and parks where it could be done without injury to the covert for his venison. The instructions for the inquest included these questions:

1) an estimate of how many acres of waste on the king's own lands could be sown and rented and the money that could be obtained from entry fees and subsequent rents; 2) the number of acres and value of the underwood that could be sold; 3) the amount that could be obtained from selling dead trees; 4) the amount that could be obtained by selling oaks for lumber without manifest destruction; and 5) the number of acres of other land that could be rented along with the entry fees and estimates of rents from that land.[30]

Several accounts recorded in the Pipe Rolls for 1298 to 1301 illustrate this policy of Edward I in attempting to make the forest a profitable venture while disputing with his barons the question as to the proper extent of the royal forests. In 1298 Richard Oysel was commissioned to sell trees, wood, and underwood up to two thousand pounds in the forests, hayes, chaces, parks, and woods of the king south of the Trent. In Sherwood Forest he sold almost six thousand oaks along with other wood and underwood for almost £718, and in various other royal woods and parks his sales amounted to three hundred pounds. Three years later he added another £273 from woods and parks in Northamptonshire and Lincolnshire.[31] The account of John de Crokesle for wood sold south of the Trent in 1299 lists many kinds of trees, with the largest number of beech, a substantial number of oaks, and smaller numbers of maple and apple.[32] Master Richard de Abyndon, William de Hardene, and Nicholas de Pershute were assigned in 1301 to sell wood up to the limit of fifty pounds in Guilford Park and one hundred pounds in the forests of Chute, Clarendon, Bere, and Pamber, but they failed to reach their limits with sales of only about one hundred pounds in all.[33] That same year, sales by Walter de Ayllesbury in parks and forests in Oxford brought in about £320.[34]

Of course, later kings continued to take timber from the royal forests to supplement their income from other sources, and there are many scattered references to this activity. The instructions given two men in charge of cutting trees in Wolmer and Aliceholt forests in 1332 were especially precise, specifying that they had been assigned one hundred trees not bearing fruit or leaves to be marked with a special iron made for this purpose. The marking of the dead trees for cutting was to take place with the warden of the forest or his deputy, the verderers, and the regarders as witnesses. Finally, the trees were then to be cut and valued in order that the profits would be available before 21 December, but they were warned not to include any oak, beech, ash, or apple, and no live trees or any trees more than the one hundred that had been allowed.[35]

An extensive series of accounts survives for sales of underwood in the park and forest of Clarendon, a small forest in Hampshire, for the years 1337 to 1359.[36] Although the income fluctuated, it began with a usual total of about eighteen pounds, rose after 1343 into the mid-twenties, and again after 1355 into the upper thirties. Exceptions to the trends were a low of only nine pounds in 1354 and a high of sixty-two pounds in 1357. The main conclusion from these figures is that these sales provided a consistent income year after year and one that could be expanded with inflation or unusual need. However, all of the money from sales of underwood was not profit, for the expenses ran from twenty to thirty percent of the totals collected. These expenses included the wages of the men felling the trees, the cost of constructing hedges around the cut-over areas to allow for new growth, and the wages of the sellers themselves calculated at two pence a day and extending over 161 days from December to May during the year 1340, for example. Some of the money was diverted for work on a castle, royal houses, and bridges and never reached the royal coffers in the form of hard cash. Receipts given to the sellers also show the delivery of money for wages of foresters, repairing manor houses and lodges, wages of a fence keeper in the park, wages for several men cutting brush for the sustenance of the deer during the winter, and repairs to the fence around the park.[37] The basic continuity of the forest economy is illustrated by similar payments being made in a similar record in 1434.[38]

Scattered royal letters and accounts for particular forests add detail to the general picture of wood sales from the forests. Letters close to the warden of Dean in 1255 and 1256 are quite explicit about the king's urgent need for money and the necessity of the warden's supplying the Wardrobe immediately with whatever had been collected from sales of wood in that forest.[39] Other accounts from Dean serve as a reminder that the king's gifts of trees to individuals, duly recorded among the sales, added to the quantity of timber actually removed from the forest during the course of the year, but the gifts were always small in comparison to the number of trees sold and were only ten percent of the number sold in a detailed account submitted in 1280.[40] In Dean, sales of underwood were directly connected with making charcoal for the iron smelting that was an important part of the economy of that particular forest.[41] In one instance we are told that the sales resulted from a salvage operation and would not have taken place "except by reason of an unlucky fire that partially burned the wood."[42] In fact, much of the evidence for sales deals with windblown trees or overaged oaks, rather than trees in their prime, and should be considered as an aspect of prudent management rather than a lumbering operation.[43] Because sales of wood involved produce from the land, a tithe was due the church, and the tithe could be paid by reserving some of the trees to be cut separately instead of paying it from the money received from the sales.[44] In an exceptional year there were even times when no buyers were forthcoming for the trees authorized to be sold, and the royal warrant to make the sales had to be surrendered without being used.[45] Much more usual was the problem of overcutting, with or without authorization, as exemplified in Rutland in 1258 when the king cancelled a sale because the warden had reported that the cutting was causing a deterioration of the forest.[46] On other occasions the problem was caused by unauthorized cutting and selling by individuals acting on their own or in defiance of the king, as Richard Malebisse did against King John in Galtres Forest.[47]

Often joined with the commission for selling wood from royal lands in the forest was the task of renting wastes. The procedure for renting wastes was begun with an inquest to determine the advantages and disadvantages of the proposed rental by means of the sworn testimony of the foresters, verderers, regarders, and other men in the forest. The questions were whether it would be to the advantage of the king to rent the land if it were to be cultivated and enclosed with a ditch and low hedge according to the assize of the forest in a manner by which a deer with a fawn could enter and leave the enclosed area and, if so, how large the area was, how much each acre could be expected to bring in exits each year, and how much profit there would be for the king.[48] Inquests were sometimes held later to determine if the commissioners appointed for renting the wastes had faithfully carried out their duties.[49] The standard practice was to collect a small fee for entering into the use of the waste and an annual rent of from two to four pence an acre depending upon the value of the land. For these sums the tenant received a royal charter confirming the right to use the land that was being rented. The commissioners were also authorized to rent lands for other persons along with the king's own lands within the forest if the owners wished them to do so.[50]

Even though most of the wastes rented were small plots of only a few acres, the total income could be significant. In the small forest of Savernake, the commissioners rented 827 acres in 1300 for entry fines of thirty-nine pounds and annual rents of nearly fourteen pounds.[51] In 1281 the commissioners in Windsor Forest rented 380 acres of waste to the bishop of Bath and Wells from his own land for half pence an acre on three hundred acres and a farthing an acre on the remainder at the same time they rented about twenty-six acres from the king's land in that forest.[52] The account made on the death of John de

Crokesle, who rented lands in various forests during the years 1299 to 1303, provides a good indication of the sizable sums that were collected from entrance fees alone even from small plots. The fees were £76 15s. 6d. for Windsor Forest and £158 17d for Clarendon and Pewsham in Hampshire. Fees for ten other lands rented in Bere and Chute were included, and other areas rented in Windsor and Salcey were not listed at all because John had died before the wastes being rented there could be measured.[53]

Constant vigilance by royal officials was necessary to insure that lands brought under cultivation by renting of wastes conformed to the area rented and to prevent additional lands from being used under cover of the rental charter. An inquest made in February 1315 reached back through the years to 1281 to determine the details of a rental for twenty acres of waste at a time when the commissioners and the original tenant were dead and the tenant's son petitioned to have the land. Earlier in 1285 the amount of land being cultivated had been questioned and the rent raised by fifty percent to the twenty shillings a year by which the original tenant's son sought to rent it in 1315.[54] However, it was not unusual for rentals of wastes to turn into long leases, as illustrated from the transcripts of rentals prepared for a forest eyre in 1348 with rentals made as early as 1300 and revisions after an inquest in 1313.[55] By the early fourteenth century, some of the rentals specified that the rents for wastes were to be paid in perpetuity to the king at the Exchequer.[56] Another variation was the grant which Edward I made to Newstead Priory of one hundred eighty acres of waste in Sherwood Forest to be used as pasture for an annual rent of four pounds and which Edward III in 1330 changed to a holding by "pure and perpetual alms."[57]

The most systematic forest records with economic information over long periods are those for agistment, and they are primarily of value because of the overview they provide rather than for the total income they brought the king from the royal forests. During the last years of Henry III's reign, there are agistment figures for twenty-four of the approximately forty-five royal forests then existing south of the Trent.[58] In addition, there are figures for Sherwood Forest from north of the Trent.[59] Agistment figures are also preserved for sixteen forests in Edward I's reign, five in Edward II's reign, and fourteen in Edward III's reign.[60] With the exception of a seven-year gap at the beginning of Edward I's reign, the agistment figures for the small forest of Groveley in Hampshire are complete for the period 1247 to 1332. For Clarendon in the same county, the figures are from 1247 to 1337 with the gap widened to twelve years at the end of Henry III's reign and beginning of Edward I's and a period of twenty-nine years when there was no agistment after Edward I cut all the oaks in 1299. For north of the Trent there are figures for Inglewood for only 1273 to 1285 and for Sherwood from 1264 to 1333 except for one gap of seven years.

The income reported as agistment might include fees for pasturing domestic animals (herbage) and fees for allowing pigs to forage in the woods (pannage). It is not always clear whether both types of income have been totaled for the record, but this seems to have been the usual practice, and the figures used are considered to be totals for agistment in the year. Another problem when the agistment figures are listed by subdivisions of the forest is that it is not always possible to be certain that all subdivisions have been included, and in a few cases the total may have been larger than that used. Although nearly all forests had years when no agistment was made because of the lack of mast from the trees, this omission was duly reported in the records.

Because of the fluctuations in agistment figures from year to year, the average for several years gives a better picture of trends. The more complete figures from Henry III's reign show an average annual revenue for agistment of over eighteen pounds from the fourteen to seventeen forests with figures during the period 1249–53, and an average annual revenue of about ten pounds from the seventeen to twenty forests with figures for the years 1266–71. Between the two periods there had been no decrease in the area of the forests and there were more forests reporting in the later period. The decline may represent a shift in use in areas of the forest from pasturage and foraging for domestic animals to assarting for cultivation. The intensive sales of wood by Henry III about 1260 may have also taken their toll. With the extreme fluctuations from year to year it would not be wise to place much significance upon the decline between these two periods in any event. In either period the total from agistment was relatively low as a portion of total income from the forests.

In the small forest of Groveley, the annual income from agistment averaged only six shillings four pence for the seventy-five years for which there are records from 1247 to 1338, and for Clarendon the average annual income was £1 15s. 10d. for the forty years from 1248 to 1298. The following year there appears for the first time the notation that because the king had had all the oaks cut and sold no agistment had been made, and the clerks continued to make this entry until 1337 when agistment was once again collected, presumably because the replacement oaks had reached sufficient maturity to warrant agistment of the forest.[61] Agistment in the larger Sherwood Forest to the north was more profitable, yielding an average annual income of £3 12s. 6d.

for the sixty-three years between 1264 and 1334, and the average is lowered because of years in which there was nothing from agistment because of lack of mast in the forest. Nevertheless, even small sums over these periods of time did add up to respectable totals of more than 23 pounds for Groveley, 71 pounds for Clarendon, and 211 pounds for Sherwood.

The careful recording of agistment returns over the years is itself an indication that agistment warranted the attention of forest officials perhaps mostly because it provided a regular income available to the king. In fact, the administrative machinery set in motion by a royal order to agist the king's lands within the royal forests was itself an elaborate undertaking from the selection of new agisters, a report of the names of agisters, the response from the executors or heirs of dead agisters, the obtaining of sureties for the agisters, and the final payment into the Exchequer of what the agisters had managed to collect.[62] Sometimes payments were made into the Wardrobe for immediate use by the royal household; at other times, the king preferred payment for pigs being agisted in the forest to be made in kind if possible in order to meet the immediate needs of the table.[63] Money from agistment could also provide a means for the king to pay for some urgent business or for a building project.[64] In 1256 Henry III even managed to pay Master Thomas his surgeon by assigning him fifteen marks from the next agistment of Cannock Forest.[65] In spite of the evident convenience of income from agistment as a ready source of cash, the royal administration did show a sense of responsibility in realizing the danger of overuse to the detriment of food for deer and other beasts of the forest. An inquest illustrating careful management sought to determine whether the proposed agistment would leave sufficient pasture for the king's wild beasts, required the pigs being agisted in Clarendon Forest to have rings in their noses to prevent their digging up the pasture there, and set a moratorium on agistment when it threatened the pasture for the deer.[66]

Unfortunately, in spite of the survival of many records from the royal forests, the records are not adequate to form any estimate of the annual income the king could expect from his forests. In fact, the income from any one forest is almost as difficult to calculate, but Margaret Bazeley's detailed analysis of Dean Forest is the best single study available. She concluded that for the period 1195 to 1307, the king received from that forest the upkeep of St. Briavels Castle, considerable purveyance, some contributions to general expenses, and some ready money paid to the Exchequer averaging £4 10s. in the years 1195–1232, £24 5s. for 1232–72, and more than £57 for 1272–1307.[67] Her summary for the entire period stresses the cumulative value of the income from this one forest:

To conclude—the profits derived from the Forest, including rents, sales and fines, should have amounted during the period to at least £20,000 odd, a sum almost equal, perhaps, to the annual revenue of Henry II, and more than half that of Henry III. To this must be added profits in kind and fines of a miscellaneous description, whose value has not been computed.[68]

Another measure of the economic importance of the royal forests is the variety of the products obtained from the forests. Timber would obviously rank high on any list, and because of the forest regulations against cutting trees without license, there are records even when trees were cut for constructing or repairing various royal houses, for work on royal castles, and for the chapel at Westminster.[69] Similarly, an abbot obtained a royal charter to permit him to cut 6,083 oaks in his own woods within a royal forest for buildings he wished to construct both within and without the forest.[70] Small trees and limbs from older, less valuable trees could be used to fuel the kiln for the king's works at Devizes.[71] Wood from the royal forest also had a military application in supplying fittings for ships of the navy, making mangonels and other siege engines, providing parts and quarrels for crossbows, and making saddlebows.[72] Various orders to prepare wood or to make charcoal before a royal visit to a place serve as a reminder that wood was also an important source of fuel for heating and was needed in large quantities for this purpose.[73]

The produce from royal forests included the animals that subsisted there, both wild and domestic. In addition to the pleasure of hunting, the king's deer provided a valuable source of meat for the royal table, and they were slain in vast quantities for this utilitarian purpose. For example, in 1251 a justice of the forests was ordered to kill one hundred bucks in Galtres and another hundred elsewhere in royal forests south of the Trent for use of the king and to notify him when they had been killed and well-salted, in order that instructions could then be given for delivery to various places.[74] Similarly, the forester of Dean was directed to allow the king's huntsman to take one hundred bucks in that forest and to deliver them salted down in barrels for the king's use at Westminster.[75] Earlier that year another forester had provided sixty does from Chute Forest for the royal Christmas feast, and wild sows were also in demand.[76] Cumulatively, records like these demonstrate that the forests were a source for meat both on a regular basis and for special occasions, but they were also valuable for pasture for various domestic animals belonging to the king, allowed in the forest by grant from the king, and living in the forest by right of common. The domestic animals legally within the forest included pigs, other farm animals, sheep, and cattle, and the agistment payments came from those animals allowed within the forest by grant of the king.[77] As a reference to the stud in the New Forest indicates, the royal forests were also used for raising horses for the king's needs.[78] Deer within the parks carved out of the forest were managed to the extent that supplementary feeding of hay might be necessary during the winter months.[79] Hawks breeding within the royal forests were protected for the king's exclusive use, and a question about location of eyries was regularly asked at the regard.[80]

In the Forest of the Dean there were forges for working the iron ore being mined there and owned by private landowners, as well as those owned by the king, from as early as the reign of Henry II. Although the private forges were supposed to operate only under license from the king, the regulations were not always carefully enforced even after stricter regulations were adopted in 1217. The nominal rent of seven shillings a year from a licensed forge compares with the consumption of wood valued by contemporaries from twelve to seventy pounds needed to work a forge. In fact, the private forges could be worked at a profit only because the underwood used for making the charcoal to fuel them was usually obtained at the king's expense.[81] One estimate based upon an annual production of from two and one-half to three tons of iron per forge and about sixty forges in Dean Forest would put the total production in 1282 of some 150 to 180 tons, and this production of iron implies the mining of iron ore in approximately five times that amount.[82] Lead mining and smelting in the forest of High Peak presented the same problems of where to locate the mines in order to bring maximum profit to the king with the least damage to the forest from the actual mining operation and the destruction of wood needed for the smelting process.[83] Charcoal was used as a fuel for the forges, but was also a product in its own right either for the king's use or through the leasing of charcoal pits for the use of other persons.[84] Other extractive operations within the forest were quarries and turbaries where turf was cut under royal license.[85] Salt-making in the forests along the southern coast was important to the preservation of meat for the royal larder at Clarendon, and the failure to supply this essential item brought the king's rebuke on more than one occasion.[86] The lawns within the royal forests furnished not only pasture but were sometimes mown for hay in significant quantities to list this as another forest product.[87]

In addition to the sales, rents, and licenses that provided income from the forests, the gifts that kings made from the forest in both vert and venison should be considered as indirect income. These gifts were numerous and enabled the king to provide largess to the recipients by permitting them to take a specified number of trees or of deer or by arranging for these forest products to be given directly to the recipients by officials of the forest. Conspicuous among the hundreds of references to gifts of trees are those to religious houses to supply wood for their fires and lumber for the construction of their buildings.[88] Even the solitary anchorite received the odd tree to help keep away the chill of an English Spring.[89] Less frequently, laymen received gifts of timber for their building projects and trees for the enclosure of their deer parks.[90] In a gesture of charity in 1343, the king granted five hundred oaks from Galtres because the sea had carried away many of the houses of a village and threatened to obliterate the rest unless the quays were repaired.[91]

These gifts, whether oaks or less desirable trees for the hearth, were taken from the demesne woods of the king, and the grants usually specified that the removal was to be effected with the least possible damage to the forest. A curious mistake occurred in 1235 when Henry III gave away twenty-five oaks which he thought to be in his demesne woods but which, in fact, belonged to the manors his father had granted to the bishop of Bath. The bishop objected that the king had no interest in those particular woods except for the general jurisdiction over vert and venison, and the forester in the area confirmed that the woods in question belonged to the manor rather than to the king.[92] The usual procedure was for the cutting of the trees to be carried out under the view and testimony of the verderers, but some cheating obviously took place when Robert de Hampton, who had a writ allowing him to cut eight oaks for his house in Carlisle, managed to cut thirty-six instead.[93]

In contrast to the gifts of trees, which went mostly to clerical recipients, the gifts of deer were made almost exclusively to laymen. These gifts fall into three categories: one or two deer meant for meat for the table, larger numbers given live to stock parks, and an intermediate range that may have been as much a quota for hunting as actual gifts.[94] Although the gifts were made by letters close, local forest officials had to keep records of the total for the purpose of accounting at the next forest eyre for deer removed in accordance with these writs. In Sherwood the cumulative figures for the last ten years of Henry III's reign are for ten harts and three hinds of the red deer and sixty-one bucks and twelve does of the fallow deer. During the first fifteen years of his son's reign, the figures are for one hart, sixty-one bucks, and forty-three does.[95] In spite of the careful accounting for all removals of deer, some flexibility was allowed in a writ allowing Robert de Brus to take one or two more than the authorized twelve bucks and does in the forest of Essex for stocking his park if they happened to be caught along with the specified number; the king did not want Robert brought before the justices of the forest for a minor discrepancy.[96] Entries that should be close to the hearts of historians are those in which the king gave bucks to his clerks who incepted in theology at Oxford University and celebrated a feast in honor of the occasion.[97]

Already in the twelfth century the royal forests had begun to assume an economic importance primarily through the imposition of monetary penalties under the close administration of the forest law. In the thirteenth and early fourteenth centuries the economic aspect of the royal forests had changed by their being drawn more directly into the agricultural and industrial life of the country, with land being put under cultivation by assarting and the renting of wastes. Sales of wood and other forest products provided significant royal income along with some mining and other extractive industry. Livestock operations coexisted with the king's wild beasts, which were themselves an important source of food. The forest records give a picture of the royal forests in general like that which R. Cunliffe Shaw gives in his study of Lancaster, where he found a "complex system of instauration with its precise methods of accountancy," grange farms with yields as high as those in southern England, and cattle and horse breeding in vaccaries and stud farms with a pronounced expansion of animal husbandry and agriculture in the thirteenth century.[98] Not only was there a careful system of accounting, there was an explicit recognition of the potential economic gain for the king from the royal forests. Orders such as that in 1237 for a survey of a part of the royal demesne with a view to increasing its value to the royal treasury are explicit in the desire to increase the profit. With the help of the foresters and verderers, a view was to be taken to see in what places the underwood or other wood could be sold, how many acres in each instance, where the demesne of the king could be enlarged by making purprestures and assarts, and how many acres could be gained in this way to the profit of the king without damage to the royal forest.[99] The same desire for profit underlies another order in 1283 to enclose the lawns in Dean Forest for their maximum utilization.[100] During the thirteenth century, the royal forests were not exempt from the expanding economic activities in England; on the contrary, they were closely absorbed as an integral part of the agrarian life of the time.

7
Political and
Constitutional Struggles,
1258–1327

The royal forest as a political and constitutional issue had been only one among many when the barons sought relief from the abuses of King John, and it remained a background issue in later struggles between the king and barons. The unique attribute of the forest as a political dispute raised in 1215 was that it lasted for another century and a quarter as an issue that remained unresolved and festering beneath the surface of other issues. One factor in the later thirteenth century that brought sporadic attention to the forest was that the Charter of the Forest after 1217 became linked with Magna Carta as a standard of legitimacy for the conduct of a king. In addition, the forest administration was an arbitrary jurisdiction of the king subject to abuse and an obvious and unpopular target for any group that might wish to restrict the power of the king. Throughout the thirteenth and fourteenth centuries, the two charters were always confirmed together, with the Forest Charter sometimes mentioned first.[1] Although most of the confirmations became a matter of form, the association of the two did keep the royal forests connected with the idea of reform, as best exemplified when baronial demands to Edward I in 1297 took the form of seeking a confirmation of the charters as the touchstone of reform.

The role of the forest as a "sleeper" issue emerged during the struggle between the barons and King Henry III in the decade after 1258 without ever becoming a major point of contention. When the huge debt incurred by the king in his quixotic pursuit of the Sicilian crown led the pope to lay down an ultimatum for payment, the king was forced to turn for financial support to his barons in a cause they had repudiated. He was forced to agree in May to a council of twenty-four barons, half chosen by the barons and half by the king, to draw up a list of needed reforms. The twelve chosen by the barons drew up a petition for the Parliament called to meet at Oxford which became the basis for the legislation that emerged from the controversy. The petition had twenty-nine clauses, but it contained only seven major topics, of which one dealt with the forest. The ground for complaint lay in the new perambulations and reafforestment that had taken place when Henry III had confirmed the charters in his own right in 1225. The barons claimed that the king had used the occasion to reafforest arbitrarily some areas that had been found to lie outside the forest bounds during the perambulation, that he claimed custody of heirs to the newly arrented assarts the barons had been allowed to make on their own lands within the forest, and that grants of warren interfered with the free hunting in places disafforested by royal charter after payment of a fine by the whole community of the realm.[2] These were serious complaints placed within the first third of the petition, but there is no reason to think they were considered especially important among the many complaints the barons listed. At the height of baronial influence over the king provision was made for a general inquest into the state of the forests, but this provision was dropped from the final resolution of the dispute after the king regained control with the defeat of the barons at Evesham.[3] The Dictum of Kenilworth in 1266 provided only that the king would "fully protect and observe the liberties of the Church, and the charters of liberties and of the forest, which he is expressly bound to keep and hold by his own oath." The following year this provision carried over into the Statute of Marlborough when it provided that "the Charter of the Forest shall be observed in all its Articles."[4]

Although the charters were confirmed in a routine fashion early in the reign of Edward I, the forest did not become involved as an issue again until the constitutional crisis raised over the confirmation of the charters in 1297. This crisis has been the subject of some controversy among historians who have examined it in detail, and to trace the role of the forest during this period is further complicated by the fact that military service and taxation were the principal questions at issue rather than the forest. However, the forest assumed more importance as the contest wore on because the barons came to see the carrying out of new perambulations as a test of the king's good faith in fulfilling his other promises as well. During this period, the issue of the forest was twofold: the question of the legitimate boundaries of the royal forests and the correction of abuses by forest officials at all levels. In 1293 the king had taken a hardline approach toward the enforcement of forest law, but he had done so at the request of his magnates, when he provided that any evildoers in the forest who resisted the hue and cry with force and arms could be killed with impunity without having to answer to the king or his justices. Because the potential for abuse was recognized, the foresters were warned not to use this authority as a cover for action against their enemies.[5] Throughout the entire dispute after 1297 the king's policy showed a willingness to curb abuses, but he agreed to new perambulations only when he was hard-pressed and forced to make this concession. As far as abuses were concerned, both sides were agreed upon the Forest Charter as the standard to be applied, and Edward I's Forest Ordinance of 1306 was an elaboration on some of its principles rather than a new departure in forest law. In fact, this crisis centering at the beginning upon the demand for a confirmation of the charters proved to be the last time that the charters were an active issue in constitutional debate, for the terms of attempted reform that next came to the fore in 1311 were new and unrelated to the charters.[6]

The differences between Edward I and his barons in the beginning had nothing to do with the forests. In the early summer of 1294, war developed between the kings of France and England over the English province of Gascony, and Edward summoned the host to meet at Portsmouth on 1 September for an expedition to the continent. Before the expedition could form, a rebellion by the Welsh broke out and distracted the efforts of the English king. Edward also was involved in dealing with the Scots, who entered into an alliance with France, and in trying to win allies of his own for a major attack upon King Philip IV of France in Flanders. It was not until 22 August 1297, that the English expedition, only a diminished shadow of what had been envisioned, set sail for Flanders and the indecisive campaign that followed. The enthusiasm of 1294 had vanished and the situation at home had deteriorated, as summarized by Sir Maurice Powicke:

> The difficulties which had delayed Edward's passage to Flanders and pursued him across the Channel were due to his exactions from the clergy, his prises of food and stores, his seizure of wool and hides, the *maltote* of 1294–7, and his attempt to enlist military aid, paid and unpaid, on an unprecedented scale for foreign service.[7]

The grievances of the barons at the time of the king's departure are preserved in a document known as the "Monstraunces," which was copied by several chroniclers in French and in Latin translation. Possibly this statement originated among the smaller landholders being called for extraordinary military service—the twenty-pound men—and was then taken up by the barons. In any event, scholars agree that it is the clearest statement of baronial grievances in the subsequent crisis.[8] Among the many complaints, there is a passage about the forests: "Also the community of the land feel themselves too much oppressed in that the Assize of the Forest is not kept as it used to be; nor are the Charters of the Forest observed; but attachments are made at will, outside the assize, otherwise than used to be."[9] The baronial complaints were placed on a higher level of principle by focusing upon a demand for the confirmation of Magna Carta and the Charter of the Forest rather than any particular grievance. The military situation for Edward I had deteriorated dramatically shortly after his departure for the continent with the rebellion of William Wallace in Scotland and Wallace's victory over English forces at the battle of Stirling Bridge on 11 September.

Dependent upon the support of the barons, the royal government had little choice but to agree to the confirmation of the charters, and the prince, as regent for his absent father, made the confirmation on 10 October. The first stage of the struggle between king and barons terminated with the confirmation by the regency being reinforced on 5 November by the confirmation of the king himself from Flanders.[10] Among other provisions, the confirmations included "that the Great Charter of Liberties and the Charter of the Forest, which were drawn up by the common assent of the whole kingdom in the time of King Henry, our father, are to be observed without impairment in all their particulars," that copies were to be sent to all royal officials, "and that our justices, sheriffs, mayors, and other ministers, whose duty it is to administer the law of the land under us and through our agency shall cause the same charters in all particulars to be admitted in pleas and judgment before them—that is to say, the Great Charter of Liberties as common law and the Charter of the Forest according to the assize of the forest, for the relief of our people."[11]

Problems arose in determining what keeping the Forest Charter in all its particulars meant, and these continuing problems helped bring the issue of the forest to the forefront as a prime issue between king and barons in the next several years. Because the first five chapters of the charter called for disafforestation and set the legitimate bounds of the forest, if these stipulations were to be brought into effect in 1297, new perambulations of the forests would be necessary to insure the legitimate bounds were being kept and, more importantly in baronial eyes, to place outside the forest those areas over which King

Henry III had regained control after 1217. After a false start by issuing writs that referred to a previous perambulation under Henry III instead of the Forest Charter itself, the regency set in motion a perambulation by sending out the necessary commissions for the justices who would carry it out. The standard to be applied as to the legitimate bounds of the forests was that of the Charter, disafforesting any lands made through royal power by King Henry II during his reign or by any of his successors.[12] Although some perambulations were made, it is clear that there was no sense of urgency on this subject, and subsequently the perambulations were allowed to languish.

The royal position was somewhat strengthened by the return of the king to England on 14 March 1298, having abandoned his futile efforts in Flanders against the French king. After a period of preparation, he was able to lead an army into Scotland where he defeated William Wallace on 22 July. Royal policy toward the forest changed with the improving royal fortunes abroad. In November 1298, Edward I ordered an inquest into abuses of the forest probably as a means of answering criticisms that he was not living up to his confirmation of the Forest Charter, but even a conscientious inquest would not answer the question of legitimate bounds that a perambulation was meant to solve.[13] Meanwhile the king delayed, and when he did renew the promise of a new perambulation there were significant changes. On 2 April 1299, in the statute "De Finibus Levatis," King Edward acknowledged the confirmation of 1297, explained that important other business had interfered with the perambulation being made, and again confirmed the Forest Charter. He reiterated the promise for a perambulation as soon as business expected with the arrival of messengers from Rome had been completed, on the ground that the presence of the whole council would be needed to deal with that business.

In addition to this leisurely approach to the problem, other parts of the statute show that Edward's stand had stiffened—it omitted the first five chapters of the Forest Charter from the confirmation which had set the standard for forest bounds and it included reservations with the phrases "Saving always our Oath, the right of our Crown, and our Exceptions and Challenges, and those of all other Persons: So that such Perambulation be reported unto Us, before that any execution or anything else be done thereupon."[14] The significance of these changes was not lost upon those who heard the statute read publicly at St. Paul's in London, for the reading touched off an uproar of immediate protest. Shortly afterward, the king was even forced to issue a mandate for London to order the arrest of all persons speaking ill of the king.[15] There may well have been protests in other sections of the country as well, for the king also ordered all persons making the perambulations to report to him by Michaelmas or sooner because he wished to stiffle the rumor that the king was not going to keep the charters or to allow a perambulation to be made.[16]

Neither the king's order nor the facts of perambulation reassured the critics, and the issue came to a head when the Parliament was called to meet in March 1300. Probably the king's attempt to raise money by renting the waste in the forest as one means of exploiting his prerogative and avoiding the issue of taxation with Parliament contributed to the emphasis upon the forest as an issue at this Parliament.[17] Immediately there was a demand for a new confirmation of the charters. After a short delay in which there were some differences about the form the new confirmation should take, the king agreed to a full *inspeximus* of the charters with no chapters omitted from the Forest Charter, and this confirmation was sealed on 28 March 1300. Further insurance for those who protested that the king had failed to live up to his previous confirmation lay in the long list of witnesses to the *inspeximus* charter as a kind of guarantee, but the king had successfully resisted attempts to have it issued with the seals of the barons in addition to his own as an infringement upon the rights of the Crown. He also won this point by inserting a phrase saving the rights of the crown and the legal actions and claims of the king and others in both the confirmation charter and the commissions for new perambulations.[18]

The perambulations seem to have been carried out as carefully as possible considering that the jurors were being asked to establish whether land had been within the forest almost one hundred fifty years earlier.[19] There were exceptions where mistakes were made and where the jurors made questionable returns. An example of the latter is when the jurors of Warwick stated that there had been no forest in that county at the time of the first coronation of King Henry II and that the hated King John had been responsible for the afforestation that had taken place in the county since that time. When challenged by the suspicious commissioners as to the basis for their statements, the best they could do was to say that was what had been related by their ancestors and what was the common talk of the county.[20] In any event, these perambulations, which were nullified within a few years, would have been little more than a curious episode in the long history of the forest had it not been that they were summoned from the dustbin of history as the basis for forest boundaries under the grandson of Edward I. The king's political position continued to improve and his legal obligations under the confirmations were nullified by a bull he obtained from the new Pope Clement V in 1305 releasing him from the oaths he had taken under duress when he confirmed the charters. What limited use he made of this papal bull was to quash the perambulations of the forest, which had evidently resulted in disafforesting considerable areas.[21]

The final statement of Edward I's policy was embodied in his Forest Ordinance of 1306. The king had only agreed to perambulations when he was forced to do so until he was in a position to set his own policy, and he tried to minimize the effect of the perambulations of 1300 by his responses to the petitions on forest grievances that came before the king in Parliament. The petitions reflect disputes over woods and lands disafforested by the perambulations when the foresters continued to demand forest payments and to impede cutting trees even after an area had been disafforested. In addition to answering specific petitions, the king made a general response relative to the questions being raised by recent disafforestment. As far as the royal demesne lands that were now placed outside the forest were concerned, he declared them covered by the restrictions of a free chace and free warren, thus continuing restrictions upon hunting in these lands as if they had remained within the forest. For lands belonging to others, he accepted that they should be quit of payments demanded by the foresters, but he also pointed out the holders of these disafforested lands should no longer have any right of common or other customs they had enjoyed unless they requested their lands be placed back within the bounds of the forest.[22] Finally, he dropped these indirect measures to minimize the effect of the perambulations and, citing his own dissatisfaction about the state of the forests and the papal bull releasing him from his oaths, he nullified the perambulations made since 1297 in his Ordinance of the Forest on 28 May 1306.[23]

The surprising thing about the Ordinance is how little emphasis is placed upon the nullification. It seems obvious that the intention was to portray the king as zealous for reform because the main thrust of the document is to attack headon the abuses by foresters and other ministers of the forest that had been the subject of complaint. As given in the Ordinance and with the eloquence of its nineteenth century translation, the basic purpose was stated thus: "We have indeed learned, from the information of our faithful Servants and the frequent cries of the oppressed, whereby we are disturbed with excessive Commotion of Mind, that the People of the said Realm are, by the Officers of our Forests, miserably oppressed, inpoverished, and troubled with many wrongs, being everywhere molested." In spite of the verbiage, the willingness to correct abuses had been a consistent royal policy throughout the struggles over the forest, even when that policy vacillated over the question of bounds depending upon how bad the king's political situation with his barons was at any given time. It is also clear that the perambulations had resulted in some disafforestment to which the king could not agree when he was in a position to assert his authority. Nevertheless, his policy after the Ordinance was not vindictive, for he pardoned those persons who had made trespasses of vert and venison during the time certain areas had been disafforested, and he nullified a park enclosed by royal charter when that area reverted to forest by the Ordinance.

The permanent decline in the area and importance of the royal forests came late in the reign of King Edward II and was confirmed in the first years of Edward III. It is a truism that Edward II was not the man his father had been, but his policy toward the forest was similar, and he made concessions only when forced to do so. One of the positions to which he appointed his Gascon favorite, Piers Gaveston, was that of justice of the forests south of the Trent. In fact, along with the office went a grant of special authority not given his predecessors: the right to remove verderers and appoint his own men in their places, to enclose wastes within the royal forest and to rent them for life or for a term, and to audit the accounts of agisters since the last forest eyre.[24] Because verderers were always elected in county court, the provision regarding this office is particularly arbitrary. This kind of exceptional treatment was indicative of the hold the favorite had over his royal patron, and the removal of Gaveston became a key point in the baronial plan of reform when the king was forced to turn to his barons for the taxes he desperately needed.

In March 1310, the barons chose a committee to draw up a list of ordinances for the improvement of the realm, and their work received the royal seal of approval the following year. James Conway Davies, who made a detailed study of these plans, described their significance:

> Of all the experiments in the constitution made during the reign the Ordinances of 1311 were the most important. They were a serious attempt at constructive statesmanship on the part of the barons. They were at once a definition of baronial objects and a program of reform. All subsequent attempts to restrain the king were based upon them or drew a considerable amount of inspiration from them.[25]

The Ordinances that concerned the forest attempted to improve the administration: all forest offices were to be taken into the king's hand pending a general inquest into abuses, and guilty officials were to be removed and the others reinstated after the inquest had been taken. The premise was that the Ordinance of the Forest of 1306 was not being observed. Among the ministers of the forest the chief offenders were the wardens of forests who had been abusing their power to make arrests and to imprison offenders, and the Ordinances placed restrictions upon this power in the future. In addition to these specific problems, part of the general attack on royal prerogative was the claim advanced that the barons would assert their authority to interpret any doubtful chapters in Magna Carta or the Charter of the Forest at the next Parliament.[26] The principal weakness in the Ordinances was that there was no method for enforcement provided, but later Ordinances were drawn up as examples of the way in which the principles should apply to particular cases. The only reference to the forest in these additions was that forest officials who had not yet rendered an account were to be distrained to appear before the Exchequer on 14 January.[27]

It was not until 4 December that the justices of the forest took the forest offices into the king's hands preparatory for a general inquest. The king had opposed the parts of the Ordinances relating to appointments to office, and his handling of the two justices of the forest is a good illustration of how he managed to frustrate the baronial attempt to control the king through controlling appointments. In both cases, he made interim appointments and was able to return his favorite Piers Gaveston for south of Trent on 3 April 1312, and Hugh Despenser for north of Trent on 14 June, even though other Ordinances had been directed specifically to the perpetual exile of Gaveston.[28] It is not too much to say that the Ordinances on the whole had no more than a temporary effect, depending upon whether the king or the barons were in the ascendancy.

The period of 1315–16 was more important than the Ordinances for the status of the forests, because the question of new perambulations became the focus of the demand for reform. The king's fortunes were at a low ebb during those years with the disastrous defeat at Bannockburn in 1314 and famine and economic hardship resulting from bad weather and catastrophic crop failures in those years. Politically, he was at the mercy of his opponents within the baronage. When Edward II summoned Parliament to meet on 27 January 1316, he stated that he wished the ordinances and the perambulations of Edward I to be observed "saving to the king his reasons against the perambulations."[29] Conditions attached to the promise to observe his predecessor's perambulations were given in a letter patent of 16 February as being that any demesnes, forests, or lands which had been in the forest at the time of King Henry II and excluded under Edward I should be reafforested. In order not to cause damage before a special inquest could be started after Easter into the king's rights, it was provided that no cutting of woods or hunting should be done in woods now in forest, whatever their status may have been under the perambulations.[30] In return for a tax of a twentieth, on 20 April the king proclaimed his intention to observe Magna Carta and the Charter of the Forest and announced that he was appointing commissioners for the perambulation.[31] On 10 May the writs of commission were finally sent.[32] However, not everyone had the patience to await the slow-moving efforts of the king to make good his promises. A group of men in Galtres Forest preempted the royal commissioners by making an unsanctioned perambulation of their own and boastfully proclaiming in the city of York that any forester entering the forest would lose his head. In Staffordshire and Shropshire, various persons prevented the collection of the twentieth on the ground that it had only been granted on the condition that Magna Carta, the Charter of the Forest, and the ordinances made in Parliament be observed and that the perambulations of the forest be made. In the writ of 8 June, the king protested rather lamely that he could not understand why the perambulations had not been made because he had ordered them as he had promised to do.[33]

The summons to an Easter Parliament in 1316 again listed the perambulations of the forest as the principal item of business. The king also expanded on his "reasons" against the perambulations of Edward I by explaining that he had agreed at the Lincoln Parliament to observe the perambulations except that any royal demesne lands or the woods belonging to others that were in the forest before the afforestations of Henry III should remain in the forest even if placed outside by the perambulations of Edward I. He also invited anyone who wished to put forward claims about their lands that were afforested to appear at the Parliament.[34] Subsidiary writs indicate that a comprehensive effort was made to collect all the records made during the time of Edward I in preparation for the Parliament. A reply prepared for the knights of the shire for Staffordshire concluded that so many errors had been made in placing areas outside the forest that nothing of the perambulations of Edward I should be kept in that county.[35] Apparently the business of the forests could not be completed in this session of Parliament, for it was not until 5 August at another Parliament meeting at Lincoln that the king confirmed the perambulations and ordered delinquent perambulations to be completed in return for the grant of a sixteenth as an aid for the war in Scotland. This time the king agreed to observe the bounds of Edward I's perambulations without qualification, except that he reserved the right to hunt for forty days in any area disafforested by his confirmation. He also ordered the justices of the forest to attempt to drive the deer from any area disafforested within the new bounds.[36] With these small exceptions, the king had been forced to accept a policy reflecting the reform purposes of the barons who for a time were held together by Thomas, earl of Lancaster, one of the more extreme party in curbing the power of the king.[37] A further commentary on this confirmation, indicating the king's lack of enthusiasm for forest reform, is provided in November 1318 when new commissioners were appointed in Devon and Nottinghamshire because the original commissioners had not made the perambulations.[38]

If such delay seems to imply a certain lack of aggressiveness on the part of the royal government, the resistance to disafforestment became open after the Battle of Boroughbridge on 16 March 1322. Thomas, earl of Lancaster, who was executed after the defeat of his party in that battle, had been a supporter of the Ordinances in general and of forest reform in particular, and with his death a reaction set in that brought the two Despensers, father and son, back to power and foreshadowed a reversal in policy toward the royal forests. On 8 April, the king ordered an inquiry into the renting of wastes within the forest as fixed by Edward I with the explicit purpose of discovering whether some of the tenants had exceeded the amounts of land they were authorized to cultivate.[39] The inquiry, at the very least, can be seen as an attempt to tighten the administration of the forest, and it undoubtedly gave an opportunity to put pressure upon tenants who had been using the land since 1300 by forcing them to justify their activities before a hostile group of forest officials intent upon exploiting all royal rights to the utmost. The changed climate at court was revealed more openly a year later in a writ to the justice of the forests north of the Trent and another in September to the justice south of the Trent, directing them that all royal demesne woods that had been forest in 1217 should be reafforested in spite of any perambulation of Edward I or confirmation of that perambulation by the present king that may have disafforested any demesne woods.[40] The justices, taking their cue from the king and his prominent advisors, followed orders with a vengeance. According to the petitions to Parliament, the petitioners complained they had granted many taxes to secure the Charter of the Forest only to have royal ministers of the forest take towns, woods, and lands into the forest contrary to the charter and, in the process, destroy ditches and interfere with cultivation to the great damage of the people.[41] The king's answer to these petitions was that the forest officials should be heard before a special panel of three judges headed by the chancellor, a man whose loyalty to the king was later demonstrated by his accompanying Edward to the bitter end when they both were captured by the king's opponents, can hardly have been reassuring to the petitioners.

With the fall of the Despensers from power in 1326 in the face of the invasion led by Queen Isabella, charges were drawn up against them and their agents. Because the elder Despenser, among his various roles, had been justice of the forests south of Trent, his deputy in this position and the deputy of the other justice both faced charges of having abused their authority. These charges drawn up by the Commons were the same that had been lodged in the earlier petitions to Parliament. Furthermore, it was charged that the deputy of Hugh Despenser simply disobeyed any chancery writs that were sent to him to correct any of the wrongs he committed. Persons living outside the forest were amerced for not attending the forest eyre, and regarders were forced to make the regard in areas that had been disafforested. He even sent writs to the wardens of the forests under his jurisdiction that he would not recognize a royal charter or writ or any franchise if the people did not bow to his will, and he made these threats in areas where the franchises should have been outside forest jurisdiction. Although provision was made for redress, the general opinion seems to have been that the deputies were only carrying out the orders of the justices of the forest and were not engaging in personal abuse of office.[42] The handling of these charges shows a general recognition of the changed policy toward the forest after the partial failure of baronial reform and the reaction that took place under the influence of the Despensers.

The fall of the Despensers was only part of the circumstances leading to the deposition of Edward II, and once again policy toward the royal forest was drastically changed by events that had nothing directly to do with abuses in the administration of the forest. Petitions to the Parliament called by Queen Isabella and Roger Mortimer to consolidate their control over the kingdom raised the question of the royal forest because they contained grievances against Edward's forest policy.[43] For the new regime, an obvious choice as a bid for support was to use these petitions as a reason for reverting to the more lenient policy of 1315–16, when the barons had pressed Edward II for reform. The new policy was embodied in a statute providing that Magna Carta and the Forest Charter were "to be observed and kept in every article" and that the perambulations of Edward I's reign were to be kept as the legitimate boundaries of the forests.[44] In fact, these provisions were somewhat contradictory because the perambulations had disafforested some areas that were legitimate forest after the charter in 1217, but together they surrendered the policy toward the forest based upon resistance to any encroachment upon royal rights that had been taken by the first two Edwards whenever they could act independently of baronial pressure for reform. The statute, in returning to the perambulations of Edward I, also brought disafforestment to areas returned to forest during the last quarter of a century.

Unlike the reluctance of the earlier kings to carry out the perambulations even during the periods they had been forced to accept this policy, there are several indications that the royal government under the control of Isabella and Mortimer now proceeded to make good the promise of the statute. In five cases involving the forests of Essex, Rockingham, and Feckenham, the deputy of the justice of forests south of Trent was ordered to answer before king and council the claims that he had taken woods into the forest that had been disafforested. On the ground that the perambulations of Edward II had never been placed in effect, the new regime ordered that all perambulations of Edward I should be observed and that in any area where a perambulation had not been made under Edward I a new perambulation should be made as quickly as possible.[45] The exception is the opposite attitude that pervades writs concerning the chace of Knaresborough, which had been given to Queen Isabella. These aimed at stopping unauthorized perambulations and other encroachment upon the chace, but there was no attempt to press claims of the forest in adjoining Wharfedale when the men there were able to present a charter of disafforestment by King John.[46]

The year of this statute in 1327 may be taken as a turning point leading to the decline of the royal forest in the later fourteenth and fifteenth centuries.[47] Although there was later confusion over some of the boundaries of certain forests—and this was inherent in the contradictory passages of the statute itself—the perambulations of Edward I were confirmed in general terms later in the fourteenth century. In a further change from the rigidity of enforcement of forest policy, King Edward III in June 1369 granted a special pardon to all except forest officials themselves who had committed forest offences as recognition for the "great aids" the Parliaments had granted him.[48] The major problem, surfacing in Commons petitions in 1372 and again in 1376, was disagreement over jurisdiction by foresters who harassed men of the *purlieu*, the area disafforested by returning to the perambulations of Edward I.[49] In 1377 there was a petition for a general inquest into the conduct of forest officials, but the king only replied that he would make inquests from time to time and that anyone could bring a charge against any particular official in the normal routine.[50]

In 1383 a statute of Richard II on the forests provided a simple confirmation of the Forest Charter, protection for juries against coercion by officials, and a reemphasis that arrests could only be made by proper indictments. The penalty for any official violating that provision was to pay a double indemnity to the damaged party and a fine to the king.[51] The complete contrast between the spirit of that provision and the savage penalties of forest law in the twelfth century, when the balance was entirely in favor of the officials and against those who fell afoul of the restrictions that were part of forest law, is a measure of the change that had occurred in two centuries. The explanation of this change can probably be found in the fact that the royal forests at the end of the fourteenth century no longer had the importance they had had in the twelfth and thirteenth centuries. Never again was the issue of the forest a major question of political and constitutional significance in medieval England.

8
The Later Middle Ages

The history of the royal forests in England during the later Middle Ages is that of a long, slow decline with no special crises to measure the stages in that decline. In fact, the fifteenth century could best be described as a period in which the royal forest was an institution in decay. However, there was no end to that history, for there was some revival in efficiency of the forest administration under the Tudors, a desperate attempt to exploit the royal prerogative over the forests by the early Stuarts, and continuity through the centuries in many instances to the present Forestry Commission, which has exercised authority over the national forest since 1919. Nevertheless, the purposes served by the royal forests changed from the demand for timber for the dominant English fleet in the seventeenth and eighteenth centuries to the present concern with the environment and twentieth-century needs for recreation. Like many other vestiges of the Middle Ages, the curious survival of some medieval forest law in rights of common and quaint verderers' courts in a few areas should not obscure the reality that the royal forests as a significant legal jurisdiction had ended long before John Manwood in 1598 wrote the epitaph in the form of the first general treatise on the royal forests.[1] Basically the royal forest was a part of medieval England that was distinctive to the period, reaching a height in importance during the thirteenth century but remaining significant in some areas subject to its jurisdiction throughout the fourteenth and fifteenth centuries.

The question of the extent of the royal forests is a difficult one that

149

has been considered in several of the earlier chapters. Even where perambulations of individual forests survive, it may not be possible to trace the "metes and bounds" in today's landscape, and perambulations for all the forests at the same time no longer exist if they were ever made that systematically. Nevertheless, the general contours of the curve that would trace the expansion and contraction of the royal forests has been made fairly clear, mainly through the work of scholars with local knowledge and interest to ferret out references to their parts of the country. It would begin with a baseline at the time when William the Conqueror gathered the woods and hunting preserves of the Saxon kings into a jurisdiction under the forest law he brought from Normandy and added new forests to that core. His youngest son, Henry I, brought organization to the royal forest and added something to its extent. Henry II, not content with merely reestablishing the royal forests and rights that had lapsed during the reign of Stephen, added large areas to the forest, which reached its greatest extent during his reign. The reigns of his two sons brought some gradual disafforestment through grants of exemption made in a haphazard manner by both kings. The minority of Henry III began with some disafforestment after the issuance of the Forest Charter in 1217, and his reign continued with some reafforestment with the confirmations of 1225 and 1227 and his overturning some of the perambulations. During his time, the differences between the court view that the maximum royal rights should be maintained and the view of the juries who sought to minimize the area under forest law revolved about the afforestations of Henry II and whether they represented an illegitimate expansion of the forest or the unfinished restoration of the forest to its rightful limits. The last chapter discussed the fluctuations under the first two Edwards and the acceptance of the perambulations of 1300 by Edward III in his statute of 1327. These boundaries were confirmed by Richard II at the close of the century, and they remained the basic limits except for particular disafforestment by charter when Manwood was writing in 1598. Moreover, an examination of the printed calendars of charter rolls and fine rolls proves that disafforestment by royal grants was not significant in the later Middle Ages.

The fate of some forests after 1300 is illustrative of the process of decay by which the royal forests of medieval England survived the centuries as attenuated ghosts of what they had been in the thirteenth century. Some forests, such as those in Leicestershire, had already been disafforested in 1225 and came to an end with the confirmation of that disafforestment in 1235.[2] In 1327 Edward III followed the trend set by his predecessors and finally declared all of Surrey to be outside the forest.[3] Although the extant records prove that the jurors in Cannock in Staffordshire were making a false claim that much of that forest had been created unjustly by Henry II, their claim was accepted in 1327 and the boundaries of the forest much reduced. For all practical purposes the forest had ceased to exist there by the end of the sixteenth century. Kinver in the same county survived nominally into the seventeenth century, but it was much diminished by the reign of Elizabeth I.[4] By 1331 Savernake Forest had been reduced from an estimated ninety-eight square miles at the end of John's reign to a mere thirteen square miles.[5] In 1341 Edward II admitted that Dean had been reduced by about one-fourth, and the farm owed by the warden was officially adjusted downward from £160 to £120 to reflect this reduction.[6] One of the best accounts of local forests deals with those in Wiltshire—Braydon, Chippenham, Melksham, and Selwood in the west and Savernake, Chute, Clarendon, Melchet, and Groveley in the east—and there Edward III in 1330 accepted the bounds of 1300. As described by the author of the county history, "All that remained under the forest law were scattered areas of royal demesne lands and woods, including lands and woods which in the past had been seized for assart, waste, or purpresture. These areas were to be clearly delimited by digging pits along the boundaries."[7]

Scholars have generally agreed to use 1327 as the date to mark the decline of the royal forest, and that date is as relevant as most dates for tracing the history of complex institutions. When Richard II accepted the same bounds and confirmed the action of his grandfather in 1383, the statute of 1327 was reinforced.[8] Its effect when studied from the viewpoint of individual forests clearly meant considerable disafforestment and, in some cases, the end of the royal forest. However, what makes the overall decline of the forest impossible to follow is that more significant than the application of the bounds drawn under Edward I in the decline of the royal forest was the gradual failure of effective administration in areas still nominally within the royal forest and the process by which the impotent forest law was being superseded by common law courts with more narrowly defined jurisdiction. The eyre for forest pleas, already irregular in its frequency in the thirteenth century, was replaced by inquests into the state of the forests by Edward III, and these inquests became completely haphazard. When it is considered that the lower forest courts depended upon the eyre to make final disposition of all but minor transgressions against the forest, the decline of the forest eyre marks the decline of the royal forest just as John Manwood thought.[9] Even in an area where reafforestation was ordered by a writ of 1347, there was a different attitude

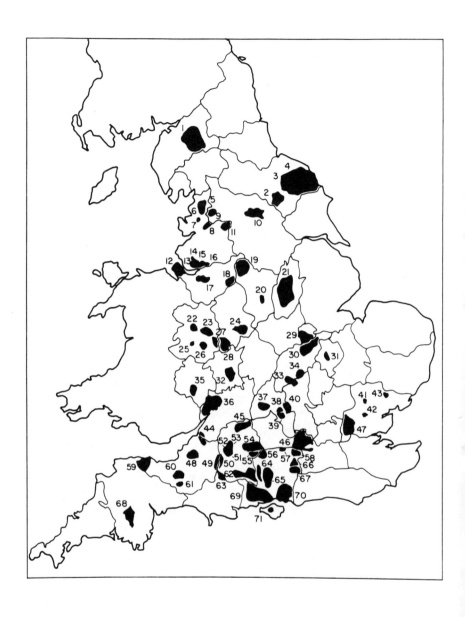

The Royal Forests
1327–1336

66	Alice Holt	22	Lithewood
58	Bagshot	18	Macclesfield
70	Bere by Porchester	51	Melksham
65	Bere by Winchester	48	Mendip
40	Bernwood	27	Morfe
11	Blackburn	7	Myerscough
6	Bleasdale	61	Neroche
9	Bowland	69	New Forest
45	Braden	60	North Petherton
64	Buckholt	57	Pamber
24	Cannock	52	Pewsham
53	Chippenham	4	Pickering
56	Chute, Hampshire	5	Quernmore
55	Chute, Wiltshire	30	Rockingham
62	Clarendon	29	Rutland (or Leighfield)
16	Croxteth	34	Salcey
68	Dartmoor	54	Savernake
36	Dean	49	Selwood, Somerset
17	Delamere	50	Selwood, Wiltshire
20	Duffield	21	Sherwood
47	Essex	26	Shirlet
59	Exmoor	38	Shotover
32	Feckenham	14	Simonswood
8	Fulwood	3	Spaunton
2	Galtres	39	Stowood
63	Gillingham	25	Stretton
41	Hatfield	15	Toxteth
35	Hereford Hay	31	Wauberghe
19	High Peak	23	Wellington
1	Inglewood	13	West Derby
71	Isle of Wight	33	Whittlewood
43	Kingswood, Essex	46	Windsor
44	Kingswood, Somerset	12	Wirral
28	Kinver	67	Woolmer
10	Knaresborough	42	Writtle
		37	Wychwood

Based on Nellie Neilson, "The Forests," in James F. Willard and W. A. Morris, eds., *The English Government at Work, 1327–1336* (Cambridge, Mass., 1940), Vol. 1, map V by permission of The Mediaeval Academy of America.

toward the royal forest under Edward III compared to that mirrored by the records of his father and grandfather. In this writ he corrected his own officials by announcing that it had not been his intention to prevent men from cutting woods or using pasture in the area being reafforested except for what was necessary for the deer.[10] In effect, the implications of this writ virtually restricted the forest law concerning vert to the coverts within the forest of Porchester rather than rigorously applying the law to the entire royal forest then being reafforested.

The infrequency of the eyre for forest pleas had already begun to affect the operations of the royal forest in the latter half of the thirteenth century, and that capstone of the forest courts deteriorated entirely by 1368. Commissions for forest eyres were sent to only three counties in 1329, four in 1330, and two in 1339 and 1348. Other years saw a commission for only one county, and there was no consistency in the coming of the eyre to any county. Only Yorkshire had as many as four eyres in the fourteenth century (1334, 1336, 1337, and 1339), Hampshire had two (1330 and 1354), and Northamptonshire had two (1330 and 1348). Still, royal writs to Nottingham in 1385 speak of putting a man on bail until the coming of the justices for forest pleas, even though that county had not had an eyre since 1334.[11] Thus, there was no statute nor even any policy decision to end the forest eyre, but the last commission for an eyre found in the *Close Rolls* was for Lancashire in 1368.

In view of the uncertainty of the eyre, it is not surprising that it had lost its effectiveness long before it fell into complete disuse. In 1330 the new king Edward III ordered the Exchequer to give the justices all the rolls from the previous two reigns, and a surviving roll for the New Forest from that time illustrates the problems the justices had to face.[12] For example, on the opening day of the session thirty-four men were present, but ninety-six other men had died before the coming of the justices. An indictment concerning one of the deceased was for the offense of shooting a deer with a bow and arrow in 1289, more than forty years before the eyre made a final disposition of the case. The next case listed on the roll occurred only three years later, and other cases dated from the reign of Edward II early in the fourteenth century. Similarly for Clarendon Forest in Wiltshire, there were listed 56 as present in 1330 and 104 as essoined by death.[13] One plea for killing deer went back to the year 1292, and other cases were complicated by the principals having died, by trespasses having continuously taken place over intervals of as long as twelve years, and by areas where trespasses occurred having been placed within and then without the forest by perambulations before the case came before the justices. Perhaps the low esteem for the forest eyre explains a writ of 1331 to the justices in Hampshire ordering them to suspend the eyre because people in those parts needed to attend to their own affairs for the common utility of the king's people.[14]

Another indication of the general breakdown of forest administration is the number of accustomed malefactors reported at the eyre who had not been effectively restrained from continuous violations of forest law: twelve in Braden, forty-eight in Savernake, eleven in Clarendon, nine in Chute, and twenty-one in Melksham, Chippenham, and Pewsham.[15] In Wiltshire the number of foresters reported as themselves accustomed malefactors of the vert within their bailiwicks going back from the present holding by Edward III, through the period under Queen Isabella, and to the time of Hugh Despenser the Elder, who was overthrown in 1326, included the present two chief foresters and came to a total of ninety-seven.[16] At the same time, there was remarkable continuity in the nature of the eyre as long as it lasted as illustrated by the foresters in Salcey and Whittlewood in 1348 responding to the same articles of the Assize that had been used in the late thirteenth century.[17]

A roll of forest pleas for Sherwood Forest in 1334 is particularly valuable for recording the attempt of the justices to clear up arrears in a systematic way since 1317 with one case from 1306. The various fines and amercements for pleas of the venison are listed and then neatly totalled at the bottom of each membrane. In presenting one case for killing a deer in 1317, the jurors said they did not know whether the defendant had been attached and security taken for his appearance at the eyre or not because the verderers had not delivered their roll of mainprises for that year. The roll of attachments for vert is stated to include those of more than four pence because cases involving over that figure could only be decided at the eyre. Amercements of verderers for the attachments of vert or because they failed to produce their rolls went back to 1288, and the amounts were grouped by reign: £54 13s. 4d. for the years 16–35 Edward I, £39 12s. 10d. for 1–20 Edward II, and £6 3s. 8d. for 1–8 Edward III. The regarders were still reporting rents for the "old assarts" going back as far as 1217, but many of the older assarts were reported as being wasted in 1334. Rents of wastes and assarts are listed as having been recorded before Geoffrey de Langeley in the Pipe Roll of 1254—recorded before William de Vescy in the Pipe Roll of 1289—ordered by a letter patent in 1298, and listed in the particulars of account submitted to the Exchequer by John de Crumwell in 1317.[18]

After the last forest eyre of 1368, the functions of the eyre in setting amercements to settle cases involving trespass of vert and venison and in supervising the ministers of the forest either ceased or devolved to other administrative arrangements. The most obvious replacement came from inquisitions *de statu foreste*, which had been a method regularized by Edward I's Ordinance of the Forest of 1306. The Ordinance provided that indictments were to be made by the foresters within whose bailiwicks the trespasses had taken place, who were to present the cases at the next general inquisition before the foresters, verderers, regarders, agisters, and other ministers of the forest and a jury of the neighborhood.[19] Clearly this procedure provided a regular method of indictment, and the evidence is that this method superseded the holding of special inquisitions on the occasion of a suspected crime, but it was no real substitute for the final determination that the eyre had provided. Some of the surviving inquisitions parallel the eyre in their scope, dealing with both vert and venison and with the abuses of foresters, but most did not extend over as long a period of time as the eyres of the fourteenth century did and, therefore, do not include many cases.

Perhaps the indictment by a general inquisition with the need to provide mainpernors who would insure that the defendants appeared at the eyre, surviving from the time when eyres were held, may have served as some sort of penalty and deterrent. Certainly, there is evidence that imprisonment was used until the king would order release of the prisoners when they found mainpernors.[20] Nevertheless, the absence of the eyre was a fundamental weakness in the functioning of the general inquisition. There are also some indications that a type of administrative justice was practiced by the wardens of the forests, probably acting through the swanimotes or attachment courts, arrogating to themselves the authority to go beyond indictment to assessing punishment.[21] In 1376 the Commons petitioned Edward III that several persons, including bailiffs of fees, had forfeited their bailiwicks by indictment before the justices of the forest without judgment and response. The petition asked for the right to have a Chancery writ to be mainprised until the coming of the eyre, as guaranteed by the ordinance of 1311, and to make a fine for the restoration of their bailiwicks, but the king's answer was that an individual with a grievance should make his own case which would be determined on its merits.[22] The implication of another petition of 1383 is that men were being imprisoned without indictment and distrained by ministers of the forest until they paid fines for redemption, but the king's response—setting a penalty on the forester of double damage to the aggrieved party and a fine to the king—should have curtailed this abuse of office after this time, unless it was ignored as the provisions of 1311 had obviously been.[23]

At least in an emergency situation following the disturbances of 1323, forest offenses were considered alongside other offenses by a justice of common pleas acting on a royal writ for a general inquiry and the results entered on the *Coram Rege Roll.*[24] Some other cases with forest offenses found their way into common law courts, but this did not happen in a general way and never replaced the eyre for forest pleas in keeping forest law alive. Commissions of *oyer et terminer* sometimes were made for matters dealing with royal lands within forests, but these commissions by their nature were directed only against specific problems.[25] Another outlet for aggrieved individuals, as well as the Commons in general, was to petition the king in Parliament over injustices of the forest, and this was done in many cases involving personal and rather insignificant matters as well as problems of general concern.[26] However, the thrust between the two laws was not all one way, for the wardens of forests were so far asserting their jurisdiction that the king in answer to a petition to Parliament in 1334 had to order them to keep their officers from extortion and to allow the coroners to execute their office within the forests.[27] The most difficulty came from the disafforested areas known as *purlieu* when foresters attempted to assert their authority over the men living in those areas.[28] This evidence points again to the development of a kind of administrative justice by the foresters when the older system of forest law was breaking down. Presumably, in other areas where the wardens and foresters were less assertive, the royal forest as an administrative-judicial area for all practical purposes ceased to exist.

Another indication of the decline of the royal forest in the fourteenth century can be seen in what happened to the regard, an institution that provided a general survey of the vert and of encroachments upon the forest. According to the Forest Charter of 1217, the regard was to be made every third year in areas where it had been made before the first coronation of King Henry II. Because commissions for making the regard were issued as letters close to the sheriffs, some idea of the continuity of this aspect of the forest administration can be derived from the Close Rolls. In the 1340s and 1350s the number of counties in which regards were held declined, then almost disappeared south of the Trent after 1360, and ended completely in the south after 1387. The three forests north of the Trent in which regards were made regularly were Inglewood, Pickering, and Sherwood. In these forests the same old chapters of the regard were used and information compiled from the inquiries about assarts, purprestures, and waste along with the more specific questions as had been done for centuries.[29]

The disappearance of the eyre after 1368 and the termination of the regard in the south after 1360 are symptoms of the decline of the royal forest in the later fourteenth century that point to a lack of attention from the governments of Edward III and Richard II. Of course, these breakdowns of the forest law and administration contributed to the decline of the royal forest, but they were not themselves the cause of that decline. For some reason, the forest no longer was important enough to get the attention and effort required to solve the administrative problems. The explanation for this neglect can be found in the changing nature of the royal forest beginning in the twelfth century and continuing in the thirteenth when the royal forest was primarily significant for its economic contribution to the royal government. One of the basic changes in England during the fourteenth century was the development of a system of public finance based upon taxes that could be levied on the growing commercial wealth of the nation. Born of the necessity of war first with Edward I and later during the first phase of the Hundred Years' War, and continued into the interval of peace begun by the Treaty of Brétigny in 1360, these taxes brought the royal government an amount of revenue that completely eclipsed that obtained from the royal forests.[30] This was especially true with the reduced area through disafforestation by the perambulations of Edward I and the stabilization of income from assarts and the farming out of other sources of revenue. The stabilization of income in itself in a period of inflation would have caused a drop in the relative value of forest revenue.

The crisis faced by Edward I in 1294 and the following years had as its primary ingredients the disputes over military service and taxation. The movement toward a system of national taxation had a profound effect upon the history of the royal forest, even though it was indirect, and the concession made by Edward I for new perambulations that brought extensive disafforestment, which he hoped would be temporary but which proved to be permanent under Edward III and Richard II, was a second element stemming from the same crisis. The development of a national taxation opened up such new possibilities for royal income that the attenuated royal forests were neglected and, having become insignificant for the economy, they declined into the hunting preserve from which they had begun.

Nevertheless, the administrative structure of the forests in the later Middle Ages remained basically unchanged. There continued to be two justices of the forest for those north and south of the Trent, wardens of individual forests, and subordinate foresters within individual forests. The major change in this organization was the length of terms that commonly extended to life and often, in practice, became hereditary.[31] In addition, there were the foresters in fee within individual forests whose positions were formally hereditary. The references to foresters of all kinds reflect an emphasis upon these offices as property to be described explicitly at the time of appointment and to be defended in court if need be. The overall impression is that of an administrative system that had become rigid and whose participants viewed their offices as a source of income rather than a responsibility to administer the forest law effectively. Commissions of forest officials show that this was an attitude shared by the king and council.[32] In the fourteenth century with the growth of parliamentary taxation, the income from forests decreased in importance, and appointments of foresters were matters of patronage to the king valued primarily for that reason.

However, the office of forester could be valuable to the recipient both as an honor and for the income it carried. Payment to a justice of the forests north of the Trent was managed by an allowance at the Exchequer from the forest income the justice collected and reported during his accounting, but lesser foresters were granted a *per diem* wage.[33] One list of wages in 1322 set the wages of the chief forester of Windsor at twelve pence a day, whereas the porter of the gates at the castle got only four pence a day, and lesser servants including the viewer of the king's works got only two pence or less a day.[34] In addition, the chief forester received certain fees, but letters to the constable in 1337, 1344, and 1346 concerning John Brocas who had been appointed chief forester for life suggest that obtaining the wages must have been something of a problem, for they all order the payment of arrears in wages and fees. An earlier letter about his predecessor refers to twelve pence a day as the customary wage, but it also was occasioned by arrears in wages.[35]

The property element in an office of forester was enhanced by the fact that many offices were attached to other holdings that were conferred as a group. At Kinver Forest, the manor of Kinver and custody of the forest went together for the payment to the king on nine pounds annually. In 1340 Henry de Mortuo Mori had to get a special letter from the king to the Exchequer to avoid making his payment because he had spent a year trying to get his predecessor to relinquish the holding, even though he had a grant from the king for it.[36] A royal letter to the escheator in 1347 emphasizes the property aspect and reveals that Henry had granted the manor and forest at the terms of the annual nine pounds payment to the Exchequer to Edward atte Wode for the term of Henry's life, and that the manor and forest now fell to Edward's heir because he died before Henry, even though the heir was a daughter Margaret only seven weeks old at her father's death.[37] Another letter in November 1349 points up that the sums due for holding a forest were more than customary figures when the forester holding the castle of St. Briavels and the forest of Dean was given an adjustment of £50 for the previous year and the same for the current year against a farm of £120 because the issues and profits were cut so badly by the Black Death and other causes that they would not cover the amount of the farm.[38] In 1380 the appointment of a forester for life took the form of an indenture with the king recording the £85 in annual farm for the town and park of Devizes; the forests of Melksham, Chippenham, and Persham; and the manor of Roude in the county of Wiltshire.[39] Usually royal appointments of foresters did not go beneath that of the warden of an individual forest, but in 1401 the king appointed a riding forester in the New Forest with an allowance of one hundred shillings a year and one in Windsor Forest with wages of three pence a day, which was one-fourth that of the warden in that forest.[40] Normally the king's interest in the lesser forest offices extended only to regulating the number of foresters that could be appointed by the warden as in the appointment in 1403 of a warden in Pickering Forest who was allowed to appoint his own subordinates.[41] A memorandum of 1372, when Richard de Pembrugge refused to go to Ireland as the king's lieutenant there, listed the various gifts and rewards the king was revoking because of his disobedience. The wardenship of a forest occurs among a list of other offices and holdings: constable of Dover Castle, warden of the Cinque Ports, warden of Bamburgh Castle, farm from the town of Bamburgh, keeper of the New Forest and the manor of Brockenhurst in it, one hundred pounds annually from the farm of the New Forest for life, and the wardship of an heir.[42]

With the office of forester considered as property there were disputes about the title to that property. An order to the escheator in August 1346 seems quite straightforward. An inquest had shown that John de Haudlo had held for life a messuage, two bovates of land, 622 acres 3½ roods of pasture, 115 shillings 5 pence in rent, and the forestership of Bernwood for the service of a serjeanty in keeping the forest of Bernwood and accounting for 50 shillings at the Exchequer. Now the property and office were ordered to be delivered to Edmund, son of Richard de Haudlo, who was apparently a grandson of the John who had obtained the original grant, and Edmund had pledged fealty to the king for the lands and bailiwick. Two weeks later, lands and the forest offices of Shotover and Stowood were ordered to be delivered jointly to a new husband and the widow of Richard, son of John de Haudlo. However, by June of the following year the king had begun the process of reclaiming the land and forestership of Bernwood from Edmund Haudele and his wife on the ground of Edmund's minority, and the inquest by the escheator turned up evidence that complicated the whole situation. It was found that Edmund's grandfather had granted the entire holding to two other men, receiving it back from them for life on the basis of a license from the king when Edmund was seven years old, and further examination into the rolls of Edward I showed that the grandfather's interest had only been through the inheritance of his wife from her father and that the king's license to him allowing him to enfeoff the two men had been based on an error. Next a general search of all the rolls of the forest eyres going back to the reigns of Henry III and Edward I failed to show the right of the warden of Bernwood to take any payments in that forest, and, therefore, the fees claimed by later wardens were based upon a usurpation. The investigation continued when other perquisites of the warden came under question. Finally, the king regained possession in a case before the bench and granted the lands and wardenship to another party.[43] Although the various letters close relating to this case made the documentation more full than in most, there is other evidence to prove that the office of the forest could be revoked for malfeasance of duty and that the possession of an office could be contested between rival claimants as a matter of law to the point of voiding a royal grant when it had been based upon error.[44]

The property element in the office of forester could also be reflected in the types of courts that might deal with disputes. A suit between a forester in fee within Savernake Forest and Henry Sturmy, warden of that forest, first came before the justices in eyre headed by Robert de Ufford in 1334. There the dispute was ordered to be tried in Parliament, but a petition sought to have the case returned for trial to Robert de Ufford. In responding to this petition the king reserved determination of the substance of the case to himself and appointed Robert de Ufford and two others with a commission of *oyer et terminer* to end transgressions that the warden of the forest had made on the forester in fee by virtue of his office and otherwise. The basis of the dispute was the refusal of the warden to give seisin to the forester in fee on the grounds that the profits involved were part of the perquisites belonging to his own office of warden. When the dispute came before the king and Great Council, they ordered the justice of the forest to inform himself through the records of previous eyres and otherwise about the contradictory claims of the parties and to decide according to the Assize of the Forest and to seek the king's advice if the decision proved difficult. Only in the last step in the tortured progress of the dispute did a forest court and forest law enter into a case that had previously been considered purely a question of seisin.[45]

It is obvious from such cases that the holding of a forest office had become hereditary in fact even when the royal grants in each instance were made only for the life of the individual grantee. The distinction between these foresters with grants for life and hereditary wardens or foresters and the foresters in fee is blurred, but some families had managed to perpetuate themselves in office over many generations whatever the exact legal status of their tenure may have been. There may have been some confusion among contemporaries. Even a member of the Sturmy family, which had held Savernake Forest since the early twelfth century, during a case in 1338 was said to have held the bailiwick jointly with his son and daughter-in-law by knight's service created by a fine to the king not "as of fee" for the service of keeping the forest, and, six months later, he claimed payments for lawing of dogs as belonging to him because he and his ancestors held the forest "in fee."[46] In 1345 the wife of Bartholomew de Lisle was expected to swear fealty through the royal escheator for the bailiwick of Chute Forest when an inquest had shown her husband at his death had held no lands in chief but that his holdings were joint with his wife "in chief by serjeanty," by which they kept the forest at their own cost.[47] Other wives similarly did fealty for offices of wardens of forests, but the justice north of the Trent balked in assigning dower from lands in Inglewood Forest to a widow and insisted that only his own ministers could minister in that forest.[48] Normally the hereditary wardenship of a forest was delivered to either male or female heirs by the escheator upon order from the king, but a feud over the office of warden in Knaresborough Forest and chace lasted four years and grew into a rebellion in 1387.[49]

The holding of an inquest was the best way to settle disputes over the right to forest offices or to the income from the forest that pertained to the office. In 1323 Edward II ordered William de Vescy and his fellow justices to hold an inquest into the office of the warden of Sherwood Forest. The jurors responded that the warden by virtue of his office should have: the right to hunt hares, wolves, bucks or harts, and cats in the forest; bark and branches from oaks that the king gives from his demesne woods; retropannage; three shillings from each dog lawed at three-year intervals; and cheminage from carts passing through the forest. He held ten knights' fees in chief, and all his lands were outside the regard and his dogs exempt from being lawed. At the last eyre it had been determined by William and his fellow justices that the bailiwick was held by the warden and his heirs in perpetuity.[50] Eleven years later an examination of rolls by the treasurer and chamberlains proved equally effective in determining why the office of a forester in fee within Sherwood had been taken into the king's hands by Edward II and remained there under his son. This searching of the records showed that the man's father had appeared before William de Vescy and fellows in a forest eyre to account for his tenure and that of his father by producing rolls in which he was found to have made erasures to the great damage of the king and, thus, forfeited his office.[51] Even the jurors in an inquest could cover long periods, as in 1346 when the listing of foresters in fee and their rights in High Peak reached back more than sixty years to the year 1285 for some of the answers. The transfer of a bailiwick to the heir of a forester in fee was the responsibility of the justice of the forest north or south of the Trent, and the royal escheators were prohibited from intervening once it had been determined the office was held "in fee."[52]

In the middle of the fourteenth century there are references to a new official known as a ranger. Although there is no question of the duties of an official with this title in the post-medieval period, the earliest references give no indication that the office had the same function in its origin. In later times the rangers were charged with driving the deer from the *purlieu,* the disafforested areas around the remaining forest after the perambulations of Edward I, back into the safety of the royal forest where they were protected by forest law from all except the king and his friends.[53] The earliest letter patent that I have found commissioned a ranger in 1341.[54] The early commissions all describe the ranger as an officer of the forest—Shotover, Wolmer and Aliceholt, and Chute.[55] In 1393 an official with this title was over Chaspell, Ivesley, and Asshewood within Kinver Forest.[56]

Sometimes the office of ranger was combined with other duties, as illustrated by the ranger in Chute who was also responsible for keeping the king's game of Harewode and the one in Kinver who was also bailiff of Chaspell. Another letter granted for life the office of forester of Savernake along with the office of ranger of the same forest.[57] By 1465 the office of ranger may have become a sinecure, for the king's servant and the king's servant yeoman of the kitchen were granted for life the wages of six pence a day with the office of ranger in Dean and in Groveley respectively.[58] There are earlier references that show the ranger was a forester paid daily wages of three pence either from the revenues of the forest or from those of the county and that the office was being held by men of less than knightly rank. One grant of the office of ranger in 1371 to Henry Dolying was made because of his long service as one of the foresters of the New Forest; this was to be held as William Dolyng, deceased, had held it for six pence a day.[59] Presumably, the permanency of the office and the higher rate of pay made it more valuable than the office of an ordinary walking or riding forester subject to the whims of the warden of the forest. Although none of the medieval evidence contradicts the later functions of the ranger, the close connection with the forests at least suggests that the early rangers had functions within the forest not found after the medieval period.

One of the important influences of the medieval royal forest was the creation of a large administrative class. In the twelfth and thirteenth centuries, the men who staffed the offices of the forest performed administrative, economic, and judicial functions equal to other governmental positions in responsibility; by the fourteenth century many of the forest officials were performing their duties by deputy while enjoying the income from the offices. Both because of the authority of their offices and the abuses of power, the foresters earned for themselves a bad reputation. Yet the development of the special forest law paralleled the development of the common law, and in the twelfth century there was considerable overlap in personnel among the justices who administered both systems of law. The forest law abandoned its harsh physical penalties by the later twelfth century and its burden was moderated also by numerous exemptions. However, exemptions were mostly purchased, and the practice of giving fines to obtain exemptions added to the mercenary image of the foresters and forest law. Whatever may have been the period when the Robin Hood legend formed and whatever may have been the class to which the audience belonged, one theme of the stories is the hatred of the officials of the royal forest, and there is adequate evidence from the king's own records to show this attitude in reality as well as in fiction.

Yet it may be doubted that the forest law and foresters were any more oppressive than other aspects of the royal government. Use of the forest law as a means of raising money in large quantities whether by the Angevins or by Henry III at the suggestion of Robert de Passelewe was bitterly resented. More fundamental in arousing a hatred of the forest law for landowners in the thirteenth century was the opposition between the restrictions of forest law to protect the vert and the necessity to expand the arable as part of the agricultural expansion in that century. The demands for disafforestation came from the landowners who were more concerned in being able to use their land to their own best advantage than with the restrictions against hunting. At the same time, a smaller group among the landowners, those who held administrative offices within the royal forest, profited from it. As forest offices tended to become hereditary, the treatment of them as property valued for the income they represented became more open. Forest administrators as a class might be disliked, but they felt no reluctance to fight to obtain and to keep their offices.

The tenacity of the administrative system of the forests was demonstrated by its continued functioning in the fourteenth century without the corrective supervision of the forest eyre on a regular basis. The nature of the evidence, reflecting mainly the instances in which this or that forester failed in his duties, makes any firm generalization about the quality of that administrative performance impossible, but there are a few instructions from the royal government that seem to imply an attempt to deal with widespread administrative problems within the forest system. In fact, the task of keeping track of all the forest ministers was itself a large one as shown by Edward II's order in 1316 to the sheriffs of all counties in which there were royal forests to get lists of all forest ministers since his accession and their replacements if they had died, in order that the king would know who was supposed to appear before the Exchequer to account for income from sales of pasture and wood.[60] In 1320 letters close directed the executors of the will of William de Vescy to send all his rolls to the Exchequer from his period in office as justice of the forests north of the Trent some twenty-three years after his death, and Hugh Despenser that year had not yet surrendered his rolls for the south side of Trent some five years after he had been forced from office.[61]

Outside events affected foresters along with other subjects of the English king, but administrative records reflect these events only rarely. In 1322 the justice of forests south of Trent was ordered to bring a number of foresters suitably armed to set out in the king's service in Scotland, and the other justice of forests in 1339 had difficulty in obtaining an allowance from his account for his fee of office in 1339 because of a royal order not to pay the fees of any of the king's ministers during an emergency when the king's need for money was critical.[62] In 1330 John Mautravers, justice south of the Trent, was sent into exile, presumably caught on the wrong side in the move by Edward III to take power into his own hands, and twenty-five years later a forest eyre was attempting to find his rolls while in office, even though it was found that he had surrendered those rolls to the justices in eyre in Wiltshire who had exiled him in 1330, and the king had recorded that fact.[63] The inability of the royal government to safeguard the records of one of the two most important officers in the forest administration in itself provides a sad commentary on the efficiency of the forest administration under Edward III.

Even in the thirteenth century, many foresters conducted their offices through deputies, and this practice was accepted by the royal government as evidenced by writs regularly directed to a forest official "or his deputy." However, King Richard II in a letter patent of 10 December 1390 attempted to require more personal accountability. He empowered the justice north of the Trent to examine every forest within his jurisdiction and to order every forester to execute his office in person under pain of forfeiting his office if he appointed a deputy. Exceptions were made for foresters in fee and for those foresters who had obtained the royal license to execute the office by deputy.[64] In practice, there was probably little change because most grants after this time included the right to exercise office by deputy.[65]

Both the abuse of office and the dangers and difficulties in performing the duties of a forester continued to be exemplified during the fourteenth century. Foresters were involved in illegal hunting on their own and in corruption when they permitted illegal hunting by others within their bailiwicks. Similarly, the foresters' offenses against the vert consisted of cutting oaks and other trees or underbrush for their own use and in ignoring transgressions by other men. At a forest eyre in 1355 the jurors presented a long list of criminal activities by Giles Beauchamp, the warden of the forest of Groveley and keeper of Clarendon Park, that can serve as an inventory of the types of abuses possible to a corrupt forester. In the order presented, the abuses were: devastation of oaks and underwood creating waste to the value of twenty pounds, oaks taken from park for three years for repair of his houses, permitting his servant to cart off oaks for two years, taking hay for his own animals, giving tree trunks to two men, giving a cartload of underbrush, allowing the bishop of Salisbury to take five does in the park over a two-year period, allowing a knight to take two does, taking the trimmings from trees for his own use, allowing assarts for fourteen years to the damage of ten pounds, permitting various men to pasture their animals in the park for three years, gathering all the honey for his own use throughout his term of office, extorting payments for hay and forage in areas outside the metes of the forest against the "great charter of the forest," arresting a man for killing a deer and then accepting a fine from him, preventing the regarders and other ministers of the forest from exercising their offices within the forest, extorting fees including cheminage even in fence month during the entire twenty-three years he held office, hunting in the forest and forcing men to make a buckstall for him, not accounting to the king for agistment during the term of his office to the value of ten pounds for each of twenty-three years, collecting money from those men pasturing animals in the forest and not accounting to the king for twenty years, allowing some men special privileges in taking underbrush, keeping cattle and pigs of his own in the forest, collecting small payments in kind from villagers that should belong to foresters in fee, and failing to account to the king for an estimated £99 14s. 3d. collected in amercements and attachments at swanimotes held during his time in office. It should also be noted that the same jurors presented similar charges against two of Giles' predecessors, who seem to have been almost as bad in their conduct of the office.[66]

It is obvious from this long list of offenses that the office of warden provided an opportunity for abuses not possible to men in other occupations. The crimes of Giles Beauchamp were exposed by a forest eyre and even the office of warden failed to protect him from punishment for abuses that he had committed throughout the entire twenty-three years he held office. In other cases, an inquest commissioned by the king might deal with offenses being committed by foresters. When the regard continued to be held, it provided another occasion for the ministers of the forest and twenty-four jurors to bring to light the transgressions of a warden of the forest as they did those of Henry Sturmy in Savernake in Edward III's time. This long list of charges against Henry Sturmy provides conclusive evidence of the importance of the forest eyre, for in several places it is emphasized that the offenses cover a period of fifty-one years since the last eyre.[67] With the cessation of the eyres and decline and cessation of regards in many areas in the latter half of the fourteenth century the control over the conduct of foresters was sadly diminished. No quantitative assessment of how this relaxation of control affected the conduct of foresters is possible because the evidence on malfeasance in office itself resulted only from corrective action taken mainly at the eyre, but the natural assumption is that foresters who committed crimes when the eyre still functioned would certainly have felt free to do so even more when that restraint was removed.

However, the abuses of foresters should be balanced somewhat by a reminder that they had their problems, too. Eight foresters failed in an attempt to force a township to pay the king what they owed over a seven-year period before 1374.[68] One of the woodwards in the forest of Galtres was granted three pence per day for life because while in the king's service he had had his eyes gouged out, and his tongue and fingers cut off by evildoers in the forest.[69] Resistance to foresters in the exercise of their office easily took a violent turn, sometimes leading to death of a forester when he attempted to arrest armed men caught in the act of killing deer.[70]

As long as the organization of the royal forest continued to function, the element of hunting and that of economic returns both existed, and the records of some economic aspects of the royal forest are more complete for the later Middle Ages than they are for the thirteenth century. Comparisons of various sorts have been made between Henry II and Edward I in terms of the development of the common law, but they were also similar in their great love of hunting. A panegyric on the death of Edward I emphasized that he had been a "vigorous lover of woods and wild beasts" who took delight in hunting with dogs and hawk.[71] A series of letters concerning his falcons show this interest in a more down-to-earth form.[72] The oldest book on hunting in England was produced by William Trici, the huntsman of Edward II, and another famous book by Edward, second Duke of York, writing between 1406–13, drew heavily upon a French treatise on hunting by Count Gaston de Foix.[73] When the king went hunting, the forester was expected to be of general assistance to the master of game and his hunters and especially to guide them with his special knowledge of his bailiwick and the habits of the deer within it.[74] These treatises on the art of hunting, along with descriptions of hunting in the imaginative literature of the fourteenth century, provide continuing evidence of the popularity of the sport.

Hunting within the royal forests continued to be restricted to the king and those to whom he gave license, but enforcement of this principle proved to be another matter. In July 1339 the king ordered all sheriffs to proclaim that no one shall hunt in the king's forests, parks, or chaces without special licenses because he has learned that many beasts have been destroyed in violation of this law after his departure from England. At the same time, Edward, duke of Cornwall, the king's young son who had been appointed regent during his father's absence on the continent, was specifically exempt from the terms of this proclamation as were those he should name, as long as they caused no destruction among the deer.[75] The question of a royal hunting monopoly bothered the theologians in a more personal sense because the forest law allowed for no clerical immunity, and one English theologian, Thomas of Chobham, developed a theological argument against the monopoly:

Kings and princes compel forest inhabitants to swear an oath respecting the peace of all wild animals which they enforce with severe penalties. If a subject takes a beast in secret, Thomas queried, does he sin mortally, or

must he return it to the prince? To this problem the masters had two solu-
tions. If the subject's oath to the prince was without duress, he should both
do penance for perjury and restore the animal. If, however, the subject made
the oath under threat of imprisonment or loss of possessions, he need only
do penance for perjury. Restitution is unnecessary because the prince is not
lord of the beasts but has usurped this authority. By this distinction Thomas
of Chobham offered to forest inhabitants justification for circumventing the
royal monopoly over wild animals.[76]

The other side of the king's interest in hunting, in which he exercised
the monopoly protected by the forest law, is shown in an order of
1375 for the sheriff to prepare for the king's coming to his forest of
Rutland for the hunting season by having men concentrate the deer so
that there could be no failure when the king went hunting.[77]

A statute of Richard II in 1390 brought a fundamental change in the
English laws about hunting which had been a monopoly for the king
within the royal forest; a monopoly for the wealthy landowners who
had obtained licenses from the king for their parks, chaces, and warrens; and free to everyone in all other places outside those areas. The
statute stated that artificers, laborers, servants, and grooms kept greyhounds and other dogs with which they go hunting on holy days when
good Christian people are in church. Therefore, it was ordained that
no artificer, laborer, or other layman with lands or tenements valued
at less than forty shillings a year nor any priest or clerk with a prefer-
ment not worth ten pounds a year should hunt deer, hares, conies or
any other "gentlemen's game" on penalty of one year in prison.[78] The
English game laws from that time marked a change from the medieval
pattern and formed an alliance of king and landed gentry to protect
their privileges from the lower classes.

The economic side of the royal forest in the later Middle Ages could
be illustrated by the variety of uses to which the forests were put, as
they had been in the thirteenth century, and by the money the forests
continued to bring as rents. These examples are spread throughout the
Forest Proceedings and the Close Rolls in particular, and they serve as
a reminder that even in decline the royal forest never completely lost
its value to the crown. Two types of income from the forests were reported in the Pipe Rolls in addition to the usual farms listed there:
rent of wastes and sales of underwood. The figures from the first are
for a few pounds only and from a handful of forests in the South with
the exception of Windsor Forest which had a total of £41 2s. 11d. from
rent of wastes in 1299. In subsequent years, the rent from Windsor was
usually from one to three pounds, but that was the only forest where
rent of wastes was reported annually over a period of several years, in

this case from 1299 to 1306. Rent of wastes in twelve forests during the years 1299 to the end of Edward I's reign in 1307 provides a dramatic illustration of his efforts to exploit this source of revenue in spite of the low sums forthcoming, an effort which is emphasized by the extremely fragmentary reports of income scattered in the early years of his son's reign.[79] On the other hand, the income from sales of underwood reported in the accounts of those men commissioned to this work by the king returned substantial sums in the later fourteenth and early fifteenth centuries. The amounts from this source were variable with the largest amount of £236 16s. 3d. reported for Buckholt Forest in 1368 in the aftermath of a destructive storm that had prostrated many of the trees so that they were sold as wood in the cleaning-up operation. Sales of underwood were reported more frequently for Clarendon than for any other forest beginning in 1357 and extending through 1431. The amounts in 1357 and 1359 were more than forty pounds, but the returns from 1422 to 1431 were from ten to twenty pounds.[80]

These two types of income, highly developed during the thirteenth century and continuing into the fifteenth, are indicative of a changed attitude toward the royal forests. When Richard fitz Nigel discussed "waste" in the later twelfth century, he was talking about a violation of the forest law that essentially destroyed the forest in one area. Although the outlines of forest law as expressed in the assizes of the twelfth century and the chapters of the regard remained, the royal forest in practice proved to be a flexible institution. With the development of its economic potential during the thirteenth century, the administrative direction of the royal forest was toward a managed resource from which the maximum revenue could be attained with some attention to the limits upon use that could destroy the forest in the process. One of the indirect effects of the royal forest was that a qualified type of conservation was practiced within its bounds during the period of maximum pressure for the expansion of arable land. The forest law, usually thought to have been especially repressive and an evil contribution of the Normans, operated to some extent as a deterrent to the widespread deforestation accompanied by a spread of agriculture into areas unsuited for agriculture and unable to sustain grain production over many years. Forest regulations provided for fencing an area where the woods had been cut in order to protect the new growth from destruction by animals. By a statute of Edward IV in 1482, the time limit during which an owner could maintain a fence to protect his woods with new growth was extended from three to seven years. This step was a logical development from earlier policy, rather than representing a new departure as John Evelyn thought in the seventeenth century, but it does illustrate an interest in conserving woods within a royal forest as a source of timber as well as cover for the king's deer.[81]

The royal forests came to be identified with the arbitrary authority of the king, and this identification led the barons to use the forest as an issue in their struggles to control royal power. Throughout the Middle Ages the royal forest was an issue of the upper landholding classes and not to be identified as an issue of the lower classes. Both in the execution of the forest law dealing with venison where the amercements were higher in relation to the defendant's ability to pay and where the impoverished were excused their payments, and dealing with vert where the law restricted the use to which the landowner might wish to put any land he held within the areas of a royal forest, the heaviest burden of the royal forest fell upon the upper class. Viewed in this light, the victory ultimately went to the barons, not through the dramatic crises of 1215, that of Edward I after 1294, or the Ordinances of 1311. That victory came with the recognition and confirmation of the areas under forest as perambulated under Edward I and a changed attitude in administering the forest law more leniently under Edward III and Richard II. The statute of 1390 giving protection to the wealthier landowners and excluding the lower classes from the right to hunt game throughout England emphasized the alliance that had developed between the aristocracy and the king. The recognition of this alliance paralleled what had happened in the broader sense as expressed by G. L. Harriss "From the middle of the fourteenth century we begin to discern a political society, composed of King and nobility (in its widest sense), whose community of interests and common assumptions were to ensure the stability of English political life until the seventeenth century."[82]

The royal forest which had so long been an issue between the king and the landowners was not an obstacle to the alliance that developed in the fourteeneth century mainly because it had so declined in importance as to no longer be of great value to the crown. The decline of the royal forest in an absolute sense was less significant than the relative increase in taxation which eclipsed the forest in the economic aspect that had been emphasized in the thirteenth century and led to the neglect of the royal forest in the later fourteenth century. These late medieval trends led directly to the lament of John Manwood, who wrote in 1598 in a time when "the Forrest Lawes are growen clean out of knowledge in most places in this Land, partly, for want of use." His view of the purpose of the royal forests had come full circle from the time of William the Conqueror, who "loved the stags as much as if he were their father" and had lost all understanding of the height of the medieval royal forest in the thirteenth century when the emphasis was primarily upon the economic benefit of the forest to the crown:

I do not speak this to that end, that I would haue Forrest Lawes rigorously executed upon offenders in Forrestes, but to haue them so executed, that Forrests may be still knowen for Forrestes, and the game preserved for her Maiestie; for otherwise, it were better to disafforest them altogether, and then her Maiestie shal be discharged of the great fees that are yeerely payed to Officers of the Forrest, out of her Maiesties Court of Exchequer.[83]

Long before Manwood's epitaph, the royal forests of medieval England had undergone a fundamental change in the fourteenth century that marked the end of what they had been at their height and a return toward the hunting preserve that they had been under the Normans.

Notes

Introduction

1. H. C. Darby, *Domesday England* (Cambridge, 1977), p. 171; H. C. Darby, ed., *A New Historical Geography of England* (Cambridge, 1973), pp. 29–35; Maurice Keen, *The Outlaws of Medieval Legend* (Toronto, 1961), pp. 1–2.

2. Charles Higounet, "Les Forêts de l'Europe occidentale du Vᵉ an XIᵉ siècle," *Agricoltura e Mondo Rurale in Occidente nell L'Alto Medioevo*, Settimane di Studio del Centro Italiano di Studi sull' Alto Medioevo, 13 (Spoleto, 1966), pp. 376–77.

3. *The Anglo-Saxon Chronicle*, ed. Dorothy Whitelock (New Brunswick, N.J., 1961), p. 165.

4. Richard fitz Nigel, *Dialogus de Scaccario*, ed. and trans. Charles Johnson (London, 1950), p. 60.

5. G. J. Turner, ed., *Select Pleas of the Forest*, Selden Society, vol. 13 (London, 1901), p. ix.

6. Ibid., x–xiv.

7. F. M. Stenton, *Anglo-Saxon England* (2d ed.; Oxford, 1962), pp. 674–75; David C. Douglas, *William the Conqueror* (Berkeley and Los Angeles, 1967), p. 372.

8. David C. Douglas and George W. Greenaway, eds., *English Historical Documents 1042–1189* (London, 1953), p. 430.

9. H. C. Darby and Eila M. J. Campbell, *The Domesday Geography of South-East England* (Cambridge, 1962), p. 265.

10. Charles Petit-Dutaillis, "Les origines franco-normandes de la 'forêt' anglaise," in *Mélanges d'histoire offerts à M. Charles Bémont* (Paris, 1913),

pp. 59–76; Charles Petit-Dutaillis and Georges Lefebre, *Studies and Notes Supplementary to Stubbs' Constitutional History* (Manchester, 1930), p. 166.

11. H. W. C. Davis et al., eds., *Regesta Regum Anglo-Normannorum 1066–1154* (Oxford, 1913–69), 1: xxxi; Léopold Delisle, *Études sur la condition de la classe agricole et l'état de l'agriculture en Normandie au moyen âge* (Evreux, 1851), pp. 336–90.

12. Margaret Bazeley, "The Extent of the English Forest in the Thirteenth Century," *Transactions of the Royal Historical Society*, 4th series, 4 (1921): 146.

13. Robert S. Hoyt, *The Royal Demesne in English Constitutional History: 1066–1272* (Ithaca, N.Y., 1950), pp. 2–3. Although B. P. Wolfe more recently has taken issue with Hoyt's terminology in his *The Royal Demesne in English History* (Athens, Ohio, 1971), he would not include royal forests as part of the demesne.

14. *Close Rolls 1231–34*, p. 506; *Close Rolls 1234–37*, pp. 521–22; *Calendar of the Patent Rolls 1232–47*, pp. 186–87, 216.

Chapter 1

1. F. H. M. Parker, "The Forest Laws and the Death of William Rufus," *The English Historical Review* 27 (1912): 26–38; F. H. Baring, "The Making of the New Forest," *The English Historical Review* 27 (1912): 513–15; C. Warren Hollister, "The Strange Death of William Rufus," *Speculum* 48 (1973): 637–53.

2. Darby and Campbell, *The Domesday Geography of South-East England*, p. 324.

3. H. C. Darby, *The Domesday Geography of Eastern England* (Cambridge, 1952), pp. 56, 124, 126, 182, 234–35, 300, 335. See also Reginald Lennard, "The Destruction of Woodland in the Eastern Counties under William the Conqueror," *The Economic History Review* 15 (1946): 36–43.

4. Ibid., pp. 234, 338.

5. Darby and Campbell, *The Domesday Geography of South-East England*, p. 167.

6. Ibid., p. 214.

7. Ibid., pp. 264–65, 389, 446; H. C. Darby and I. B. Terrett, *The Domesday Geography of Midland England* (Cambridge, 1954), pp. 31, 89; H. C. Darby and I. S. Maxwell, *The Domesday Geography of Northern England* (Cambridge, 1962), pp. 259, 409.

8. Darby and Campbell, *The Domesday Geography of South-East England*, p. 166.

9. Davis et al., *Regesta*, 1: xxxi; 2: xx. The general administrative practice of the Norman kings in maintaining royal rights as described by B. P. Wolffe was to use the "normal national apparatus of central control, working through the shires and hundreds. The king's own lands like the royal fiefs were subjected at the same time, and by the same methods and machinery,

to one system of undifferentiated government." See his *The Royal Demesne in English History* (Athens, Ohio, 1971), pp. 34–35.

10. Davis *et al.*, *Regesta*, 1: #332.

11. Ibid., 1: #51, #457.

12. Petit-Dutaillis and Lefebre, *Studies and Notes*, pp. 152–56; Turner, *Select Pleas*, pp. cxxiii–cxxxiv.

13. Eadmer, *Historia Novorum in Anglia*, trans. by Geoffrey Bosanquet (Philadelphia, 1965), p. 106.

14. Douglas and Greenaway, *English Historical Documents*, pp. 400–02.

15. Davis *et al.*, *Regesta*, 2: xxi.

16. William of Newburgh, "Historia Rerum Anglicarum," in R. Howlett, ed., *Chronicles of the Reigns of Stephen, Henry II., and Richard I.*, Rolls Series (London, 1884–89), 1: 30.

17. Douglas and Greenaway, *English Historical Documents*, p. 403.

18. Davis *et al.*, *Regesta*, 3: #382.

19. H. A. Cronne, *The Reign of Stephen, 1135–54* (London, 1970), p. 233.

20. H. A. Cronne, "The Royal Forest in the Reign of Henry I," in H. A. Cronne *et al.*, *Essays in British and Irish History in Honour of James Eadie Todd* (London, 1949), p. 2.

21. *Leges Henrici Primi*, ed. L. J. Downer (Oxford, 1972), p. 120.

22. Cronne, "The Royal Forest," p. 2.

23. *Pipe Roll 31 Henry I*, p. 77.

24. Cronne, "The Royal Forest," p. 22; Doris M. Stenton, *English Justice between the Norman Conquest and the Great Charter 1066–1215* (Philadelphia, 1964), pp. 62–63.

25. *Pipe Roll 31 Henry I*, pp. 13, 21, 57, 74, 106.

26. Ibid., pp. 16, 38, 87.

27. Ibid., pp. 106–7.

28. Davis *et al.*, *Regesta*, 2: #1518; 3: #41.

29. Cronne, "The Royal Forest," p. 19.

30. *Leges Henrici Primi*, p. 145.

31. Cronne, "The Royal Forest," p. 10.

32. *Pipe Roll 31 Henry I*, p. 17.

33. Ibid., pp. 2, 3, 17, 26, 48, 77, 82, 101, 106, 127.

34. Ibid., p. 39. Raoul Croc farmed these vaccaries, and on p. 72 Walter Croc is listed as keeping two vaccaries in Staffordshire.

35. Davis *et al.*, *Regesta*, 1: #319, #347; 2: xx, #616.

36. Nellie Neilson, "The Forests," in James F. Willard and William A. Morris, *The English Government at Work, 1327–1336* (Cambridge, Mass., 1940–), 1: 458.

37. Davis *et al.*, *Regesta*, 2: #594, #696, #935, #1047, #1162; Cronne, "The Royal Forest," p. 14.

38. Davis *et al.*, *Regesta*, 2: #708.

39. Ibid., #1818.

40. *Pipe Roll 31 Henry I*, p. 58.

41. Davis *et al., Regesta,* 2: #853.
42. Ibid., 3: #274.
43. Ibid., 3: #459.
44. Ibid., 3: #565.
45. Ibid., 2: #774, #1753; 3: #422, #647, #839, #851, #977, #972.
46. Ibid., 3: #574.
47. Ibid., 2: #577.

Chapter 2

1. W. L. Warren, *Henry II* (Berkeley and Los Angeles, 1973), pp. 332–33. A recent article pertinent to the interpretation of Stephen's reign is Thomas Callahan, Jr., "The Notion of Anarchy in England 1135–1154: A Bibliographical Survey," *The British Studies Monitor* 6 (1976): 23–35.
2. Warren, *Henry II,* p. 263.
3. Margaret Bazeley, "The Extent of the English Forest in the Thirteenth Century," *Transactions of the Royal Historical Society* 4th series, 4 (1921): 146; James C. Holt, *Magna Carta* (Cambridge, 1965), p. 35.
4. Richard fitz Nigel, *Dialogus de Scaccario,* ed. and trans. Charles Johnson (London, 1950), pp. 58–59; *Pipe Rolls 12–16, 18, 20–21 Henry II;* Warren, *Henry II,* p. 390.
5. Public Record Office, Chancery Miscellanea, 11/1 #10, 14–16, 20–21.
6. Ibid., 11/1, #5, 6, 9–10, 14–17, 19–22; Exchequer, Treasury of Receipt, Forest Proceedings, 339.
7. Chancery Miscellanea, 11/1 #9, 15.
8. Ibid., 11/1, #22.
9. *Pipe Roll 2 Richard I,* pp. 67, 145; *6 John,* pp. 32, 40, 85, 189; *9 John,* p. 66; Holt, *Magna Carta,* pp. 52–53 comments: "All this was additional to a large number of individual licenses to assart which the king or Hugh de Neville granted at this time. Here, if anywhere, the Crown was squandering its resources."
10. *Pipe Roll 2 John,* pp. 18, 237; *5 John,* p. 6; *11 John,* p. 64; *14 John,* p. 32; G. J. Turner, ed., *Select Pleas of the Forest,* Selden Society, vol. 13 (London, 1901), pp. 9–10; *The Cartae Antiquae Rolls 1–10,* ed. Lionel Landon, Pipe Roll Society, vol. 71 (London, 1960), p. 136; Walter of Coventry, *Memoriale,* ed. William Stubbs, Rolls Series, vol. 58 (London, 1872–73), 2: 126.
11. *Rotuli Chartarum,* ed. Thomas D. Hardy, Record Commission (London, 1837), 1: pt. 1, 40b, 42b, 43a–b, 122a–b, 123a, 126a, 128a, 132a–b, 153b, 155a, 176b, 194b, 206a–b; *Rotuli Litterarum Clausarum,* ed. Thomas D. Hardy, Record Commission (London, 1833–44), 1: 10b, 11a, 15b, 33a, 197a.
12. *Rotuli Chartarum,* 1: pt. 1, 1–2.
13. Public Record Office, Exchequer, King's Remembrancer, Forest Proceedings, 2/22.
14. *Pipe Roll 11 John,* p. 138.

15. Ibid., pp. xxvi, 92; *Rotuli Litterarum Patentium,* ed. Thomas D. Hardy, Record Commission (London, 1835), 1: pt. 1, 40a.

16. Turner, ed., *Select Pleas,* p. 6.

17. Richard fitz Nigel, *Dialogus de Scaccario,* p. 60.

18. Ibid., pp. 59–60.

19. Warren, *Henry II,* pp. 306–7.

20. Benedict of Peterborough (*sc.* Roger of Howden), *The Chronicle of the Reigns of Henry II. and Richard I.,* ed. William Stubbs, Rolls Series (London, 1867), 2: 74, and repeated in Roger of Howden, *Chronica,* ed. William Stubbs, Rolls Series (London, 1868–71), 3: 4.

21. Walter Map, *De Nugis Curialium,* trans. Montague R. James, Cymmrodorion Record Series, vol. 9 (London, 1923), p. 261; Peter of Blois, *Opera Omnia* in J. P. Migne, ed., *Patrologiae,* Series Latina (Paris, 1904), vol. 207, col. 198, Ep. LXVI.

22. *Pipe Roll 13 Henry II.*

23. David C. Douglas and George W. Greenaway, eds., *English Historical Documents 1042–1189* (London, 1953), p. 440.

24. Benedict of Peterborough (*sc.* Roger of Howden), *Chronicle,* 1: 92, 94, 99; Ralph de Diceto, "Ymagines Historiarum" in *Historical Works,* ed. William Stubbs, Rolls Series (London, 1876), 1: 402.

25. Diceto, "Ymagines Historiarum," pp. 402, 410; Benedict of Peterborough (*sc.* Roger of Howden), *Chronicle,* 1: 105.

26. William of Newburgh, "Historia Rerum Anglicarum" in *Chronicles of the Reigns of Stephen, Henry II., and Richard I.,* ed. R. Howlett, Rolls Series (London, 1884–89), 1: 280.

27. Holt, *Magna Carta,* p. 38.

28. W. L. Warren, *King John* (New York, 1961), p. 152.

29. Roger of Wendover, *Chronica,* ed. Henry O. Coxe (London, 1841), 3: 227; Sidney Painter, *The Reign of King John* (Baltimore, 1949), p. 207.

30. Roger of Howden, *Chronica,* 4: 144–45.

31. Walter of Coventry, *Memoriale,* p. 207.

32. Benedict of Peterborough (*sc.* Roger of Howden), *Chronicle,* 1: 323.

33. Roger of Howden, *Chronica,* 2: 289–90.

34. James C. Holt, "The Assizes of Henry II: The Texts" in D. A. Bullough and R. L. Storey, eds., *The Study of Medieval Records. Essays in Honour of Kathleen Major* (Oxford, 1971), pp. 97–98.

35. H. G. Richardson and G. O. Sayles, *The Governance of Mediaeval England* (Edinburgh, 1963), pp. 444–46.

36. Holt, "Assizes," p. 101.

37. Warren, *Henry II,* pp. 602–3.

38. A convenient translation is in Douglas and Greenaway, *Documents,* pp. 418–20.

39. Holt, "Assizes," pp. 99–100.

40. Roger of Howden, *Chronica,* 2: 243–44.

41. Ibid., 4: 62–66.

42. Richard fitz Nigel, *Dialogus de Scaccario,* pp. 57–58.

43. Elizabeth Cox Wright, "Common Law in Thirteenth Century English Royal Forests" in *Dissertation Collection, University of Pennsylvania* (Philadelphia, 1928), 31: no. 2, 191 or the article with the same title in *Speculum* 3 (1928): 168–91. For the older view see Charles Petit-Dutaillis and George S. Lefebre, *Studies and Notes Supplementary to Stubbs' Constitutional History* (Manchester, 1930), p. 165. S. B. Chrimes accepted the revision in his introduction to Sir William Holdsworth, *A History of English Law* (7th ed.; London, 1956), 1: 20. For the areas under forest law, see Margaret Bazeley, "The Extent of the English Forest in the Thirteenth Century," pp. 140–72.

44. *Pipe Roll 6 Henry II*, pp. 20, 42; *13 Henry II*, pp. 102, 138; *16 Henry II*, pp. 102, 107; *17 Henry II*, p. 50; *25 Henry II*, pp. 86, 89; *1 Richard I*, p. 77; *8 Richard I*, p. 31, for forest pleas included with other pleas.

45. *Pipe Roll 13 Henry II*, p. 182; *24 Henry II*, p. 52; *8 Richard I*, pp. 152, 266; *10 Richard I*, p. 105.

46. Douglas and Greenaway, *Documents*, p. 419.

47. *Curia Regis Rolls of the Reigns of Richard I. and John* (London, 1922–72), 3: 145; 4: 274; 6: 85–86.

48. Doris M. Stenton, ed., *Pleas before the King or His Justices 1198–1202*, Selden Society, vols. 67–68, 83 (London, 1952–67), 3: "Introduction," *passim*.

49. The names of forest justices are all based on the Pipe Rolls. These names were also checked against lists given in James H. Ramsay, *A History of the Revenues of the Kings of England 1066–1399* (Oxford, 1925).

Chapter 3

1. *Pipe Roll 6 Henry II*, p. 20.

2. *Pipe Roll 8 Henry II*, pp. 16, 29, 32, 52, 57, 59, 61.

3. Doris M. Stenton, *English Justice between the Norman Conquest and the Great Charter 1066–1215* (Philadelphia, 1964), p. 73.

4. Benedict of Peterborough (*sc.* Roger of Howden), *The Chronicle of the Reigns of Henry II. and Richard I.*, ed. William Stubbs, Rolls Series (London, 1867), 1: 323. See J. C. Holt, "The Assizes of Henry II: The Texts" in D. A. Bullough and R. L. Storey, eds., *The Study of Medieval Records. Essays in Honour of Kathleen Major* (Oxford, 1971), p. 91.

5. *Pipe Roll 12 Henry II*, pp. 61, 107; *13 Henry II*, pp. 50, 140, 174, 182, 204.

6. *Pipe Roll 15 Henry II*, p. 23.

7. *Pipe Roll 13 Henry II*, p. 205.

8. *Pipe Roll 12 Henry II*, pp. 54, 82.

9. *Dialogus de Scaccario*, ed. and trans. Charles Johnson (London, 1950), p. 61.

10. *Pipe Roll 15 Henry II*, pp. 39, 82.

11. *Pipe Roll 14 Henry II*, p. 44.

12. *Pipe Roll 13 Henry II*, pp. 93, 174, 182.

13. *Pipe Roll 14 Henry II*, p. 138.

14. *Pipe Roll 13 Henry II*, pp. 56, 174; *14 Henry II*, pp. 119, 173, 176; *16 Henry II*, p. 48.

15. *Pipe Roll 14 Henry II*, p. 44. Later the smaller offenses were grouped in the Pipe Roll entry, but the sheriff or the treasury was provided with a list of names and particulars by the justices. See *Pipe Roll 1 Richard I*, p. 140 and *3 Richard I*, pp. 27, 96.

16. *Pipe Roll 15 Henry II*, p. 54.

17. Ibid., p. 82.

18. *Pipe Roll 14 Henry II*, pp. 137–38.

19. *Pipe Roll 15 Henry II*, p. 23.

20. *Pipe Roll 12 Henry II*, pp. 61, 101.

21. *Pipe Roll 16 Henry II*, p. 49.

22. *Pipe Roll 12 Henry II*, p. 36; *14 Henry II*, p. 215.

23. *Pipe Roll 17 Henry II*, p. 40.

24. *Pipe Roll 13 Henry II*, p. 138; *18 Henry II*, p. 10.

25. W. L. Warren, *Henry II* (Berkeley and Los Angeles, 1973), p. 355.

26. *Pipe Roll 18 Henry II*, p. 43.

27. *Pipe Roll 14 Henry II*, p. 158.

28. Benedict of Peterborough (*sc.* Roger of Howden), *Chronicle*, 1: 92.

29. James H. Ramsay, *A History of the Revenues of the Kings of England 1066–1399* (Oxford, 1925), 1: 124; *Pipe Roll 22 Henry II*, pp. 51–53.

30. Doris M. Stenton, ed., *Pipe Roll 23 Henry II*, p. xxi.

31. Ramsay, *History of the Revenues*, 1: 191; B. P. Wolffe, *The Royal Demesne in English History* (Athens, Ohio, 1971), p. 31.

32. *Pipe Roll 23 Henry II*, p. 94.

33. *Pipe Roll 27 Henry II*, p. 30.

34. *Pipe Roll 29 Henry II*, p. 47.

35. *Pipe Roll 1 Richard I*, p. 173.

36. *Pipe Roll 1 John*, p. 33. Although Alan de Neville the younger was a forest justice, he never was on an eyre in Essex, and this reference must be to his father.

37. *Pipe Roll 26 Henry II*, p. 7; *The Memoranda Roll . . . of the First Year . . . of King John (1199–1200)*, Pipe Roll Society, n.s. vol. 21 (London, 1943), p. 83.

38. *Pipe Roll 31 Henry II*, p. 168.

39. Ibid., pp. 171, 211.

40. Ibid., p. 193.

41. Ibid., pp. 51, 103, 121, 194.

42. Ibid., p. 114.

43. Ibid., pp. 18–19, 152.

44. Ibid., pp. 20, 54, 207.

45. Ibid., pp. 167, 171.

46. Ibid., p. 147.

47. Ibid., pp. 18, 19.

48. Ibid., p. 186.

49. *Pipe Roll 1 John*, p. 217.

50. *Pipe Roll 1 Richard I*, p. 165; *3 Richard I*, p. 94; *8 Richard I*, p. 266; *10 Richard I*, p. 175; *1 John*, p. 51; *14 John*, p. 82.

51. *Pipe Roll 1 Richard I*, p. 23; *3 Richard I*, p. 82.

52. *Pipe Roll 5 Richard I*, p. 135.

53. *Pipe Roll 4 Richard I*, p. 177; *11 John*, p. 123.

54. *Pipe Roll 4 Richard I*, p. 199.

55. *Pipe Roll 1 John*, pp. 83, 226.

56. G. J. Turner, ed., *Select Pleas of the Forest*, Selden Society, vol. 13 (London, 1901), pp. 2, 5.

57. Ibid., p. 1.

58. Ibid., p. 4.

59. *Pipe Roll 2 Richard I*, p. 13.

60. *Pipe Roll 1 John*, p. 237.

61. *Pipe Roll 2 John*, pp. 18, 188.

62. *Pipe Roll 6 John*, p. 172.

63. *Pipe Roll 3 John*, p. 96.

64. *Pipe Roll 2 John*, p. 254.

65. Benedict of Peterborough (*sc.* Roger of Howden), *Chronicle*, 1: 224. For a summary of canons against hunting by the clergy, see Rudolph Willard, "Chaucer's 'Text that seith that hunters ben nat hooly men.' " in University of Texas, *Studies in English*, 1947, pp. 209–251.

66. *The Cartae Antiquae Rolls 11–20*, ed. J. Conway Davies, Pipe Roll Society, vol. 71 (London, 1960), p. 133.

67. For examples of the type, see *The Cartae Antiquae Rolls 1–10*, ed. Lionel Landon, Pipe Roll Society, vol. 55 (London, 1939), p. 62; *Rotuli Chartarum*, ed. Thomas D. Hardy, Record Commission (London, 1837), 1: pt. 1, 6a, 12a, 42b, 43a, 101a; *Rotuli Litterarum Clausarum*, ed. Thomas D. Hardy, Record Commission (London, 1833–44), 1: 25b, 189b. The practical effect of these charters can be seen when fines were mistakenly assessed to these monasteries and they were able to obtain quittance by proving their exemption by charter: *Pipe Roll 14 John*, pp. 98, 127. R. A. Donkin has emphasized that for many years after its foundation a monastic community had a great need for timber and has illustrated this with figures from the thirteenth century in "The Cistercian Settlement and the English Royal Forests I," *Citeaux: Commentarii Cistercienses* 11 (1960): 39–55.

68. *Cartae Antiquae Rolls 11–20*, p. 102.

69. *Pipe Roll 3 Richard I*, p. 115; *Cartae Antiquae Rolls 1–10*, p. 49.

70. *Cartae Antiquae Rolls 1–10*, p. 45.

71. Ibid., p. 146.

72. Ibid., p. 5; *11–20*, p. 133.

73. *Dialogus de Scaccario*, pp. 103–4.

74. Turner, *Select Pleas of the Forest*, pp. cxv–cxxii gives a general discussion of parks in the thirteenth century.

75. *Rotuli Litterarum Patentium*, ed. Thomas D. Hardy, Record Commission (London, 1835), 1: pt. 1, 178b; *Pipe Roll 26 Henry II*, p. 137.

76. *Pipe Roll 6 John*, pp. 33–34; *10 Richard I*, p. 107.

77. *Pipe Roll 9 John*, p. 178.

78. Ibid., p. 109.

79. See Turner, *Select Pleas,* pp. cix–cxv.

80. *Cartae Antiquae Rolls 1–10,* p. 134.

81. Margaret L. Bazeley, "The Extent of the English Forest in the Thirtenth Century," *Transactions of the Royal Historical Society,* 4th series, vol. 4 (London, 1921), pp. 140–41. When King John in 1199 granted Henry de Gray the right for him and his heirs to hunt hares and wolves throughout England except in the king's demesne hayes, the charter referred to these hunting privileges as a grant of a *"chacia,"* a quite different use of the term. *Rotuli Chartarum,* 1: 6.

82. *Rotuli Chartarum,* 1: 66b; Turner, *Select Pleas,* pp. cxxiii–cxxxiv; Charles Petit-Dutaillis and Georges Lefebre, *Studies and Notes Supplementary to Stubbs' Constitutional History* (Manchester, 1930), pp. 152–56.

83. Turner, *Select Pleas,* p. 10.

84. Cyril E. Hart, *The Commoners of Dean Forest* (Gloucester, 1951), pp. 3, 7.

85. *Pipe Roll 2 John,* pp. 18–19.

86. *Dialogus de Scaccario,* p. 57.

87. Ibid., pp. 58–59.

88. *Cartae Antiquae Rolls 1–10,* p. 139; *11–20,* pp. 125, 179, 189.

89. Public Record Office, Chancery Miscellanea, 12/4 contains copies of twelve charters of Henry II granting quittances of payment for assarts and includes two thousand acres assarted by the Templars in Wales. *Pipe Roll 9 John,* pp. 109–10; *12 John,* p. 36.

90. Public Record Office, Exchequer, Treasury of Receipt, Forest Proceedings, 144, 235.

91. *Dialogus de Scaccario,* pp. 58–59.

92. Cited in Warren, *Henry II,* p. 390.

93. *De Nugis Curialium,* trans. Montague R. James, Cymmrodorion Record Series, vol. 9 (London, 1923), pp. 5–6.

94. Benedict of Peterborough (*sc.* Roger of Howden) *Chronicle,* 1: 93–94.

95. Chapter 11 of the Assize in William Stubbs, *Select Charters* (8th ed.; Oxford, 1905), p. 159; Benedict of Peterborough, (*sc.* Roger of Howden), *Chronicle,* 1: 323.

96. Sidney Painter, *The Reign of King John* (Baltimore, 1949), p. 60.

97. A convenient translation of the Assize of Woodstock may be found in David C. Douglas and George W. Greenaway, eds., *English Historical Documents 1042–1189* (London, 1953), pp. 418–20.

98. *Pipe Roll 1 Richard I,* p. 9.

99. *Pipe Roll 7 Richard I,* p. 16.

100. Painter, *Reign of King John,* p. 67.

101. Matthew Paris, *Chronica Majora,* ed. H. R. Luard, Rolls Series (London, 1872–83), 3: 71; *Rotuli Chartarum,* 1: 111b–112a.

102. *Rotuli Litterarum Clausarum,* 1: 3a, 6b, 15b, 35b, 37a, 38b, 65b, 71a–b.

103. *Rotuli Litterarum Patentium*, 1: pt. 1, 27a–b; *Pipe Roll 5 John*, p. 160; *Rotuli de Liberate ac de Misis et Praestitis*, ed. T. D. Hardy, Record Commission (London, 1844), p. 23.

104. *Rotuli Litterarum Patentium*, 1: pt. 1, 31b; *Pipe Roll 4 John*, pp. 19, 57; *12 John*, p. 203.

105. *Pipe Roll 5 John*, pp. 160–61; *10 John*, pp. 202–5.

106. *Pipe Roll 14 John*, p. 157.

107. *Pipe Roll 16 John*, p. xx; James C. Holt, *Magna Carta*, pp. 125–26.

108. Painter, *Reign of King John*, p. 70; W. L. Warren, *King John* (New York, 1961), p. 252.

109. *Rotuli Litterarum Patentium*, 1: pt. 1, 185a.

110. Ibid., p. 73a.

111. Ibid., pp. 153a, 188b, 193a.

112. Ibid., pp. 88b, 150a.

113. *Pipe Roll 6 John*, pp. 143–44. The grant was subsequently enrolled in *Rotuli Chartarum*, 1: 132a.

114. *Pipe Roll 10 John*, p. 45.

115. *Pipe Roll 9 John*, p. 149.

116. *Pipe Roll 3 Richard I*, p. 88; *4 Richard I*, pp. 214, 297; *8 Richard I*, p. 14; *2 John*, p .48.

117. *Curia Regis Rolls of the Reigns of Richard I. and John*, Deputy Keeper of the Records (London, 1922–   ), 1: 469.

118. *Pipe Roll 2 John*, p. 6; *3 John*, p. 159; *Rotuli Chartarum*, 1: 86b, 101a.

119. *Pipe Roll 17 Henry II*, p. 83; *9 John*, p. 163; *16 John*, p. 121.

120. *Pipe Roll 1 John*, pp. xxiv, 238; *Rotuli Litterarium Patentium*, 1: pt. 1, 68b; *Rotuli Chartarum*, 1: 130a.

121. *Curia Regis Rolls*, 1: 213.

122. *Pipe Roll 12 John*, p. 67.

123. Margaret L. Bazeley, "The Forest of Dean in its Relations with the crown during the twelfth and thirteenth centuries," *Transactions of the Bristol and Gloucestershire Archaeological Society* 33 (1910): 169–76.

124. Ibid., pp. 187–91, 218.

125. Ramsay, *History of the Revenues*, 1: 191, 261.

126. Richard fitz Nigel, *Dialogus de Scaccario*, pp. 30–31.

127. *Pipe Roll 31 Henry II*, pp. 206–7.

128. *Memoranda Roll 1 John*, pp. 7–8.

129. The Sturmy (or Esturmy) family had an association with Savernake Forest over the centuries from a mention in Domesday Book to the end of the seventeenth century, and members of the family were foresters there from the early twelfth through the fourteenth century. See [Charles S. C. Bruce], earl of Cardigan, *The Wardens of Savernake Forest* (London, 1949).

130. *Curia Regis Rolls of the Reigns of Richard I. and John* (London, 1922–72), 4: 147.

131. *Pipe Roll 14 Henry II*, p. 190; *3 John*, p. xiv. Letters close that carried orders for transportation of venison during John's reign can be seen in *Rotuli Litterarum Clausarum*, 1: 48b, 52b, 58a, 141a.

132. *Pipe Roll 16 Henry II*, p. 73; *24 Henry II*, p. xxi; *25 Henry II*, p. 14; *27 Henry II*, p. xxiii; *29 Henry II*, pp. 6, 141; *30 Henry II, pp.* 60, 144; *8 Richard I*, p. 81; *8 John*, pp. xvi, xviii.

133. "Expugnatio Hibernica" in *Opera*, ed. J. S. Brewer, Rolls Series (London, 1861–91), 5: 302. Translation by Thomas Wright, *The Historical Works of Giraldus Cambrensis* (London, 1863), p. 250.

134. *De Nugis Curialium*, p. 261.

135. See chapter 15 of the Assize of Clarendon in Douglas and Greenaway, *English Historical Documents 1042–1189*, p. 410.

136. Turner, *Select Pleas*, pp. 1–3, 5.

137. "Vitae S. Roberti Knareburgensis," *Analecta Bollandiana* 57 (1939): 368–69.

138. "The Legend of Fulk fitz-Warin," in Ralph of Coggeshall, *Chronicon Anglicanum*, ed. Joseph Stevenson, Rolls Series (London, 1875), pp. 331, 337, 386. Real charcoal burners did occasionally find their way into the records: *Pipe Roll 31 Henry II*, p. 148.

139. Matthew Paris, *Chronica Majora*, 3: 12.

Chapter 4

1. J. C. Holt, *The Northerners* (Oxford, 1961), p. 195.

2. Ibid., pp. 85–86, 157–58; *Pipe Roll 14 John*, pp. xxiv, xxvi; J. C. Holt, *Magna Carta* (Cambridge, 1965), pp. 125–26.

3. Walter of Coventry, *Memoriale*, ed. William Stubbs, Rolls Series (London, 1872–73), 2: 207, as translated by Holt, *Magna Carta*, p. 128.

4. There has been no agreement in dating the charter. Discussions of the problem with different conclusions may be found in William S. McKechnie, *Magna Carta* (2nd ed.; Glasgow, 1914), pp. 171–75; Holt, *Northerners*, pp. 114–16, 119; and Holt, *Magna Carta*, pp. 296–300.

5. The texts of these documents are conveniently gathered together in the appendices of McKechnie and of Holt, *Magna Carta*. I have followed the conventional numbering of clauses and chapters that editors added to the original documents.

6. My account owes a great deal to the discussions of the forest by Professor J. C. Holt in his *Northerners*, pp. 113–21 and *Magna Carta*, pp. 235–37.

7. Holt, *Magna Carta*, pp. 205–6.

8. Richard fitz Nigel, *Dialogus de Scaccario*, ed. and trans. Charles Johnson (London, 1950), p. 60.

9. *Rotuli Litterarum Patentium* (Record Commission: London, 1835), 1: pt. 1, 180b.

10. Holt, *Northerners*, p. 121 and *Magna Carta*, pp. 246–47.

11. Printed in McKechnie, *Magna Carta*, pp. 496–97 and Holt, *Magna Carta*, pp. 348–49.

12. Printed in Holt, *Magna Carta*, pp. 350 ff.

13. Ibid., p. 273, n. 1.

14. The rediscovery of the original charter is described in Richard Thom-

son, *An Historical Essay on the Magna Charta of King John* (London, 1829), p. 434: "On a re-arrangement of these manuscripts, about sixty years before the Commissioners' visit in 1806, the Forest Charta was not found in its proper drawer, and was considered lost; but on a diligent search then made, it was discovered in a box in a closet in the Chapter-Room, with several deeds concerning the possessions of the Chapter." The provisions of the charter are discussed in Charles Petit-Dutaillis and Georges Lefebvre, *Studies and Notes Supplementary to Stubbs' Constitutional History* (Manchester, 1930), pp. 187–98.

15. Holt, *Magna Carta*, p. 274.

16. Holt in ibid., p. 275 makes the interesting observation that "The Forest Charter and the particular issue of disafforestation helped to keep Magna Carta alive." See also Faith Thompson, *The First Century of Magna Carta* (Minneapolis, 1925), p. 89.

17. *Close Rolls 1227–31*, p. 100.

18. *Patent Rolls 1216–25*, pp. 162, 258. Perambulations from this time survive for forests in three counties in P.R.O., Chancery Miscellanea, 11/1/5, 6, 9, 10.

19. *Patent Rolls 1216–25*, pp. 174, 190, 193, 197. The case of Sherwood Forest has been studied by J. C. Holt in "Philip Mark and the Shrievalty of Nottinghamshire and Derbyshire in the Early Thirteenth Century," *Transactions of the Thoroton Society* 56 (1952): 8–24.

20. *Patent Rolls 1216–25*, p. 231.

21. Roger of Wendover in Matthew Paris, *Chronica Majora*, ed. H. R. Luard, Rolls Series (London, 1872–83), 3: 76.

22. *Patent Rolls 1216–25*, p. 491.

23. Roger of Wendover in Matthew Paris, *Chronica Majora*, 3: 91–92. See the final paragraph of the 1225 Magna Carta printed in Holt, *Magna Carta*, p. 357.

24. *Patent Rolls 1216–25*, pp. 512, 567–68; Roger of Wendover in Paris, *Chronica Majora*, 3: 94.

25. "Annales de Theokesberia" in Henry R. Luard, ed., *Annales Monastici*, Rolls Series (London, 1864–69), 1: 68.

26. *Patent Rolls 1225–32*, p. 69.

27. *Patent Rolls 1216–25*, pp. 288–89.

28. Roger of Wendover in Paris, *Chronica Majora*, 3: 122; Kate Norgate, *The Minority of Henry the Third* (London, 1912), p. 266.

29. *Patent Rolls 1225–32*, pp. 109–10, 184, 225. Perambulations at this time, including the confession of error by the jurors of York, are preserved in P.R.O., Chancery Miscellanea, 11/1/14, 15, 16, 19–22.

30. P.R.O., Exchequer, Treasury of Receipt, Forest Proceedings, 339, m.2–3; Chancery Files (Tower and Rolls Chapel), Recorda, 90/39.

31. *Close Rolls 1227–31*, p. 90.

32. Ibid., p. 59.

33. Ibid., p. 58.

34. Ibid., p. 220; *Pipe Roll 14 Henry III*, pp. 71, 312.

35. *Pipe Roll 14 Henry III*, p. 81; *Close Rolls 1231–34*, p. 86.

36. *Close Rolls 1227–31*, pp. 579–80.

37. Ibid., p. 101.

38. *Close Rolls 1234–37*, pp. 51, 82, 304–05; *Curia Regis Rolls* (London, 1922–72), 15: 323.

39. *Close Rolls 1227–31*, p. 101.

40. Matthew Paris, *Chronica Majora*, 3: 380–83; *Close Rolls 1234–37*, pp. 421, 426; *Close Rolls 1237–42*, p. 22; Thompson, *First Century of Magna Carta*, p. 94.

41. *Close Rolls 1234–37*, p. 541. Margaret Bazeley discussed the effect of the various perambulations of the forest and grants by Henry III and concluded there was a net loss in forest area during his reign in "The Extent of the English Forest in the Thirteenth Century," *Transactions of the Royal Historical Society*, 4th series, vol. 4 (1921): 149, 154.

42. *Close Rolls 1247–51*, p. 539; *Close Rolls 1251–53*, p. 88.

Chapter 5

1. G. J. Turner, ed., *Select Pleas of the Forest*, Selden Society, vol. 13 (London, 1901), pp. xiv–xv; "The Justices of the Forest South of Trent," *English Historical Review* 18 (1903): pp. 112–16; T. F. Tout, *The Place of the Reign of Edward II in English History* (2nd ed.; Manchester, 1936), pp. 318–20.

2. *Patent Rolls 1216–25*, p. 124; *Close Rolls 1237–42*, p. 437; *Close Rolls 1256–69*, p. 486.

3. *Close Rolls 1254–56*, pp. 373–74; *Close Rolls 1264–68*, p. 44. An example of an account for the forests north of Trent for 1257–61 is P.R.O., Pipe Roll/105, m.20d.

4. *Calendar of the Patent Rolls 1272–81*, p. 335.

5. *Calendar of the Patent Rolls 1247–58*, p. 162; *Close Rolls 1254–56*, p. 101.

6. *Calendar of the Patent Rolls 1266–72*, p. 96.

7. *Calendar of the Patent Rolls 1247–58*, p. 204.

8. Turner, *Select Pleas*, p. xv; P.R.O., Duchy of Lancaster, Forest Proceedings, 1/3.

9. *Calendar of the Close Rolls 1279–88*, p. 404.

10. *Close Rolls 1268–72*, p. 291.

11. *Close Rolls 1251–53*, p. 408.

12. *Close Rolls 1254–56*, pp. 160–61.

13. *Close Rolls 1231–34*, p. 506; *Close Rolls 1234–37*, pp. 521–22; *Calendar of the Patent Rolls 1232–47*, pp. 186–87, 216; "Annales de Burton" in Henry R. Luard, ed., *Annales Monastici*, Rolls Series (London, 1864–69), 1: 251–52.

14. Turner, *Select Pleas*, p. xv.

15. Maurice Powicke, *The Thirteenth Century* (2nd ed.; Oxford, 1962), pp. 51–52; Ralph V. Turner, *The King and His Courts* (Ithaca, N.Y., 1968), pp. 209–10.

16. Matthew Paris, *Chronica Majora*, ed. H. R. Luard, *Rolls Series* (Lon-

don, 1872–83), 4: 400, 426–27. The articles for this inquest are found in the "Additamenta," *Chronica Majora,* 6: 94–99.

17. P.R.O., Chancery Miscellanea, 11/3 (9).

18. Matthew Paris, *Chronica Majora,* 4: 401.

19. *Close Rolls 1242–47,* pp. 416, 475.

20. Robert Grosseteste, *Epistolae,* ed. H. R. Luard (Rolls Series: London, 1861), 353–55.

21. Turner, *Select Pleas,* pp. xvi–xix. See *Close Rolls 1231–34,* p. 472 for the appointment of John de Neville to succeed his deceased father Hugh de Neville in this position for annual payment of twenty pounds.

22. *Close Rolls 1247–51,* p. 43.

23. *Calendar of the Patent Rolls 1272–81,* p. 3.

24. *Calendar of the Patent Rolls 1232–47,* p. 81; *1258–66,* p. 279; *1272–81,* p .127.

25. *Patent Rolls 1216–25,* p. 47; *Calendar of the Patent Rolls 1266–72,* pp. 61, 342.

26. *Pipe Roll 14 Henry III,* pp. 35, 85.

27. *Calendar of the Patent Rolls 1247–58,* pp. 59, 627; *1258–66,* pp. 557–58.

28. *Calendar of the Patent Rolls 1247–58,* p. 450.

29. P.R.O., Exchequer, Treasury of Receipt, Forest Proceedings, 11, m. 5v.

30. *Curia Regis Rolls* (London, 1922–72), 15: 342.

31. P.R.O., Chancery Miscellanea, 11/5 (1).

32. P.R.O., Exchequer, Treasury of Receipt, Forest Proceedings, 13, m. 36.

33. P.R.O. Chancery Miscellanea, 11/4 (23).

34. P.R.O., Duchy of Lancaster, Forest Proceedings, 1/3, m. 12–12v.

35. P.R.O., Exchequer, King's Remembrancer, Forest Proceedings, 2/26.

36. Turner, *Select Pleas,* p. xxii.

37. Ibid., pp. xxiv–xxv; P.R.O., Exchequer, Treasury of Receipt, Forest Proceedings, 13, m. 11, m. 25; 30, m. 8v.; 41, m. 4; 70, m. 1; 76, m. 14; 78, m. 4; 126, m. 2; *Calendar of the Charter Rolls,* 1: 468; *Close Rolls 1254–56,* p. 296; *Close Rolls 1256–59,* p. 437.

38. *Calendar of the Patent Rolls 1258–66,* p. 228; P.R.O., Exchequer, Treasury of Receipt, Forest Proceedings, 156, m. 3; Turner, *Select Pleas,* p. 28.

39. P.R.O., Exchequer, Treasury of Receipt, Forest Proceedings, 153, m. 4.

40. P.R.O. Chancery Miscellanea, 11/2 (11).

41. P.R.O., Exchequer, Treasury of Receipt, Forest Proceedings, 161, m. 10.

42. Ibid., 127, m. 3v.

43. Turner, *Select Pleas,* pp. 44–53. See also *Close Rolls 1268–72,* p. 158 and *Close Rolls 1272–79,* p. 6, where there is an order in 1273 to release Peter from prison to enable him to prepare his defense with the usual pro-

vision that his friends will stand surety for his appearance before the king at the next pleas of the forest.

44. P.R.O., Exchequer, Treasury of Receipt, Forest Proceedings, 13, m. 14v.

45. Turner, *Select Pleas,* pp. 19, 24; P.R.O., Exchequer, Treasury of Receipt, Forest Proceedings, 35, m. 1v.; 161, m. 4; 184, m. 9–10.

46. Turner, *Select Pleas,* p. 21; P.R.O., Exchequer, Treasury of Receipt, Forest Proceedings, 169, m. 3; 13, m. 20; 221, m. 5; 76, m. 2v.; 29, m. 1v.

47. P.R.O., Chancery Miscellanea, 11/4 (10).

48. P.R.O., Exchequer, Treasury of Receipt, Forest Proceedings, 13, m. 17v. An example of a straightforward hunting violation is ibid., 188, m. 8.

49. Ibid., 161, m. 4.

50. Turner, *Select Pleas,* pp. 20, 128.

51. P.R.O., Exchequer, Treasury of Receipt, Forest Proceedings, 184, m. 9v.

52. Ibid., 216, m. 2.

53. Turner, *Select Pleas,* p. 49.

54. P.R.O., Exchequer, Treasury of Receipt, Forest Proceedings, 132, m. 8v.

55. Turner, *Select Pleas,* pp. 125–27.

56. P.R.O., Exchequer, Treasury of Receipt, Forest Proceedings, 76, m. 2v.; Chancery Miscellanea, 11/2 (22), m. 1–2.; 11/4 (18), m. 1–2.

57. *Close Rolls 1268–72,* pp. 492, 503.

58. Turner, *Select Pleas,* pp. xxiii–xxiv. Some foresters in fee were said to have held by serjeanty tenure, but very little is known about this. See Elisabeth Kimball, *Serjeanty Tenure in Medieval England* (New Haven, 1936), pp. 110–11.

59. P.R.O., Exchequer, Treasury of Receipt, Forest Proceedings, 229, m. 10v.

60. *Calendar of the Patent Rolls 1266–72,* p. 15.

61. *Close Rolls 1242–47,* p. 336.

62. *Curia Regis Rolls,* 15: 512; *Close Rolls 1237–42,* p. 11.

63. *Close Rolls 1227–31,* p. 35; P.R.O., Chancery Miscellanea, 11/5 (13), m. 1–2; P.R.O., Duchy of Lancaster, Forest Proceedings, 1/4, m. 1–2; *Close Rolls 1247–51,* p. 415; P.R.O. Exchequer, Treasury of Receipt, Forest Proceedings, 11, m. 4v.; *Calendar of the Charter Rolls,* 1: 68; 2: 203–4; Margaret Bazeley, "The Forest of Dean in Its Relations with the Crown during the Twelfth and Thirteenth Centuries," *Transactions of the Bristol and Gloucestershire Archaeological Society* 33 (1910): pp. 191–202.

64. P.R.O., Exchequer, King's Remembrancer, Forest Proceedings, 1/25, m. 3; Turner, *Select Pleas,* pp. 66–67, prints a list of perquisites of a forester in fee in Sherwood Forest.

65. *Close Rolls 1251–53,* p. 201; P.R.O., Exchequer, King's Remembrancer, Forest Proceedings, 2/23, m. 9.

66. P.R.O., Exchequer, Treasury of Receipt, Forest Proceedings, 127, m. 5v.

67. P.R.O., Exchequer, Treasury of Receipt, Books, 76, f. 13.

68. P.R.O., Exchequer, King's Remembrancer, Forest Proceedings, 1/25, m. 3.

69. Ibid., 3/3, m. 2–4; Exchequer, Treasury of Receipt, Forest Proceedings, 30, m. 22, 39; 31, m. 2, 9–17; 68, m. 1; 229, m. 11; *Calendar of the Patent Rolls 1258–66*, p. 472.

70. Turner, *Select Pleas*, pp. xix–xx; *Close Rolls 1231–34*, pp. 96, 269; *Close Rolls 1247–51*, p. 174; *Close Rolls 1253–54*, p. 99. For the verderers in Dean, see Bazeley, "The Forest of Dean," pp. 210–13 and Cyril E. Hart, *The Verderers and Speech-Court of the Forest of Dean* (Gloucester, 1950).

71. *Calendar of the Close Rolls 1288–96*, p. 83.

72. *Close Rolls 1231–34*, p. 33.

73. Turner, *Select Pleas*, pp. 62–64.

74. P.R.O., Exchequer, Treasury of Receipt, Forest Proceedings, 127, m. 6v.

75. Ibid., 7 is a roll of the attachment court of Inglewood Forest.

76. Turner, *Select Pleas*, p. 64.

77. *Calendar of the Patent Rolls 1232–47*, p. 172.

78. Turner, *Select Pleas*, p. 12.

79. Ibid., p. 26; P.R.O., Exchequer, Treasury of Receipt, Forest Proceedings, 172, m. 2v.; 13, m. 15, 17v.; Duchy of Lancaster, Forest Proceedings, 1/3, m.8.

80. P.R.O., Exchequer, Treasury of Receipt, Forest Proceedings, 198, m. 10v.; Turner, *Select Pleas*, pp. 1, 4, 7.

81. P.R.O., Chancery Miscellanea, 11/4 (1).

82. P.R.O., Exchequer, Treasury of Receipt, Forest Proceedings, 68, m. 1.

83. Ibid., 127, m. 1v.; 267, m. 13v.

84. Turner, *Select Pleas*, p. 101.

85. Ibid., p. lxxxvi; *Patent Rolls 1216–25*, pp. 402–03; *Patent Rolls 1225–32*, pp. 285–87, with chapters of the regard.

86. Royal writs to sheriffs ordering regards listed in the Close Rolls for the last quarter of the thirteenth century are frequent, but they do not come at regular three-year intervals.

87. P.R.O., Exchequer, Treasury of Receipt, Forest Proceedings, 12, m. 8; 152, m. 2; 68, m. 6; *Close Rolls 1242–47*, pp. 125–26.

88. *Close Rolls 1247–51*, p. 289.

89. Turner, *Select Pleas*, pp. lxxvi–lxxviii. *Close Rolls 1242–47*, p. 125 and *1259–61*, pp. 140–41 provide nearly identical versions of the chapters.

90. P.R.O., Exchequer, Treasury of Receipt, Forest Proceedings, 126, m. 1.

91. See the appendix to my article "The Forest Eyre in England during the Thirteenth Century," *The American Journal of Legal History*, 18 (1974): p. 331. Most of this discussion of the eyre is taken from this article.

92. P.R.O., Exchequer, Treasury of Receipt, Forest Proceedings, 145, m. 1–1v.

93. Ibid., 72, m. 1; 152, m. 4; 70, m. 4–4v.

94. Turner, *Select Pleas,* p. lvii. At the end of the sixteenth century, John Manwood pointed to the disuse of the forest eyre as the main reason for the decline of the forest system in his day, thus nicely illustrating the importance the eyre once had and the myopia of an antiquarian writer who could ignore the massive disafforestments of the fourteenth century. Cited by William Holdsworth, *A History of English Law* (7th ed.; London, 1956), 1: 104.

95. An example of a summons is *Close Rolls 1227–31,* p. 382.

96. *Close Rolls 1242–47,* pp. 416, 475; Turner, *Select Pleas,* p. lvii.

97. *Close Rolls 1251–53,* pp. 304–5; *1261–64,* pp. 117–18.

98. The description of a lengthy roll of fifty-six membranes dating from the fourteenth century will illustrate the most complete form. Copies of the royal writs of summons head the roll. Subsequent sections contain: names of those who appear and essoins for nonappearance, violators of the assize of bread and ale, amercements for failure to appear the first day of the eyre, amercements for default of the regard, mainpernors who do not present the persons for whom they had pledged, foresters who abuse the office, exemptions and privileges, pleas for offenses against the venison, pleas of the vert, exemptions from the regard, oaths taken by foresters, and an account of the lesser revenues of the forest. Of the various categories, the pleas of venison and vert are the most important, occupying twelve membranes and twenty-nine membranes written on both sides. P.R.O., Exchequer, Forest Proceedings, Treasury of the Receipt, 16.

99. Turner, *Select Pleas,* pp. lxi–lxiv, 18, 27.

100. In 1228 when the king was concerned about the forest administration, he sent a representative with instructions that he be admitted to attachments, the eyre, and swanimotes. *Patent Rolls 1225–32* (London, 1901–), p. 197. I have followed Turner (*Select Pleas,* p. xxxvi) in his use of the term "special inquisition" and his distinction between it and a "general inquisition" because both are clear and descriptive terms, even though there is no warrant for the term "special inquisition" in documents of the thirteenth century, as Turner himself pointed out.

101. Turner, *Select Pleas,* pp. xxix–xxx, xxxvi, xlvi.

102. Ibid., pp. 63–64.

103. *The Statutes of the Realm,* Record Commission (London, 1810), 1: 149.

104. E.g., P.R.O. Exchequer, Treasury of Receipt, Forest Proceedings, 7, 48, 135, and 157.

105. Ibid., 156, m. 3.

106. See rolls cited in footnote 104. These rolls, which include cases about the venison, disprove the conclusion of Turner (*Select Pleas,* p. xxx) that attachment courts had no authority relating to venison. However, R. Cunliffe Shaw, *The Royal Forest of Lancaster* (Preston, 1956), pp. 46–48, overstates the judicial function of the attachment court in disagreeing with Turner. My account further differs from Turner in assuming that most presentments by foresters and verderers represent prior consideration in the

attachment court and not just in a special inquisition. The procedure seems to have been for a special inquisition to be held when there was presumption of a forest violation and for the accused to appear at the next session of the attachment court. See Turner, *Select Pleas,* p. 114; P.R.O., Exchequer, Treasury of Receipt, Forest Proceedings, 13, m. 24; 79, m. 4; 200, m. 2; 251, m. 4.

107. Turner, *Select Pleas,* p. 3.

108. P.R.O., Exchequer, Treasury of Receipt, Forest Proceedings, 5.

109. *Close Rolls 1256–59,* p. 217.

110. *Close Rolls 1254–56,* p. 318.

111. P.R.O., Exchequer, Treasury of Receipt, Forest Proceedings, 13, m. 20v.

112. Ibid., 153, m. 6v.; 188, m. 4v.

113. Ibid., 251, m. 2; 76, m. 9; 79, m. 6.

114. Ibid., 13, m. 31v.; *Close Rolls 1251–53,* p. 295; *Close Rolls 1253–54,* p. 211.

115. P.R.O., Exchequer, Treasury of Receipt, Forest Proceedings, 153, m. 10v.–11.

116. Ibid., 30, m. 39.

117. Ibid., 156, m. 1, 3, 5; 161, m. 21; 267, m. 4; *Close Rolls 1227–31,* p. 33; *Close Rolls 1234–37,* pp. 232, 453.

118. *Close Rolls 1237–43,* p. 22.

119. Elizabeth C. Wright, "Common Law in the Thirteenth-Century English Royal Forest," *Speculum* 3 (1928): 191, and in an expanded form in *Dissertation Collection, University of Pennsylvania* (Philadelphia, 1928), 31, no. 2.

120. *Close Rolls 1231–34,* pp. 595–96. Perhaps this was the reason why two cases of hunting in the royal forest without a license appear in *Curia Regis Rolls,* 11: 238; 15: 282 rather than in forest eyres.

121. *Close Rolls 1231–34,* pp. 491, 499, 511; Ralph B. Pugh, *Imprisonment in Medieval England* (Cambridge, 1968), pp. 130–32.

122. Turner, *Select Pleas,* pp. 33–34.

123. *Curia Regis Rolls,* 15: 256.

124. *Close Rolls 1251–53,* p. 211; P.R.O., Chancery Miscellanea, 12/2/1; 11/5 (17); Exchequer, Treasury of Receipt, Forest Proceedings, 156, m. 3, 5; 161, m. 21.

125. Turner, *Select Pleas,* p. 19.

126. *Curia Regis Rolls,* 13: 40–41.

127. Ibid., 14: 128.

128. *Rotuli Parliamentorum* (London, 1767–77), 1: 15.

129. Ibid., 1: 35–36, 46, 192–93.

130. *Year Books of the Reign of King Edward the First Years XX and XXI,* ed. Alfred J. Horwood, Rolls Series (London, 1866), pp. 424–25.

131. Turner, *Select Pleas,* pp. lxxxvii, lxxxix, xci. Examples of clerical offenses against both vert and venison may be found in P.R.O., Chancery

Miscellanea, 11/1 (26), 11/2 (3); Duchy of Lancaster, Forest Proceedings, 1/3, m. 3v.; Exchequer, Treasury of Receipt, Forest Proceedings, 41, m. 3; 44, m. 7; 161, m. 9v.; *Calendar of the Close Rolls 1272–79*, p. 38.

132. Turner, *Select Pleas*, pp. 12–13.

133. *Rotuli Parliamentorum*, 1: 37–38, 163. In many royal forests religious houses had the right to a tithe of the venison taken in the forests by special grants of the king. E.g., see *Calendar of the Close Rolls 1272–79*, p. 220; *1288–96*, p. 490.

134. *Close Rolls 1227–31*, p. 520. Another Oxford example is *Close Rolls 1253–54*, p. 50.

135. P.R.O., Exchequer, Treasury of Receipt, Forest Proceedings, 267, m. 4.

136. Ibid., 30, m. 9; 36, m. 1; 76, m. 13; 251, m. 4; *Close Rolls 1247–51*, p. 416; *Close Rolls 1259–61*, pp. 356, 449; *Rotuli Parliamentorum*, 1: 55.

137. P.R.O., Exchequer, Treasury of Receipt, Forest Proceedings, 12, m. 15v. 22.

138. Turner, *Select Pleas*, pp. cxi–cxii.

139. *Calendar of the Patent Rolls 1272–81*, pp. 27–28, 30, 71.

140. P.R.O., Exchequer, Treasury of Receipt, Forest Proceedings, 188, m. 9v.; Turner, *Select Pleas*, p. 34.

141. *Calendar of the Charter Rolls*, 2: 237.

142. Typical examples of partial exemptions are *Close Rolls 1231–34*, pp. 224–25; *Close Rolls 1247–51*, p. 210; *Calendar of the Charter Rolls*, 1: 84, 114, 140, 270. After discussing exemptions, Margaret Bazeley, "The Extent of the English Forest in the Thirteenth Century," *Transactions of the Royal Historical Society*, 4th series, vol. 4 (1921): 145–46 concluded: "It is clear that the forest system was not so hard and fast as it is often pictured."

143. Turner, *Select Pleas*, pp. cxv–cxxii.

144. P.R.O., Exchequer, Treasury of Receipt, Forest Proceedings, 13, m. 12, 19, 25–25v.; *Close Rolls 1268–72*, p. 313; Turner, *Select Pleas*, p. 40.

145. *Close Rolls 1227–31*, p. 277; Turner, *Select Pleas*, p. 104.

146. *Close Rolls 1254–56*, p. 39; *Close Rolls 1256–59*, p. 194; *Calendar of the Charter Rolls*, 1: 81, 176, 311, 452.

147. P.R.O., Exchequer, Treasury of Receipt, Forest Proceedings, 136 (Woodstock).

148. Ibid., 12, m. 4, 6, 7v.; 13, m. 12, 18v., 14v.; 76, m. 2, 12v.; 158, m. 12; King's Remembrancer, Forest Proceedings, 2/23, m. 7; Chancery Miscellanea, 11/2 (13), m. 1–2; Turner, *Select Pleas*, pp. 55, 57, 58; *Close Rolls 1268–72*, p. 313.

149. *Calendar of the Patent Rolls 1272–81*, p. 69; P.R.O., Chancery Miscellanea, 12/1/4.

150. Matthew Paris, *Chronica Majora*, 3: 343.

151. Turner, *Select Pleas*, pp. cxix–cxxii.

152. Ibid., pp. cix–cxv; Shaw, *The Royal Forest of Lancaster*, pp. 231–32.

153. Turner, *Select Pleas*, pp. cxiii–cxxxiv.

154. Nigel Wireker, *Speculum Stultorum,* eds. John H. Mozley and R. R. Raymo (Berkeley asd Los Angeles, 1960), pp. 87–88.

155. P.R.O., Exchequer, Treasury of Receipt, Forest Proceedings, 68, m. 7–7v.

156. Turner, *Select Pleas,* pp. 31–32.

157. Ibid., p. 27; P.R.O., Exchequer, Treasury of Receipt, Forest Proceedings, 158, m. 2.

158. P.R.O., Exchequer, Treasury of Receipt, Forest Proceedings, 5, m. 35v.

159. Ibid., 12, m. 7; 5, m. 35v.

160. Ibid., 5, m. 35v.

161. Ibid., 13, m. 17v.; 198, m. 3; Chancery Miscellanea, 35/10, #47; *Close Rolls 1272–81,* p. 296.

162. *Calendar of the Patent Rolls 1272–81,* p. 216.

163. P.R.O., Exchequer, Treasury of Receipt, Forest Proceedings, 5, m. 35v.; 127, m. 5.

164. P.R.O., Duchy of Lancaster, Forest Proceedings, 1/3, m. 1–1v., 2v.; Special Collections, Ancient Correspondence, 45, #128; *Close Rolls 1227–31,* p. 365; *Close Rolls 1259–61,* p. 403; *Close Rolls 1264–68,* p. 434; *Calendar of the Patent Rolls 1258–66,* pp. 87, 273.

165. P.R.O., Chancery Miscellanea, 12/9 (26), (28); Exchequer, Treasury of Receipt, Forest Proceedings, 5, m. 35v.

166. Bazeley, "The Forest of Dean," p. 165.

167. *Calendar of the Patent Rolls 1266–72,* p. 581.

168. P.R.O. Exchequer, Treasury of Receipt, Forest Proceedings, 5, m. 35v.; 127, m. 5v.

169. Ibid., 152, m. 4–4v.

170. Ibid., 12, m. 3.

171. Ibid., 13, m. lv.; 127, m. 3–4; *Close Rolls 1227–31,* p. 290; *Close Rolls 1247–51,* p. 1; *Close Rolls 1256–59,* p. 217.

172. P.R.O., Exchequer, Treasury of Receipt, Forest Proceedings, 2, m. 2v.; Turner, pp. 58, 66; *Close Rolls 1242–47,* p. 417; *Close Rolls 1247–51,* p. 17; *Close Rolls 1251–53,* pp. 501–2; *Close Rolls 1254–56,* p. 341.

173. Turner, *Select Pleas,* pp. 3–4.

174. P.R.O. Exchequer, Treasury of Receipt, Forest Proceedings, 2, m. 2.

175. Ibid., 161, m. 20; *Close Rolls 1256–59,* p. 207.

176. P.R.O., Exchequer, Treasury of Receipt, Forest Proceedings, 161, m. lv., 2v., 5, 6. In this example the amercements for a baron ranged as high as £59, as compared to a similar offense by a knight who paid 100s., and an ordinary free man assessed 40s. even though he took more deer. The principle seems to be related to chapter 20 of Magna Carta which limited an amercement on a free man to the amount he could pay "saving his livelihood." The same limitation on the amercement for a forest eyre is given in *Fleta,* eds. H. G. Richardson and G. O. Sayles, Selden Society, vol. 72 (London, 1955), 2: 103. The question in relation to Magna Carta was discussed by C. A. F. Meekings in his introduction to *Crown Pleas of the Wiltshire*

Eyre, 1249, Wiltshire Archaeological and Natural History Society, Records Branch, 16 (Devizes, 1961), pp. 107–8.

177. P.R.O., Exchequer, Treasury of Receipt, Forest Proceedings, 30, m. 15v.

178. Ibid., 127, m. 2v.

179. Ibid., 76, m. 12v.

180. Ibid., 153, m. 4.

181. Ibid., 229, m. 2–2v.

182. P.R.O., Exchequer, King's Remembrancer, Forest Proceedings, 1/20, m. 4.

183. P.R.O., Exchequer, Treasury of Receipt, Forest Proceedings, 12, m. 3v.

184. *Fleta,* 2: 103.

185. P.R.O., Exchequer, Treasury of Receipt, Forest Proceedings, 84, m. 1.

186. Ibid., 83, m. 3.

187. Ibid., 41, m. 1; 68, m. lv.; 83, m. 1–2; 158, m. 11v–12v.; Turner, *Select Pleas,* p. 11.

188. *Close Rolls 1231–34,* p. 557

189. *Calendar of the Patent Rolls 1232–47,* p. 165; *Close Rolls 1237–42,* pp. 137–38, 144–45.

190. *Close Rolls 1237–42,* pp. 137–38.

191. *Curia Regis Rolls,* 10: 259; 14: 87; *Patent Rolls 1216–25,* p. 452; *1225–32,* p. 139; *Close Rolls 1247–51,* p. 248; *1256–59,* pp. 57, 165; *1272–81,* p. 218; P.R.O., Exchequer, Treasury of Receipt, Forest Proceedings, 79, m. 4.

192. *Close Rolls 1231–34,* p. 94; *1234–37,* pp. 1, 8, 105; *1237–42,* p. 239; *1261–64,* p. 120; *Calendar of the Close Rolls 1279–88,* pp. 7, 18; *Calendar of the Patent Rolls 1281–92,* p. 22.

193. P.R.O., Exchequer, Treasury of Receipt, Forest Proceedings, 13, m. 9–10.

194. R. H. Hilton, "The Origins of Robin Hood," *Past and Present* 14 (1958): 30–44 and J. C. Holt, "The Origins and Audience of the Ballads of Robin Hood," ibid. 18 (1960): 89–110.

195. *Close Rolls 1264–68,* p. 21.

196. P.R.O., Exchequer, Treasury of Receipt, Forest Proceedings, 2, m. 2; Chancery Miscellanea, 11/3 (22).

197. *Statutes of the Realm,* 1: 111.

198. Turner, *Select Pleas,* p. 99.

199. Ibid., p. 81.

200. Ibid., p. 36; P.R.O., Duchy of Lancaster, Forest Proceedings, 1/3, m. 1.

201. P.R.O., Exchequer, Treasury of Receipt, Forest Proceedings, 251, m. 2.

202. Ibid., 65, m. 1; 171, m. lv.; *Close Rolls 1227–31,* p. 568; *Close Rolls 1247–51,* p. 430; *Calendar of the Patent Rolls 1272–81,* p. 399.

203. Turner, *Select Pleas*, p. 3.

204. Ibid., pp. 16–17, 18–19, 21–22, 29, 33.

205. John West, "The Administration and Economy of the Forest of Feckenham during the Early Middle Ages" (M.A. thesis, University of Birmingham, 1964), pp. 168–75.

206. P.R.O., Exchequer, Treasury of Receipt, Forest Proceedings, 198, m. 1–1v.; 199, m. 7–7v.; 200, m. 7.

207. Ibid., 30, m. 21v.

208. *Patent Rolls 1216–25*, pp. 211–15, 217–19; *Close Rolls 1227–31*, pp. 262, 456.

209. *Close Rolls 1242–47*, p. 445; *Close Rolls 1264–68*, p. 408; *Patent Rolls, 1216–25*, p. 238. An example of arable land being termed a purpresture is *Close Rolls 1251–53*, p. 305.

210. P.R.O., Duchy of Lancaster, Forest Proceedings, 1/3, m. 16–18v.

211. Turner, *Select Pleas*, p. 18.

212. P.R.O., Chancery Miscellanea, 11/4 (15), m. 2; 11/4 (17), m. 1; *Calendar of the Patent Rolls 1272–81*, p. 173.

213. P.R.O., Chancery Miscellanea, 11/5 (9), m. 1–3; Exchequer, Treasury of Receipt, Forest Proceedings, 72, m. 8–8v.

214. P.R.O., Chancery Miscellanea, 11/1 (11); 11/2 (7); 11/2 (19); Exchequer, Treasury of Receipt, Forest Proceedings, 184, m. 10.

215. P.R.O., Exchequer, King's Remembrancer, Forest Proceedings, 1/20, m. 1–2.

216. P.R.O., Chancery Miscellanea, 11/5 (5); 35/10, #45; Exchequer, Treasury of Receipt, Forest Proceedings, 76, m. 8; Turner, *Select Pleas*, p. 60; *Close Rolls 1251–53*, p. 295; *Close Rolls 1254–56*, p. 135; *Patent Rolls 1216–25*, pp. 360–62, 368, 399–402; *Calendar of the Patent Rolls 1232–47*, p. 247; *Calendar of the Patent Rolls 1272–81*, p. 211.

217. *Rotuli Litterarum Patentium*, Record Commission (London, 1835), 1: Pt. 1, 3b; *Calendar of the Patent Rolls 1272–81*, p. 105; *Close Rolls 1247–51*, p. 180; *1251–53* p. 371; *1256–59*, p. 88; *1264–68*, pp. 314, 467; *1268–72*, p. 51; P.R.O., Exchequer, King's Remembrancer, Forest Proceedings, 2/23, m. 9 (yule logs).

218. *Calendar of the Patent Rolls 1232–47*, pp. 90–91.

219. P.R.O., Exchequer, Treasury of Receipt, Forest Proceedings, 30, m. 24–24v.; 72, m. 3; 76, m. 15; 127, m. 6.

220. Ibid., 30, m. 22; 68, m. 1; 74, m. 3; 82, m. 5.

221. Ibid., 30, m. 23v.

222. Ibid., 29, m. 2.

223. Ibid., 28, m. 5; Chancery Miscellanea, 11/4 (7); *Close Rolls 1254–56*, pp. 61, 245.

224. Bazeley, "The Forest of Dean," pp. 268–69; *Close Rolls 1247–51*, p. 282.

225. P.R.O., Exchequer, Treasury of Receipt, Forest Proceedings, 2, m. 5v.; 127, m. 12; 158, m. 17; *Close Rolls 1231–34*, p. 98.

226. *Close Rolls 1227–31*, pp. 7, 277; *1247–51*, pp. 297–309, 338; *1251–53*, p. 122; *1256–59*, p. 227; *Calendar of the Close Rolls 1307–13*, p. 2.

227. P.R.O., Chancery Miscellanea, 11/2 (6); 11/3 (1); 11/5 (6); 11/5 (18); Exchequer, Treasury of Receipt, Forest Proceedings, 188, m. 13v.; 5, m. 36v.; Turner, *Select Pleas*, pp. 25–26; *Close Rolls 1247–51*, p. 539; *1251–53*, pp. 111, 434.

228. P.R.O., Chancery Miscellanea, 11/5 (4); *Close Rolls 1251–53*, p. 122.

229. Turner, *Select Pleas*, p. xxvi.

230. Ibid., pp. xxxvii–l.

231. Matthew Paris, *Chronica Majora*, 4: 400–401, 426–27.

232. Turner, *Select Pleas*, pp. xlx–xlvi.

233. John Bellamy, *Crime and Public Order in England in the Later Middle Ages* (London, 1973), pp. 17–18.

234. Bazeley, "The Forest of Dean," pp. 162–63.

235. *Calendar of the Patent Rolls 1258–66*, p. 675.

236. Ibid., pp. 192, 237.

237. *Calendar of the Charter Rolls*, 1: 3, 4, 8, 16, 22, 122–23, 369; 2: 43; *Close Rolls 1242–47*, p. 235.

238. *Calendar of the Charter Rolls*, 2: 247; *Calendar of the Patent Rolls 1272–81*, p. 471.

239. *Close Rolls 1237–42*, p. 483.

240. *Calendar of the Charter Rolls*, 1: 75–76.

Chapter 6

1. P.R.O., Exchequer, Pipe Rolls, 105, m. 20v; 122, m. 28; 73, m. 8v.; 133, m. 29v.; 145, m. 29.

2. P.R.O., Exchequer, King's Remembrancer, Various Accounts, 136/6, m. 1.

3. P.R.O., Exchequer, Pipe Rolls, 91, m. 14v.

4. Ibid., 48, m. 8v.

5. P.R.O., Exchequer, Chancellors Rolls, 45, m. 20.

6. P.R.O., Exchequer, Pipe Rolls, 97, m. 10.

7. P.R.O., Exchequer, King's Remembrancer, Various Accounts, 131/26, m. A 1–3, B 1–3v.

8. The figures on which the graph is based come from ibid., 130/6–40; 131/1–30; 132/1–30; 133/1–22; 534/2, 5–6, 9–14.

9. P.R.O., Exchequer, Treasury of Receipt, Forest Proceedings, 64, 66, 67, 69, 72, 100, 106, 108, 109, 115, 117, 141, 142. For a discussion of assarting in some of these same forests, the problems of using the forest records, and extracts from the records, see J. A. Raftis, *Assart Data and Land Values* (Toronto, 1974), p. 98ff.

10. M. M. Postan, *The Medieval Economy and Society* (Berkeley and Los Angeles, 1972), pp. 21, 25.

11. Raftis, *Assart Data*, p. 105, found that his Northamptonshire evidence pointed to both large enterprise by whole villages and small assarts by relatively poor individuals at different times and places. Until the whole question of assarting has been studied in the same detail as he had done for Northamptonshire, short-term variations and regional differences remain obscure, but my generalization in the text reflects an overview of all the extant records with figures for assarting.

12. P.R.O., Chancery Miscellanea, 11/1/8, 11/3/10; Exchequer, Treasury of Receipt, Forest Proceedings, 170, m. 3; 183; *Close Rolls 1237–42,* p. 168; *1242–47,* p. 386.

13. P.R.O., Exchequer, Treasury of Receipt, Forest Proceedings, 36, m. 1; 152, m. 4v.; 198, m. 10v.; 207, m. 10v.; *Calendar of the Patent Rolls 1272–81,* p. 194. See also R. A. Donkin, "The Cistercian Settlement and the English Royal Forests," *Cîteaux: Commentarii Cistercienses* 11 (1960): 117–124.

14. *Close Rolls 1247–51,* pp. 413–14.

15. P.R.O., Exchequer, Treasury of Receipt, Forest Proceedings, 183; *Calendar of the Patent Rolls 1272–81,* pp. 227, 403; *Calendar of the Close Rolls 1288–96,* p. 173.

16. P.R.O., Exchequer, Treasury of Receipt, Forest Proceedings, 164, m. 7.

17. P.R.O., Exchequer, King's Remembrancer, Forest Proceedings, 1/27; *Close Rolls 1231–34,* p. 426; *1264–68,* p. 3; *Calendar of the Patent Rolls 1247–58,* p. 474.

18. P.R.O., Chancery Miscellanea, 11/2/18.

19. *Calendar of the Close Rolls 1279–88,* p. 342.

20. *Calendar of the Close Rolls 1272–79,* p. 364

21. *Calendar of the Close Rolls 1288–96,* p. 243.

22. P.R.O., Exchequer, Treasury of Receipt, Forest Proceedings, 13, m. 25; 163, m. 8v.; 310, m. 22.

23. *Calendar of the Patent Rolls 1247–58,* pp. 432–33, 436.

24. *Calendar of the Patent Rolls 1247–58,* p. 544.

25. P.R.O., Exchequer, Pipe Rolls, 84, m. 2v.

26. P.R.O., Chancery Miscellanea, 11/4/20.

27. P.R.O., Exchequer, Pipe Rolls, 105, m. 20–20v.

28. *Close Rolls 1247–51,* p. 563; *1251–53,* p. 201.

29. *Close Rolls 1251–53,* pp. 227, 243.

30. P.R.O., Chancery Miscellanea, 11/4/20.

31. P.R.O., Exchequer, Pipe Rolls, 158, m. 38v.

32. Ibid., 154, m. 52, 52v.

33. Ibid., 159, m. 19.

34. Ibid., 146, m. 50v.

35. P.R.O., Special Collections, Ancient Correspondence, 51/1.

36. P.R.O., Exchequer, Various Accounts, 139–22, 23, 24, 26, 28, 30. The total sales in pounds were as follows:

| 1337—20 | 1341—12 | 1348—24 | 1355—38 |

1338—18	1342—17	1349—32	1356—36
1339—18	1343—25	1350—19	1357—62
1340—18	1344—31	1354— 9	1358—37
			1359—34

37. P.R.O., Exchequer, Various Accounts, 140/2, 6, 7.

38. Ibid., 140/9.

39. *Close Rolls 1254–56*, pp. 89–90, 296, 425.

40. P.R.O., Exchequer, Treasury of Receipt, Forest Proceedings, 332.

41. P.R.O., Exchequer, King's Remembrancer, Various Accounts, 140/17.

42. Ibid., 140/19.

43. P.R.O., Exchequer, Treasury of Receipt, Forest Proceedings, 41, m. 5v.; 72, m. 2; 80, m. 1; *Calendar of the Patent Rolls 1266–72*, p. 220.

44. *Calendar of the Close Rolls 1409–13*, p. 423.

45. *Close Rolls 1237–39*, p. 436.

46. *Close Rolls 1256–59*, p. 345.

47. P.R.O., Chancery Miscellanea, 11/1.

48. P.R.O., Exchequer, King's Remembrancer, Forest Proceedings, 3/24.

49. P.R.O., Exchequer, Treasury of Receipt, Forest Proceedings, 88, m. 3v.

50. P.R.O., Chancery Miscellanea, 11/5/2; Exchequer, King's Remembrancer, Forest Proceedings, 1/36.

51. P.R.O., Exchequer, Treasury of Receipt, Forest Proceedings, 204.

52. P.R.O., Exchequer, Treasury of the Receipt, Books, 75, f. 8v.

53. P.R.O., Exchequer, King's Remembrancer, Various Accounts, 136/3.

54. P.R.O., Chancery Files (Tower and Rolls Chapel) Recorda, 24/24.

55. P.R.O., Exchequer, Treasury of Receipt, Forest Proceedings, 91, m. 1, 3.

56. Ibid., 101, m. 1.

57. Ibid., 134.

58. Ibid., 2, 5, 10–11, 35, 37, 41, 44, 72–73, 137, 139–140, 145, 147, 157–58, 161, 184, 187, 198–200, 227, 231.

59. Ibid., 127.

60. Ibid., 13, 44, 127, 130, 132, 161, 188, 207, 217, 260; P.R.O., Exchequer, King's Remembrancer, Forest Proceedings, 133/30; 134/1, 2, 7.

61. P.R.O., Exchequer, Treasury of Receipt, Forest Proceedings, 207.

62. P.R.O., Exchequer, King's Remembrancer, Various Accounts, 136/2.

63. *Close Rolls 1234–37*, p. 141; *1251–53*, pp. 43, 46, 49, 53.

64. *Close Rolls 1251–53*, p. 269; *1261–64*, p. 93.

65. *Close Rolls 1254–56*, p. 357.

66. P.R.O., Exchequer, Treasury of Receipt, Forest Proceedings, 199; *Close Rolls 1247–51*, p. 206; *Calendar of the Close Rolls 1288–96*, p. 296.

67. "The Forest of Dean in its Relations with the Crown during the Twelfth and Thirteenth Centuries." *Transactions of the Bristol and Gloucestershire Archaeological Society* 33 (1910): 233.

68. Ibid., p. 251.

69. P.R.O., Exchequer, Treasury of Receipt, Forest Proceedings, 11; 158; *Close Rolls 1231–34* p. 41; *1234–37,* p. 324; *Calendar of the Close Rolls 1272–79,* pp. 79, 96, 188, 298, 370; *1288–96,* p. 350.

70. P.R.O., Exchequer, Treasury of Receipt, Forest Proceedings, 127, m. 7.

71. *Close Rolls 1247–51,* p. 407.

72. *Close Rolls 1227–31,* pp. 49, 248; *1231–34,* pp. 90, 206, 352; *Calendar of the Close Rolls 1288–96,* pp. 242, 433.

73. P.R.O., Exchequer, King's Remembrancer, Forest Proceedings, 1/20, m. 2; *Close Rolls 1227–31,* p. 569.

74. *Close Rolls 1247–51,* p. 486.

75. *Calendar of the Close Rolls 1272–79,* p. 474.

76. *Calendar of the Patent Rolls 1272–81,* p. 260; *Close Rolls 1234–37,* p. 215.

77. *Close Rolls 1227–31,* pp. 182, 195; *1231–34,* pp. 71, 538, *1234–37,* pp. 105, 320; *1251–53,* p. 33; *1253–54,* p. 65; *Calendar of the Close Rolls 1302–07,* p. 494.

78. *Patent Rolls 1216–25,* p. 28. For the later period see Nellie Neilson, "The Forests" in James F. Willard and William A. Morris, *The English Government at Work, 1327–1336* (Cambridge, Mass., 1940), 1: 437–44.

79. *Close Rolls 1237–42,* p. 381; *Calendar of the Close Rolls 1296–1302,* p. 72.

80. *Close Rolls 1231–34,* p. 454; *1256–59,* p. 398.

81. Bazeley, "The Forest of Dean," pp. 266–68.

82. Rodney H. Hilton, *A Medieval Society: The West Midlands at the End of the Thirteenth Century* (London, 1967), p. 215.

83. *Close Rolls 1251–53,* p. 246.

84. *Calendar of the Close Rolls 1288–96,* p. 280; P.R.O., Exchequer, Treasury of Receipt, Forest Proceedings, 333.

85. P.R.O., Duchy of Lancaster, Forest Proceedings, 1/3, m. 12–12d.; 1/4, m. 1; *Close Rolls 1231–34,* p. 100; *Close Rolls 1234–37,* pp. 103, 141; *Rotuli Parliamentorum* (London, 1767–77), 1: 166.

86. *Close Rolls 1231–34,* p. 372; *1234–37,* p. 465; *1247–51,* p. 206.

87. *Close Rolls 1234–37,* p. 485. Extensive accounts in which sale of hay figures prominently are P.R.O., Exchequer, King's Remembrancer, Various Accounts, 133/26, 27, 29; 134/3.

88. There are 39 entries for laymen and 52 for clergy in the single volume of *Close Rolls 1227–31*. P.R.O., Exchequer, Treasury of Receipt, Forest Proceedings, 81, m. 1–2; 83, m. 12–14; 88, m. 1–4; 84, m. 1v.–2v.; 89.

89. *Close Rolls 1227–31,* p. 482.

90. Ibid., pp. 55, 189.

91. *Calendar of the Close Rolls 1343–46,* p. 184.

92. P.R.O., Exchequer, Treasury of Receipt, Forest Proceedings, 153. m.2.

93. Ibid., 5, m. 25v.

94. *Close Rolls 1227–31,* pp. 224, 277, 411, 480; *Calendar of the Close Rolls 1279–88,* pp. 33–34.

95. P.R.O., Exchequer, Treasury of Receipt, Forest Proceedings, 127, m. 5v.

96. Ibid., 13, m. 3.

97. *Calendar of the Close Rolls 1288–96,* p. 170.

98. R. Cunliffe Shaw, *The Royal Forest of Lancaster* (Preston, 1956), p. 482.

99. *Close Rolls 1234–37,* p. 519.

100. *Calendar of the Close Rolls 1279–88,* p. 210.

Chapter 7

1. Faith Thompson, *The First Century of Magna Carta* (Minneapolis, 1925), p. 89.

2. R. E. Treharne and I. J. Sanders, *Documents of the Baronial Movement of Reform and Rebellion 1258–1267* (Oxford, 1973), pp. 4–5, 81.

3. Ibid., p. 155.

4. Ibid., p. 321; *The Statutes of the Realm* (London, 1810), 1: 20.

5. *Rotuli Parliamentorum* (London, 1767–77), 1: 101.

6. H. Rothwell, "The Confirmation of the Charters, 1297," *English Historical Review* 60 (1945): 319.

7. Maurice Powicke, *The Thirteenth Century* (2nd ed.; Oxford, 1962), pp. 669–70.

8. J. G. Edwards, "Confirmatio Cartarum and Baronial Grievances in 1297," *English Historical Review* 58 (1943): 148, 152; B. Wilkinson, *The Constitutional History of Medieval England 1216–1399* (London, 1948–58), 1: 203–4.

9. Wilkinson, *Constitutional History,* 1: 221.

10. Edwards, "Confirmatio Cartarum," p. 162.

11. Wilkinson, *Constitutional History,* 1: 226–27.

12. *Calendar of the Patent Rolls 1292–1301,* p. 312; *Calendar of the Close Rolls 1296–1302,* pp. 134, 137, 186, 190–91, 396; "Annales de Wigornia" in Henry R. Luard, ed., *Annales Monastici,* Rolls Series (London, 1864–69), 4: 535–36; G. J. Turner, ed., *Select Pleas of the Forest* (London, 1901), p. ciii.

13. *Calendar of the Close Rolls 1296–1302,* p. 223; *Calendar of the Patent Rolls 1292–1301,* pp. 373–74.

14. *Statutes of the Realm,* 1: 126, 128; *Calendar of the Close Rolls 1296–1302,* p. 298.

15. Rothwell, "Confirmation of the Charters, p. 324.

16. *Calendar of the Patent Rolls 1292–1301,* pp. 424, 441, 454.

17. Ibid., p. 486.

18. *Calendar of the Charter Rolls,* 2: 483; *Calendar of the Close Rolls 1296–1302,* pp. 387, 399, 408–9; Rothwell, pp. 324–27.

19. *Calendar of the Patent Rolls 1292–1301,* pp. 506, 514, 607; *Calendar*

of the Close Rolls 1296–1302, pp. 383, 393–94, 396–97, 429, 577, 588; P.R.O., Chancery Miscellanea, 12/11/2; Exchequer, Treasury of Receipt, Forest Proceedings, 284; 225, m. 10–11. Commenting on one local example, L. M. Cantor states that Edward I's perambulations provided the first precise boundaries of Cannock and Kinver Forests which had been known previously only by prescription, in "The Medieval Forests and Chaces of Staffordshire," *North Staffordshire Journal of Field Studies* 8 (1968): p. 43.

20. Turner, *Select Pleas*, pp. 120–21.

21. Faith Thompson, *Magna Carta: Its Role in the Making of the the English Constitution 1300–1629* (Minneapolis, 1948), pp. 4–5.

22. *Rotuli Parliamentorum*, 1: 159–160, 163, 177–78; Frederic W. Maitland, ed., *Memoranda de Parliamento: Records of the Parliament . . . 1305*, Rolls Series (London, 1893), pp. 18, 67, 89, 155–56, 294–96; *Calendar of the Close Rolls 1302–07*, pp. 323, 340; *Statutes of the Realm*, 1: 144.

23. *Statutes of the Realm*, 1: 147–49.

24. *Calendar of the Patent Rolls 1307–13*, p. 295.

25. James Conway Davies, *The Baronial Opposition to Edward II* (London, 1967), p. 357. J. R. Maddicott, *Thomas of Lancaster 1307–1322* (Oxford, 1970), pp. 324–25, warns "The fallacious concept of a 'baronial opposition,' perpetually in being and holding a distinct set of policies, has vitiated much learned work on the reign. In fact baronial groupings were mostly temporary and fissiparous." For the period 1310 to 1322, reform of the royal forest was one issue that appealed to the barons as a group, but this issue was kept in the fore primarily through the interest Thomas of Lancaster took in it.

26. *Statutes of the Realm*, 1: 160–61.

27. Davies, *Baronial Opposition*, pp. 384–85.

28. Ibid., pp. 388, 393, 487.

29. *Rotuli Parliamentorum*, 1: 351.

30. *Calendar of the Patent Rolls 1313–17*, p. 398.

31. *Calendar of the Close Rolls 1313–18*, p. 224.

32. *Calendar of the Patent Rolls 1313–17*, pp. 296, 539.

33. Ibid., p. 324; *Calendar of the Close Rolls 1313–18*, p. 225.

34. *Calendar of the Close Rolls 1313–18*, pp. 272–74.

35. P.R.O., Chancery Miscellanea, 12/11/6.

36. *Calendar of the Patent Rolls 1313–17*, pp. 529–31; *Calendar of the Close Rolls 1313–18*, p. 427.

37. See Maddicott, *Thomas of Lancaster*, especially p. 179.

38. *Calendar of the Patent Rolls 1317–21*, p. 240.

39. *Calendar of the Patent Rolls 1321–24*, pp. 149–50. The execution of earl Thomas brought the afforested areas in Lancashire directly under the royal forest administration because the areas escheated to the king. See R. Cunliffe Shaw, *The Royal Forest of Lancaster* (Preston, 1956), pp. 126–28.

40. *Calendar of the Close Rolls 1318–23*, p. 634; *1323–27*, p. 22.

41. *Calendar of the Close Rolls 1323–27*, p. 539; *Rotuli Parliamentorum*, 1: 420, 430.

42. *Rotuli Parliamentorum*, 2: 10.

43. Ibid., p. 11.

44. *Statutes of the Realm*, 1: 255.

45. *Calendar of the Close Rolls 1323–27*, p. 557; *1327–30*, p. 212; *Calendar of the Patent Rolls 1327–30*, p. 39.

46. *Calendar of the Close Rolls 1327–30*, p. 124; *Rotuli Parliamentorum*, 2: 24.

47. I have found no reason to disagree with this view as expressed by Charles Petit-Dutaillis, *Studies and Notes Supplementary to Stubbs' Constitutional History* (Manchester, 1930), p. 232, and accepted by other scholars in legal and constitutional history.

48. *Statutes of the Realm*, 1: 391; *Rotuli Parliamentorum*, 2: 301.

49. *Rotuli Parliamentorum*, 2: 311, 313, 335, 367; 3: 18.

50. Ibid., 3: 18.

51. *Statutes of the Realm*, 2: 32; *Rotuli Parliamentorum*, 3: 164.

Chapter 8

1. John Manwood, *A Treatise and Discourse of the Lawes of the Forest* (London, 1598).

2. R. A. McKinley in *The Victoria History of the County of Leicester*, ed. William Page (London, 1907–   ), 2: 266.

3. J. Nisbet in *The Victoria History of the County of Surrey*, ed. H. E. Malden (London, 1902–   ), 2: 566.

4. M. W. Greenslade in *The Victoria History of the County of Stafford*, ed. William Page (London, 1908–   ), 2: 338–43, 348.

5. H. C. Brentnall, "The Metes and Bounds of Savernake Forest," *The Wiltshire Archaeological and Natural History Magazine* 49 (1940–42): 434.

6. *Calendar of the Patent Rolls 1340–43*, pp. 190–91.

7. R. Grant in *The Victoria History of Wiltshire*, ed. R. B. Pugh (London, 1953–   ), 4: 400.

8. *Statutes of the Realm*, 2: 32.

9. Manwood, *A Treatise*, fol. 51. The eyre also ceased to funciton as a part of the common law judicial administration. See C. A. F. Meekings, ed., *Crown Pleas of the Wiltshire Eyre, 1249*, Wiltshire Archaeological and Natural History Society, Records Branch, vol. 16 (Devizes, 1961), p. 8.

10. *Calendar of the Patent Rolls 1345–48*, p. 264.

11. *Calendar of the Close Rolls 1381–85*, p. 547.

12. *Calendar of the Close Rolls 1330–33*, p. 31; P.R.O., Exchequer, Treasury of Receipt, Forest Proceedings, 163.

13. P.R.O., Exchequer, Treasury of Receipt, Forest Proceedings, 207, m. 1–2, 11.

14. *Calendar of the Close Rolls 1330–33*, p. 241.

15. P.R.O., Exchequer, Treasury of Receipt, Forest Proceedings, 281, m. 2.

16. Ibid.

17. Ibid., 114.

18. Ibid., 132, m. 4, 7v., 11, 15, 20, 23.

19. *Statutes of the Realm*, 1: 148–49. In 1311 the procedure for mainprise until the eyre freely without payment of any fine to the chief justice was spelled out in detail (p. 161). The term "general inquisition" was used by G. J. Turner who discussed this institution in *Select Pleas of the Forest*, Selden Society, vol. 13 (London, 1901), pp. xlii–l.

20. *Calendar of the Patent Rolls 1370–74*, pp. 104, 475; *Calendar of the Close Rolls 1374–77*, pp. 34, 397; *1377–81*, pp. 285, 298, 413; *1402–05*, p. 403.

21. P.R.O., Exchequer, Treasury of Receipt, Forest Proceedings, 212, m. lv., 2v.; King's Remembrancer, Forest Proceedings, 1/35, m. 1. Nellie Neilson, "The Forests," in James F. Willard and William A. Morris, *The English Government at Work, 1327–1336* (Cambridge, Mass., 1940), 1: 420 raised the question whether there might have been another kind of inquest in Galtres Forest which she labelled the *turnus custodis*.

22. *Rotuli Parliamentorum* (London, 1767–77), 2: 333.

23. Ibid., 3, 164.

24. G. H. Tupling, *South Lancashire in the Reign of Edward II as Illustrated by the Pleas at Wigan Recorded in Coram Rege Roll No. 254*, Chetham Soc., 3rd serv., vol. 1 (Manchester, 1949), pp. xl, 98, 101, 104–5, 109–10.

25. *Calendar of the Patent Rolls 1361–64*, p. 148; *1367–70*, p. 64; *1370–74*, p. 472 and P.R.O., Exchequer, Treasury of Receipt, Forest Proceedings, 34 for the inquest carried out by order of this letter patent. Reference is made to this type of proceeding in R. Grant in *The Victoria History of Wiltshire*, 4: 395 and Neilson, "The Forests," pp. 421–22. Other examples of conflict between forest law and the common law are *Calendar of the Close Rolls 1333–37*, p. 148; *1389–92*, p. 489; P.R.O., Exchequer, Treasury of Receipt, Forest Proceedings, 303.

26. *Rotuli Parliamentorum*, 1: 314, 319; II, 33, 50, 80, 84, 101, 169, 203, 239.

27. Ibid., 2: 376; *Calendar of the Close Rolls 1333–37*, 307.

28. *Rotuli Parliamentorum*, 2: 388; 3: 43, 116.

29. P.R.O., Exchequer, Treasury of Receipt, Forest Proceedings, 215.

30. See G. L. Harriss, *King, Parliament, and Public Finance in Medieval England to 1369* (Oxford, 1975), pp. 466–67, 509–11 and *passim* for a thorough discussion of the development, but, of course, without reference to its effect upon the royal forest.

31. Neilson, "The Forests," pp. 402–11, has a concise discussion of the period 1327–36.

32. *Calendar of the Close Rolls 1346–49*, p. 216; *1360–64*, p. 328; *1392–96*, pp. 469–70.

33. *Calendar of the Close Rolls 1327–30*, p. 281; *1341–43*, pp. 280, 625.

34. *Calendar of the Close Rolls 1318–23*, p. 600.

35. *Calendar of the Close Rolls 1333–37*, p. 226; *1337–39*, p. 54; *1343–46*, p. 295; *1346–49*, p. 21.

36. *Calendar of the Close Rolls 1339–41*, p. 380.

37. *Calendar of the Close Rolls 1346–49*, p. 216.

38. *Calendar of the Close Rolls 1349–54*, p. 116.

39. *Calendar of the Close Rolls 1377–81*, p. 359.

40. *Calendar of the Close Rolls 1399–1402*, p. 336; *1402–05*, p. 199.

41. *Calendar of the Close Rolls 1402–05*, p. 65.

42. *Calendar of the Close Rolls 1369–74*, p. 420.

43. *Calendar of the Close Rolls 1346–49*, pp. 101, 106, 309, 312, 323, 327, 334, 385.

44. *Calendar of the Close Rolls 1343–46*, pp. 62, 183; *1405–09*, p. 28.

45. *Rotuli Parliamentorum*, 2: 78–79. The case was part of a longer struggle against Henry Sturmy that ran from 1332 to 1361 as discussed in H. C. Brentnall, "Savernake Forest in the Middle Ages," *The Wiltshire Archaeological and Natural History Magazine* 48 (1937–39): 382–85.

46. *Calendar of the Close Rolls 1337–39*, 327, 531.

47. *Calendar of the Close Rolls 1343–46*, p. 611. Elisabeth Kimball, *Serjeanty Tenure in Medieval England* (New Haven, 1936), pp. 108–13, briefly considers serjeanty tenure in the forests.

48. *Calendar of the Close Rolls 1343–46*, p. 433.

49. *Calendar of the Close Rolls 1330–33*, p. 209; *1343–46*, p. 502; *1346–49*, p. 232; *1396–99*, p. 454; John Bellamy, *Crime and Public Order in England in the Later Middle Ages* (London, 1973), p. 26.

50. P.R.O., Exchequer, Treasury of Receipt, Forest Proceedings, m. 9v.

51. P.R.O., Chancery Files (Tower and Rolls Chapel), Recorda, 44/5.

52. Ibid., 57/42B.

53. Turner, *Select Pleas*, pp. xxv–xxvi; William R. Fisher, *The Forest of Essex* (London, 1887), pp. 163–64.

54. *Calendar of the Close Rolls 1341–43*, p. 175.

55. *Calendar of the Patent Rolls 1345–48*, p. 20; *1348–50*, p. 261; *1350–54*, p. 67; *1354–58*, p. 105.

56. *Calendar of the Patent Rolls 1391–96*, p. 212.

57. *Calendar of the Patent Rolls 1391–96*, p. 216.

58. *Calendar of the Close Rolls 1461–68*, p. 291.

59. *Calendar of the Patent Rolls 1370–74*, p. 142.

60. *Calendar of the Close Rolls 1313–18*, p. 327.

61. *Calendar of the Close Rolls 1318–23*, pp. 240–41.

62. Ibid., p. 523; *Calendar of the Close Rolls 1339–41*, p. 287.

63. P.R.O., Exchequer, Treasury of Receipt, Forest Proceedings, 267, m.1.

64. *Calendar of the Patent Rolls 1388–92*, pp. 338–39.

65. *Calendar of the Patent Rolls 1391–96*, pp. 201, 270, 578.

66. P.R.O., Exchequer, Treasury of Receipt, Forest Proceedings, 267, m. 7–8, 9v., ll–llv.

67. Ibid., 217, m. 9–11. For comment, see Brentnall, "Savernake Forest," p. 382.

68. Ibid., 310/21.

69. *Calendar of the Close Rolls 1377–81*, p. 161.

70. P.R.O., Exchequer, Treasury of Receipt, Forest Proceedings, 172, m. 2v.; 303; 310/7 and 8.

71. "Commendatio Lamentabilis in Transitu Magni Regis Edwardi" in William Stubbs, ed., *Chronicles of the Reigns of Edward I. and Edward II.* (London, 1882–83), 2: 5.

72. F. J. Tanquerey, "Lettres du roi Edward I à Robert de Bavent, king's yeoman, sur des questions de vénerie," *Bulletin of the John Rylands Library* 23 (1939): 487–503.

73. J. C. Cox, *The Royal Forests of England* (London, 1905), p. 61. For an excellent overview, see Marcelle Thiebaux, "The Mediaeval Chase," *Speculum* 42 (1967): 260–74.

74. Edward, Second Duke of York, *The Master of Game*, ed. by William A. and F. Baillie-Grohman (London, 1909), pp. 188–89.

75. *Calendar of the Close Rolls 1339–41*, p. 258.

76. John W. Baldwin, *Masters, Princes, and Merchants: The Social Views of Peter the Chanter and His Circle* (Princeton, 1970), pp. 246–47, 320.

77. *Calendar of the Close Rolls 1374–77*, p. 154.

78. *Statutes of the Realm*, 2: 65; Charles Petit-Dutaillis and Georges Lefebvre, *Studies and Notes Supplementary to Stubbs' Constitutional History* (Mancester, 1930), pp. 247–48.

79. P.R.O., Exchequer, Treasury of the Receipt, Books, 75, m. 1–33v.

80. P.R.O., Exchequer, Pipe Rolls, 176, m. 65v.; 181, m. 29v.; 202, m. 37, 38v.; 204, m. 33, 41v., 43; 206, m. 54v.; 211, m. 41v.; 212, m. 41v.; Lord Treasurer's Remembrancer, Rolls of Foreign Accounts, #2, m. 2v., 4; #3, m. 6; #6, m. 3v.; #7, m. 5v.; #16, m. 6v.; #17, m. 1v.; #18, m. 1; #20, m. 7v.; #24, m. 5; #25, m. 4; #26, m. 5; #61, m. 1v.; #66, m. 1; #75, m. 2.

81. *Statutes of the Realm*, 2:474–75.

82. G. L. Harris, *King, Parliament, and Public Finance*, p. 517.

83. John Manwood, *A Treatise*, fol. 16.

Bibliography

Primary Sources

A. Manuscript

Guildford Muniment Room. Guildford, Surrey.
    Loseley Mss. 1081/1. Partial roll of forest pleas.

Public Record Office. London.

    Chancery Files.
        (Tower and Rolls Chapel) Recorda. C 260.
        Tower Series Certiorari. C 258.
    Chancery Miscellanea. C 47.
    Duchy of Lancaster
        Ancient Correspondence. D.L. 34.
        Cartae Miscellaneae. D.L. 36.
        Forest Proceedings. D.L. 39.
    Exchequer.
        Chancellors Rolls. E 352.
        King's Remembrancer. Forest Proceedings. E 146.
        King's Remembrancer. Various Accounts. E 101.
        Pipe Rolls. E 372.
        Lord Treasurer's Remembrancer. Rolls of Foreign Accounts. E 364.
        Treasury of Receipt. Forest Proceedings. E 32.
        Treasury of the Receipt. Books. E 36.
    Special Collections.
        Ancient Correspondence. S.C. 1.
        Ancient Petitions. S.C. 8.

B. Printed

The Anglo-Saxon Chronicle. Edited by Dorothy Whitelock. New Brunswick, N.J., 1961.

Blaaw, W. H. "Letters to Ralph de Nevill, Bishop of Chicester, 1222–1244, and Chancellor to King Henry III." *Sussex Archaeological Collections.* Vol. 3, pp. 33–77. London, 1850.

Blois, Peter of. *Opera Omnia. Patrologiae.* Edited by J. P. Migne. Series Latina, vol. 207. Paris, 1904.

Calendar of the Charter Rolls. The Deputy Keeper of the Records. London, 1903–   .

Calendar of the Close Rolls. The Deputy Keeper of the Records. London, 1900–   .

Calendar of the Patent Rolls. The Deputy Keeper of the Records. London, 1906–   .

Canterbury, Gervase of. *Historical Works.* Edited by William Stubbs. 2 vols. Rolls Series. London, 1879–80.

The Cartae Antiquae Rolls. Edited by Lionel Landon. Pipe Roll Society, vol. 55. London, 1939.

The Cartae Antiquae Rolls. Edited by J. Conway Davies. Pipe Roll Society, vol. 71. London, 1960.

Close Rolls of the Reign of Henry III. 14 vols. The Deputy Keeper of the Records. London, 1902–   .

Coggeshall, Ralph of. *Chronicon Anglicanum.* Edited by Joseph Stevenson. Rolls Series. London, 1875.

Coventry, Walter of. *Memoriale.* Edited by William Stubbs. 2 vols. Rolls Series. London, 1872–73.

Curia Regis Rolls. 15 vols. The Deputy Keeper of the Records. London, 1922–72.

Davis, H. W. C., *et al.*, eds. *Regesta Regum Anglo-Normannorum 1066–1154.* 4 vols. Oxford, 1913–69.

Devizes, Richard of. *Chronicle. Chronicles of the Reigns of Stephen, Henry II., and Richard I.* Vol. 3. Edited by R. Howlett. Rolls Series. London, 1884–89.

Diceto, Ralph de. *Historical Works.* Edited by William Stubbs. 2 vols. Rolls Series. London, 1876.

Douglas, David C., and Greenaway, George W., eds. *English Historical Documents 1042–1189.* Vol. 2. London, 1953.

Eadmer. *Historia Novorum in Anglia.* Translated by Geoffrey Bosanquet. Philadelphia, 1965.

Edward, Second Duke of York, *The Master of Game.* Edited by William A. and F. Baille-Grohman. London, 1909.

fitz Nigel, Richard. *Dialogus de Scaccario.* Edited and translated by Charles Johnson. London, 1950.

Fleta. Edited by H. G. Richardson and G. O. Sayles. Vol. 2. Selden Society, vol. 72. London, 1955.

Great Britain. Exchequer. *Magnum Rotulum Scaccarii vel Magnum Rotulum Pipae de Anno Tricesimo-Primo Regni Henrici Primi.* Edited by Joseph Hunter. Public Record Commission. London, 1833.

The Great Roll of the Pipe. Pipe Roll Society. London, 1884– .

The Great Roll of the Pipe for the First Year of the Reign of King Richard the First. Edited by Joseph Hunter. London, 1844.

Grosseteste, Robert. *Epistolae.* Edited by H. R. Luard. Rolls Series. London, 1861.

Guisborough, Walter of. *The Chronicle of Walter of Guisborough.* Edited by Harry Rothwell. Camden Society. London, 1957.

Howden, Roger of. *Chronica.* Edited by William Stubbs. 4 vols. Rolls Series. London, 1868–71.

"The Legend of Fulk fitz-Warin." Appendix to Ralph of Coggeshall. *Chronicon Anglicanum.* Edited by Joseph Stevenson. Rolls Series. London, 1875.

Leges Henrici Primi. Edited and translated by L. J. Downer. Oxford, 1972.

Luard, Henry R., ed. *Annales Monastici.* 5 vols. Rolls Series. London, 1864–69.

Maitland, Frederic William, ed. *Memoranda de Parliamento.* London, 1893.

Manwood, John. *A Treatise and Discourse of the Lawes of the Forrest.* London, 1598.

Map, Walter. *De Nugis Curialium.* Edited by Thomas Wright. Camden Society. London, 1850.

Map, Walter. *De Nugis Curialium.* Translated by Montague R. James. Cymmrodorion Record Series, vol. 9. London, 1923.

The Memoranda Roll . . . of the First Year . . . of King John (1199–1200). Introduction by H. G. Richardson. Pipe Roll Society. London, 1943.

Newburgh, William of. *Historia rerum Anglicarum. Chronicles of the Reigns of Stephen, Henry II., and Richard I.* Vols. 1 and 2. Edited by R. Howlett. Rolls Series. London, 1884–1889.

Paris, Matthew. *Chronica Majora.* Edited by H. R. Luard. 7 vols. Rolls Series. London, 1872–83.

Patent Rolls of the Reign of Henry III. London, 1901– .

Peterborough, Benedict of. *The Chronicle of the Reigns of Henry II. and Richard I.* Edited by William Stubbs. 2 vols. Rolls Series. London, 1867.

Rotuli Chartarum. Edited by Thomas D. Hardy. Record Commission. London, 1837.

Rotuli de Liberate ac de Misis et Praestitis. Edited by T. Duffus Hardy. Record Commission. London, 1844.

Rotuli Litterarum Clausarum. Edited by Thomas D. Hardy. Record Commission. 2 vols. London, 1833–44.

Rotuli Litterarum Patentium. Edited by Thomas D. Hardy. Record Commission. London, 1835.

Rotuli Parliamentorum. 6 vols. London, 1767–77.

The Statutes of the Realm. London, 1810– .

Stubbs, William, ed. *Chronicles of the Reigns of Edward I. and Edward II.* 2 vols. London, 1882–83.

Tanquerey, Frédéric Joseph. "Lettres du roi Edward I à Robert de Bavent, king's yeoman, sur des questions de vénerie." *Bulletin of the John Rylands Library* 23 (1939): 487–503.

Treharne, R. E. and Sanders, J. J., eds. *Documents of the Baronial Movement of Reform and Rebellion 1258–1267.* Oxford, 1973.

Turner, G. J., ed. *Select Pleas of the Forest.* Selden Society, vol. 13. London, 1901.

"Vitae S. Roberti Knareburgensis." *Analecta Bollandiana* 57 (1939): 363–400.

Wales, Gerald of. *Opera.* Edited by J. S. Brewer. 8 vols. Rolls Series. London, 1861–91.

Wendover, Roger of. *Chronica.* Edited by Henry O. Coxe. English Historical Society. London, 1841.

Wireker, Nigel. *Speculum Stultorum.* Edited by John H. Mozley and R. R. Raymo. Berkeley and Los Angeles, 1960.

Wireker, Nigel. *A Mirror for Fools.* Translated by J. H. Mozley. Notre Dame, Indiana, 1963.

Year Books of the Reign of King Edward the First Year XX and XXI. Edited by Alfred J. Horwood. Rolls Series. London, 1866.

Secondary Works

Baldwin, John W. *Masters, Princes, and Merchants: The Social Views of Peter the Chanter and His Circle.* 2 vols. Princeton, 1970.

Baring, F. H. "The Making of the New Forest." *English Historical Review* 27 (1912): 513–15.

Bazeley, Margaret Ley. "The Extent of the English Forest in the Thirteenth Century." *Transactions of the Royal Historical Society,* 4th ser., vol. 4 (1921): 140–72.

———. "The Forest of Dean in its Relations with the Crown during the Twelfth and Thirteenth Centuries." *Transactions of the Bristol and Gloucestershire Archaeological Society* 33 (1910): 153–285.

Bellamy, John. *Crime and Public Order in England in the Later Middle Ages.* London, 1973.

[Bruce, Charles S. C.], Earl of Cardigan. *The Wardens of Savernake Forest.* London, 1949.

Borenius, Tancred and Charlton, John. "Clarendon Palace: An Interim Report." *The Antiquaries Journal* 16 (1936): 55–84.

Brentnall, H. C. "The Metes and Bounds of Savernake Forest." *The Wiltshire Archaeological and Natural History Magazine* 49 (1940–42): 391–434.

———. "Savernake Forest in the Middle Ages." *The Wiltshire Archaeological and Natural History Magazine* 48 (1937–39): 371–86.

Callahan, Thomas. "The Notion of Anarchy in England, 1135–1154: A Bibliographical Survey." *The British Studies Monitor* 6 (1976): 23–35.

Cantor, L. M. "The Medieval Forests and Chases of Staffordshire." *North Staffordshire Journal of Field Studies* 8 (1968): 39–53.

Chanter, J. F. "The Swainmote Courts of Exmoor, and the Devonshire Portion and Purlieus of the Forest." *Report and Transactions of the Devonshire Association for the Advancement of Science, Literature, and Art* 39 (1907): 268–301.

Cox, J. Charles. *The Royal Forests of England*. London, 1905.

Cronne, H. A. *The Reign of Stephen 1135–54*. London, 1970.

———. "The Royal Forest in the Reign of Henry I." In H. A. Cronne *et al. Essays in British and Irish History in Honour of James Eadie Todd*. London, 1949.

Darby, H. C. *Domesday England*. Cambridge, 1977.

———. *The Domesday Geography of Eastern England*. Cambridge, 1952.

——— and Terrett, I. B. *The Domesday Geography of Midland England*. Cambridge, 1954.

——— and Maxwell, I. S. *The Domesday Geography of Northern England*. Cambridge, 1962.

——— and Campbell, Eila M. J. *The Domesday Geography of South-East England*. Cambridge, 1962.

———, ed. *A New Historical Geography of England*. Cambridge, 1973.

Davies, James Conway. *The Baronial Opposition to Edward II*. London, 1967.

Delisle, Léopold. *Études sur la Condition de la Classe Agricole et l'état de l'agriculture en Normandie au Moyen Âge*. Évreux, 1851.

Donkin, R. A. "The Cistercian Settlement and the English Royal Forests." *Cîteaux: Commentarii Cistercienses* 11 (1960): 39–55, 117–32.

Douglas, David C. *William the Conqueror*. Berkeley and Los Angeles, 1967.

Edwards, J. R. "Confirmatio Cartarum and Baronial Grievances in 1297." *English Historical Review* 58 (1943): 147–71, 273–300.

Farrer, William and Brownbill, J., eds. *The Victoria History of the County of Lancaster*. London, 1906– .

Fisher, William Richard. *The Forest of Essex*. London, 1887.

Foss, Edward. *The Judges of England*. 9 vols. London, 1848.

Greswell, William H. P. *The Forests and Deer Parks of the County of Somerset*. Taunton, 1905.

Harriss, G. L. *King, Parliament, and Public Finance in Medieval England to 1369*. Oxford, 1975.

Hart, Cyril E. *The Commoners of Dean Forest*. Gloucester, 1951.

———. *Royal Forest*. Oxford, 1966.

———. *The Verderers and Speech-Court of the Forest of Dean*. Gloucester, 1950.

Higounet, Charles. "Les Forêts de l'Europe occidentale du Vᵉ au XIᵉ siècle,"

Agricoltura e Mondo Rurale in Occidente nell L'Alto Medioevo. Settimane di Studio del Centro Italiano di Studi sull' Alto Medioevo, vol. 13. Spoleto, 1966.

Hilton, Rodney H. *A Medieval Society; The West Midlands at the End of the Thirteenth Century.* London, 1967.

———. "The Origins of Robin Hood." *Past and Present* 14 (November 1958): 30–44.

Holdsworth, Sir William. *A History of English Law.* Vol. 1. 7th ed. London, 1956.

Hollister, C. Warren. "The Strange Death of William Rufus." *Speculum* 48 (1973): 637–53.

Holt, James C. "The Assizes of Henry II: The Texts." *The Study of Medieval Records. Essays in Honour of Kathleen Major.* Edited by D. A. Bullough and R. L. Storey. Oxford, 1971.

———. *Magna Carta.* Cambridge, 1965.

———. *The Northerners.* Oxford, 1961.

———. "The Origins and Audience of the Ballads of Robin Hood." *Past and Present* 18 (November 1960): 89–110.

———. "Philip Mark and the Shrievalty of Nottinghamshire and Derbyshire in the Early Thirteenth Century." *Transactions of the Thoroton Society* 56 (1952): 8–24.

Hoyt, Robert S. *The Royal Demesne in English Constitutional History: 1066–1272.* Ithaca, N.Y., 1950.

Keen, Maurice. *The Outlaws of Medieval Legend.* London, 1961.

———. "Robin Hood—Peasant or Gentleman?" *Past and Present* 19 (April, 1961): 7–15.

Kimball, Elisabeth. *Serjeanty Tenure in Medieval England.* New Haven, 1936.

Lennard, Reginald. "The Destruction of Woodland in the Eastern Counties under William the Conqueror." *The Economic History Review* 15 (1946): 36–43.

Liddell, W. H. "Some Royal Forests North of Trent 1066–1307." M.A. Thesis, University of Nottingham, 1961.

Liebermann, Felix. *Über Pseudo-Cnuts Constitutiones de Foresta.* Halle, 1894.

Maddicott, J. R. *Thomas of Lancaster 1307–1322.* Oxford, 1970.

Malden, H. E., ed. *The Victoria History of the County of Surrey.* London, 1902– .

McKechnie, William S. *Magna Carta.* 2nd ed. Glasgow, 1914.

McKisack, May. *The Fourteenth Century.* Oxford, 1959.

Meekings, C. A. F. *Crown Pleas of the Wiltshire Eyre, 1249.* Wiltshire Archaeological and Natural History Society. Records Branch, vol. 16. Devizes, 1961.

Neilson, Nellie. "The Forests." In James F. Willard and William A. Morris, eds. *The English Government at Work, 1327–1336.* Vol. 1. Cambridge, Mass., 1940– .

Norgate, Kate. *England Under the Angevin Kings.* 2 vols. London, 1887.

———. *The Minority of Henry the Third.* London, 1912.

Page, William, ed. *The Victoria History of the County of Leicester.* London, 1907– .

———., ed. *The Victoria History of the County of Stafford.* London, 1908– .

Painter, Sidney. *The Reign of King John.* Baltimore, 1949.

Parker, F. H. M. "The Forest Laws and the Death of William Rufus." *English Historical Review* 27 (1912): 26–38.

———. "Inglewood Forest." *Transactions of the Cumberland and Westmorland Antiquarian and Archaeological Society,* New Series, 5 (1905): 36–61; 6 (1906): 159–70; 9 (1909): 24–37; 10 (1910): 1–28.

Pearsall, Derek and Salter, Elizabeth. *Landscapes and Seasons of the Medieval World.* Toronto, 1973.

Petit-Dutaillis, Charles. "Les Origines franco-normandes de la 'forêt' Anglaise." *Mélanges d'histoire offerts à M. Charles Bémont.* Paris, 1913.

——— and Lefebvre, Georges. *Studies and Notes Supplementary to Stubbs' Constitutional History.* Manchester, 1930.

Poole, Austin Lane. *From Domesday Book to Magna Carta 1087–1216.* 2nd ed. Oxford, 1955.

Postan, M. M. *The Medieval Economy and Society.* Berkeley and Los Angeles, 1972.

Powicke, Sir Maurice. *The Thirteenth Century.* 2nd ed. Oxford, 1962.

Pugh, Ralph B. *Imprisonment in Medieval England.* Cambridge, 1968.

———., ed. *The Victoria History of Wiltshire.* London, 1953– .

Raftis, J. A. *Assart Data and Land Values.* Toronto, 1974.

Ramsay, James H. *A History of the Revenues of the Kings of England 1066–1399.* 2 vols. Oxford, 1925.

Richardson, H. G. and Sayles, G. O. *The Governance of Mediaeval England from the Conquest to Magna Carta.* Edinburgh, 1963.

———. *Law and Legislation from Aethelberht to Magna Carta.* Edinburgh, 1966.

Rothwell, H. "The Confirmation of the Charters, 1297." *English Historical Review* 60 (1945): 16–35, 177–91, 300–315.

———. "Edward I and the Struggle for the Charters, 1297–1305." In *Studies in Medieval History Presented to Frederick Maurice Powicke.* Edited by R. W. Hunt *et al.* Oxford, 1948.

Shaw, R. Cunliffe. *The Royal Forest of Lancaster.* Preston, 1956.

Stenton, Doris M. *English Justice between the Norman Conquest and the Great Charter 1066–1215.* Philadelphia, 1964.

———. *Pleas before the King or His Justices 1198–1202.* 3 vols. Selden Society, vols. 67, 68, 83. London, 1952–67.

Stenton, F. M. *Anglo-Saxon England.* 2nd ed. Oxford, 1962.

Thiebaux, Marcelle. "The Mediaeval Chase." *Speculum* 42 (1967): 260–274.

Thompson, Faith. *The First Century of Magna Carta*. Minneapolis, 1925.

———. *Magna Carta: Its Role in the Making of the English Constitution 1300–1629*. Minneapolis, 1948.

Thomson, Richard. *An Historical Essay on the Magna Charta of King John*. London, 1829.

Tout, T. F. *Chapters in the Administrative History of Medieval England*. 6 vols. Manchester, 1920–33.

———. *The Place of the Reign of Edward II in English History*. 2nd ed. Manchester, 1936.

Tubbs, Colin R. *The New Forest: An Ecological History*. Newton Abbot, Devon: David and Charles, 1968.

Tupling, G. H. *South Lancashire in the Reign of Edward II as Illustrated by the Pleas at Wigan Recorded in Coram Rege Roll No. 254*. Chetham Society, 3rd ser., vol. 1. Manchester, 1949.

Turner, G. J. "The Justices of the Forest South of Trent." *English Historical Review* 18 (1903): 112–16.

Turner, Ralph V. *The King and His Courts*. Ithaca, N.Y., 1968.

Warren, W. L. *Henry II*. Berkeley and Los Angeles, 1973.

———. *King John*. New York, 1961.

West, John. "The Administration and Economy of the Forest of Feckenham during the Early Middle Ages." M.A. Thesis, University of Birmingham, 1964.

Wilkinson, B. *The Consittutional History of Medieval England 1216–1399*. 3 vols. London, 1948–58.

Willard, Rudolph. "Chaucer's 'Text that seith that hunters ben nat hooly men.'" University of Texas. *Studies in English* (1947), pp. 209–251.

Wolffe, B. P. *The Royal Demesne in English History*. Athens, Ohio, 1971.

Wright, Elizabeth Cox. "Common Law in the Thirteenth-Century English Royal Forest." *Speculum* 3 (1928): 166–91.

———. "Common Law in Thirteenth Century English Royal Forests." Ph.D. Dissertation, University of Pennsylvania, 1928.

Young, Charles R. "English Royal Forests under the Angevin Kings." *The Journal of British Studies* 12 (1972): pp. 1–14.

———. "The Forest Eyre in England during the Thirteenth Century." *The American Journal of Legal History* 18 (1974): 321–31.

Index

Abingdon Abbey, 44
Abyndon, Master Richard de, 125
administration: Henry I, 6, 12, 13;
 Henry II, 22–23, 25, 27; Richard
 I, 25; breakdown in later Middle
 Ages, 151, 154–57, 165–66
agisters, 28, 76, 79, 87, 88, 114, 130,
 142, 156
agistment, accounts for, 128–30
Ainsty, 21
Albini, William de, 13
Aldwinkle, Richard of, 86
Aliceholt Forest, 125, 163
Andevill, Ralph de, 43
Andover Forest, 57
Anglo-Saxon Chronicle, 2–3, 4
Anglo-Saxons, 1, 2, 4, 53
animals, domestic in forest, 12, 26,
 44, 46, 54, 68, 86, 87, 90, 111,
 114, 115, 131–32, 167
arrows, manufactured in forest, 54
Articles of the Barons, 64–65
Arundel, Robert, 13
assarts, 16, 29, 35, 54, 68, 75, 87,
 93, 109, 117, 121–22, 134, 158,

166; rent of, 30, 47, 50, 55, 114,
 136, 155
assize: of bread and wine, 94; of
 Clarendon, 31, 34, 37; of the
 forest, 33, 93, 127, 138, 155, 162;
 (forest 1184), 12, 27–29, 30, 31,
 40–42, 49; (forest 1198), 27, 28,
 29–30, 38, 39, 64; of William de
 Vescy, 84, 90, 92
attachment court, 86, 89–90, 92,
 100, 156
atte Wode, Edward, 160
Ayllesbury, Walter de, 125

bailiffs of royal manors and woods,
 76
Barenton, Eustace of, 14
barons, exemption from forest eyre,
 103
Basset, Ralph, 13
Bath, bishop of, 72, 110, 113, 127,
 133
Battle Abbey, abbot of, 104
beasts of the forest, 4, 10–11
Beauchamp, Giles, 166–67

213

THE MIDDLE AGES

Edward Peters, General Editor

Christian Society and the Crusades, 1198–1229. Sources in Translation, including The Capture of Damietta by Oliver of Paderborn. Edited by Edward Peters

The First Crusade: The Chronicle of Fulcher of Chartres and Other Source Materials. Edited by Edward Peters

The Burgundian Code: The Book of Constitutions or Law of Gundobad and Additional Enactments. Translated by Katherine Fischer Drew

The Lombard Laws. Translated, with an Introduction, by Katherine Fischer Drew

Ulrich Zwingli (1484–1531): Selected Works. Edited by Samuel Macauley Jackson

From St. Francis to Dante: Translations from the Chronicle of the Franciscan Salimbene (1221–1228). G. G. Coulton

The Duel and the Ooath. Part I and II of Superstition and Force, Henry Charles Lea. Introduction by Edward Peters

The Ordeal. Part III of Superstition and Force, Henry Charles Lea

Torture. Part IV of Superstition and Force. Henry Charles Lea

Witchcraft in Europe, 1110–1700: A Documentary History. Edited by Alan C. Kors and Edward Peters

The Scientific Achievement of the Middle Ages. Richard C. Dales

History of the Lombards. Paul the Deacon. Translated by William Dudley Foulke

Monks, Bishops and Pagans: Christian Culture in Gaul and Italy, 500–700. Edited, with an Introduction, by Edward Peters

The World of Piers Plowman. Edited and translated by Jeanne Krochalis and Edward Peters

Felony and Misdemeanor: A Study in the History of Criminal Law. Julius Goebel, Jr.

Women in Medieval Society. Edited by Susan Mosher Stuard

The Expansion of Europe: The First Phase. Edited by James Muldoon

Laws of the Alamans and Bavarians. Translated, with an Introduction, by Theodore John Rivers

Law, Church, and Society: Essays in Honor of Stephan Kuttner. Edited by Robert Somerville and Kenneth Pennington

The Fourth Crusade: The Conquest of Constantinople, 1201–1204. Donald E. Queller

The Magician, the Witch, and the Law. Edward Peters

Daily Life in the World of Charlemagne. Pierre Riché. Translated, with an Introduction, by Jo Ann McNamara.